SAVITRI DEVI

AND TIME ROLLS ON

THE SAVITRI DEVI INTERVIEWS

EDITED BY R. G. FOWLER

Second, Revised Edition

A Savitri Devi Archive Book
Counter-Currents Publishing, Ltd.
San Francisco
2012

Printed on acid-free paper
No animal products were used in the creation of this book.
Dust jacket and cover by R. G. Fowler and Michael J. Polignano

ISBNs:
Hardcover Edition: 978-1-935965-50-3
Paperback Edition: 978-1-935965-51-0
Electronic Edition: 978-1-935965-52-7

Library of Congress Cataloging-in-Publication Data

Savitri Devi.
And time rolls on : the Savitri Devi interviews / Savitri Devi ;
edited by R.G. Fowler. -- Second edition.
pages cm
"A Savitri Devi Archive book"--Title page verso.
An edited transcription of interviews originally taped in 1978.
Previously published: Atlanta : Black Sun Publications, 2005.
Includes bibliographical references and index.
ISBN 978-1-935965-50-3 (hardcover edition : acid free paper) --
ISBN 978-1-935965-51-0 (paperback edition : acid free paper) --
ISBN 978-1-935965-52-7 (electronic edition)
1. Savitri Devi--Interviews. 2. Savitri Devi--Political and social
views. 3. Savitri Devi--Philosophy. 4. Women intellectuals--
France--Biography. 5. Intellectuals--France--Biography. 6. Na-
zis--France--Biography. 7. National socialism--Philosophy. 8.
National socialism and religion. 9. Indo-Europeans--Ethnic
identity. 10. Indo-Europeans--Civilization. I. Fowler, R. G. II.
Title.
CT1018.S29A3 2012
324.2436'0238--dc23
2012047168

SAVITRI DEVI (1905–1982) became known as the high priestess of "esoteric Hitlerism" for her unique synthesis of National Socialism, Hindu mythology, and the Indo-European cyclical view of history in her 1958 book *The Lightning and the Sun*. In 1978, Savitri Devi recorded ten hours of interviews on her life, her thought, and her experiences in the National Socialist movement both before and after World War II. These interviews, now published as *And Time Rolls On: The Savitri Devi Interviews*, are an ideal introduction to this brilliant and controversial thinker.

"I embraced Hinduism because it was the only religion in the world that is compatible with National Socialism. And the dream of my life is to integrate Hitlerism into the old Aryan tradition, to show that it is really a resurgence of the original Tradition. It's not Indian, not European, but Indo-European. It comes from back to those days when the Aryans were one people near the North Pole. The Hyperborean Tradition."

"It suddenly dawned on me, sometime in April 1929 . . . and in Palestine of all places, that this foreign German leader who wanted all Germans in one state and wanted the abolition of the treaties of Versailles and Saint Germain, really wanted more than that, much more. And much more meaning: the freedom of Europe, the freedom of the Aryan race, from any kind of Jewish spiritual overlordship. He's the one who's going to free us from that. Well if he's that, then he's not only the Germans' leader, he's my leader too. *Mein Führer*. And from that day, I felt, not that I was becoming a National Socialist—I never became one—but that I had always been one, without knowing it. That's what I felt. And I started thinking of going to Germany and joining the movement. It was the movement of liberation."

"What I like about National Socialism is the idea of perfection. The idea that man should be perfect. There is a perfect type of each race. Every race should strive to its own perfect type. National Socialism is an Aryan racialism, but you could transpose it. I can very well imagine a non-Aryan, say a Japanese, having the same ideas as ours. . . . And that's why if to be a religion, the basic principles of the doctrine have to be universal, I can say National Socialism is a religion."

"I love all animals, especially felines. . . . The only creature that I cannot love is the stupid, average two-legged mammal who doesn't think for himself. He's supposed to think. He's supposed to look upwards. Man in Greek is called *anthropos*. Now if you decompose the word *anthropos*, it means 'the one who looks above.' If he doesn't look above, he's no *anthropos*. He's no man. And the majority of people who call themselves men, they are not men according to the Greek etymology of the word. A man is supposed to think."

"I'm for a multi-racial world in which each race keeps to itself, in harmony with the other races. Like in a garden, you have flowerbeds of roses and flowerbeds of carnations and irises and different other flowers. They don't intermarry. They stay separate, and each one has its beauty. . . . I'm against colonialism for the reason that colonialism infects the master as well as the slave. It even infects the master more."

The Savitri Devi Archive

The Centennial Edition of Savitri Devi's Works

R. G. Fowler, General Editor

Each volume will be released in a limited cloth edition of 200 numbered copies.

Volume One:

AND TIME ROLLS ON
THE SAVITRI DEVI INTERVIEWS

Volume Two:

GOLD IN THE FURNACE
EXPERIENCES IN POST-WAR GERMANY

Volume Three:

FOREVER AND EVER
DEVOTIONAL POEMS

Volume Four:

DEFIANCE
THE PRISON MEMOIRS OF SAVITRI DEVI

Volume Five:

THE LIGHTNING AND THE SUN
(complete and unabridged)

Volume Six:

PILGRIMAGE

Future Volumes:

MEMORIES AND REFLECTIONS OF AN ARYAN WOMAN

THE LOTUS POND
IMPRESSIONS OF INDIA

HARD AS STEEL

LONG-WHISKERS AND THE TWO-LEGGED GODDESS
OR, THE TRUE STORY OF A "MOST OBJECTIONABLE NAZI" AND . . .
HALF-A-DOZEN CATS

IMPEACHMENT OF MAN

A SON OF GOD
THE LIFE AND PHILOSOPHY OF AKHNATON, KING OF EGYPT
(complete and unabridged)

AKHNATON'S ETERNAL MESSAGE
(and other writings on Akhnaton)

A WARNING TO THE HINDUS
(and THE NON-HINDU INDIANS AND INDIAN UNITY)

NOT "FOR NOTHING": LETTERS OF SAVITRI DEVI, VOLUME 1

SAINT SAVITRI: LETTERS OF SAVITRI DEVI, VOLUME 2

Savitri Devi, New Delhi, 9 November 1977

To Georg and Magdlen Schrader,
Savitri's Good Friends

CONTENTS

EDITOR'S PREFACE

In November of 1978, Ernst Zündel, a leading publisher of National Socialist and revisionist literature, dispatched a young German associate to New Delhi to interview Savitri Devi on tape.[1] Zündel discovered Savitri through Adrien Arcand, a leading figure of the pre-World War II French Canadian Right. Savitri and Zündel began to correspond in 1961 and continued to do so until her death in 1982.[2]

Of Savitri's books, Zündel was most impressed with *The Lightning and the Sun* (1958), claiming that its influence on his life and thought was second only to Hitler's *Mein Kampf.* Her other National Socialist books, such as *Defiance* (1951), *Gold in the Furnace* (1952), and *Pilgrimage* (1958), struck him as merely "devotional" works. But he regards *The Lightning and the Sun* as, quite literally, a revelation. Zündel believes that Savitri Devi, like Edgar Cayce and Adolf Hitler himself, was a prophet, an oracle, a "channel" through whom revelations from a higher order of reality entered our world.

Savitri's goal was certainly that of a prophet. She wished to found a new religion for the White West. This religion was to be both a revival and a transformation of classical Aryan paganism. Its purpose was to replace Christianity and serve as a vehicle for the triumph of Savitri's National Socialist ideals. But there was some confusion as to what, precisely, this religion was supposed to be.

---

[1] "Savitri Devi" is a *nom de plume* meaning "Sun Goddess." ("Savitri" = sun; "Devi" = goddess.) It may seem like undue familiarity to refer to her, for the sake of verbal economy, as "Savitri" rather than as "Devi," but "Devi" is not a surname, but a title analogous to "Saint," and just as one refers to Saint Paul as Paul for short, rather than as Saint, one refers to Savitri Devi as Savitri, not Devi. Savitri's surname, after her marriage, was Mukherji, Mukherji being a contraction of Mukhopadhyaya.

[2] All information relating to Ernst Zündel is drawn from an interview with the editor taped on 29 October 2001.

In her book *A Son of God*, written in 1943–45 and later re-titled *Son of the Sun*, Savitri makes a case for reviving the monotheistic solar religion of the Egyptian pharaoh Akhnaton.[3] In *Impeachment of Man*, her pioneering animal rights book written in 1945–46, Savitri praises Akhnaton's philosophy in Nietzschean terms as optimistic and life-affirming.[4] However, in her book *Defiance*, written in 1950, Savitri admits that her praise of Akhnaton was not entirely in earnest. It was an attempt to package elements of Aryan paganism for a war-weary and suspicious world.[5] Furthermore, in *The Lightning and the Sun*, written between 1948 and 1956, Savitri offers a critique of the apolitical and pacifistic elements of Akhnaton's vision.[6] In *Defiance* and *Pilgrimage* (written in 1953–54), we find Savitri communing with the old Nordic gods. In *Defiance*, she recounts worshipping the Midnight Sun and praying at the Godafoss (Waterfall of the Gods) during her year in Iceland (1946–1947).[7] In *Pilgrimage*, she tells of her 1953 pilgrimage to National Socialist sites in Germany and Austria, which culminated in her visit to the Externsteine, where she spent a night in the initiation grave and greeted the rising sun in the Chamber of the Sun.[8] In *Pilgrimage*, she also addresses prayers to the Germanic "Almighty Father of Light" (*Lichtvater allwaltender*).[9] However,

---

[3] Savitri Devi, *A Son of God: The Life and Philosophy of Akhnaton, King of Egypt* (London: Philosophical Publishing House, 1946). Second Edition: *Son of the Sun: The Life and Philosophy of Akhnaton, King of Egypt* (San Jose, California: Supreme Grand Lodge of AMORC, 1956).

[4] Savitri Devi, *Impeachment of Man* (Calcutta: Savitri Devi Mukherji, 1959), ch. 3, "Joyous Wisdom."

[5] Savitri Devi, *Defiance: The Prison Memoirs of Savitri Devi*, ed., R. G. Fowler (Atlanta: The Savitri Devi Archive, 2008), 233-34.

[6] Savitri Devi, *The Lightning and the Sun* (Calcutta: Savitri Devi Mukherji, 1958), ch. 11, "Too Late and Too Early."

[7] On the visit to the Godafoss see *Defiance*, 335-36; on the worship of the Midnight Sun, see *Defiance*, 80.

[8] Savitri Devi, *Pilgrimage* (Calcutta: Savitri Devi Mukherji, 1958), ch. 9, "The Rocks of the Sun," esp. 348-54.

[9] *Pilgrimage*, 33, 52. Cf. Savitri's account of her return to India in 1957 in *Long-Whiskers and the Two-Legged Goddess, or the true story of a*

in *Gold in the Furnace*, written in 1948–49, she flatly denies that it is possible to revive the cult of Wotan—or any dead religion, for that matter, which would include Akhnaton's.[10] In her 1939 book *A Warning to the Hindus*, Savitri praised Hinduism as the last *living* remnant of Aryan paganism.[11] But in *Impeachment of Man*, she offers a Nietzschean critique of Hinduism and Buddhism as pessimistic and life-denying.[12] Yet in *Gold in the Furnace*, *Defiance*, and *Pilgrimage*, we find her meditating on the teachings of the Bhagavad-Gita and praying to the Hindu deities Shiva and Kali.[13]

Savitri also speaks of a universal or international religion in several of her books. In *Pilgrimage*, Savitri addresses prayers to an unnamed supreme deity, "the One," the "Lord of the Invisible Forces."[14] In *Gold in the Furnace*, she claims that the only rational international religion is the "Religion of Life," i.e., "the spontaneous worship of warmth and light—of the life-energy," the "supreme worship of the Godhead *in* Life." She claims, furthermore, that, "nowhere can divinity be collectively experienced better than in the consciousness of race and soil."[15]

Finally, Savitri speaks of National Socialism as a religion. In *Gold in the Furnace*, Savitri describes National Socialism as the form that "the everlasting religion of Life" takes on in the pre-

---

"most objectionable Nazi" and . . . half-a-dozen cats (Calcutta: Savitri Devi Mukherji, n.d.), 135.

[10] Savitri Devi, *Gold in the Furnace: Experiences in Post-War Germany*, ed. R. G. Fowler (Atlanta: The Savitri Devi Archive, 2006), 312.

[11] Savitri Devi, *A Warning to the Hindus* (Calcutta: Hindu Mission, 1939), ch. 3, "The Human Value of Hinduism: Indian Paganism, the Last Living Expression of Aryan Beauty."

[12] *Impeachment of Man*, ch. 2, "Pessimistic Pantheism."

[13] For Savitri's meditations on the Bhagavad-Gita see *Defiance*, ch. 12, "The Way of Absolute Detachment"; *Pilgrimage*, 189, 199; for her prayers to Kali, see *Gold in the Furnace*, 77, 173, 178; *Defiance*, 262; *Pilgrimage*, 197; for her prayers to Shiva, see *Defiance*, 308-9 and *Pilgrimage*, 197.

[14] *Pilgrimage*, 74, 93, 196-97.

[15] *Gold in the Furnace*, 216.

sent Dark Age.[16] She also claims that Adolf Hitler is a divine being and expresses the hope that someday he will be worshipped as such.[17] In *The Lightning and the Sun*, Savitri uses the framework of Hinduism to cast National Socialism as a new religion. She plays Saint Paul to Hitler's Jesus. Like Paul, who transformed Jesus from a prophet and/or failed political revolutionary into an incarnation of God himself, Savitri proclaims Hitler to be the ninth avatar of the god Vishnu, who entered into time in the present Dark Age (Kali Yuga) to combat decadence and usher in a new Golden Age (Satya Yuga, or Age of Truth). Hitler failed because he came too soon. He was, moreover, conscious that he would fail. But he fought anyway, in the spirit of the Bhagavad-Gita, because it was his duty. Although Hitler was not the chosen one, he blazed the way for the last avatar, Kalki, who will not fail.

Savitri's religious vision may be completely consistent, but she nowhere offers a synoptic overview, so its consistency is hard to grasp. Therefore, Zündel sent an agent with a tape recorder to get the oracle to clarify herself. Ten hours of interviews were recorded.[18]

Zündel was, however, deeply disappointed with the results, which he described as "stream-of-consciousness" ramblings. He suggested that Savitri, unlike Cayce and Hitler, could not control her ability to channel. He also speculated that Savitri's occasional repetitions and constant digressions were signs of the onset of senility. But in spite of his disappointment, Zündel recognized that the interviews had documentary value and marketed them as a set of five two-hour tapes.

Zündel's reaction makes perfect sense given his aims for the interviews. But in fairness to Savitri, she may have thought that she had given adequate account of her religious beliefs in her books, and she evidently had other aims in mind. Savitri was,

---

[16] *Gold in the Furnace*, 284.

[17] *Gold in the Furnace*, 222, 235.

[18] The completed tapes narrowly escaped oblivion. Zündel repeatedly impressed upon the interviewer that he was to keep the finished tapes on his person at all times.

furthermore, a brilliant and tireless talker, and the interviewer was obviously intimidated by her. He lost control of the proceedings almost from the beginning.

I am assuming that the five tapes present the interviews in chronological order. The interviewer asks no questions after the first tape and his voice is seldom heard. The first tape is the most rambling and disjointed of the five, covering such topics as Hinduism, Christianity, cruelty to animals, some virtues of the Aztecs, human and animal sacrifices, the cosmic significance of Adolf Hitler, the evil of Mother Teresa, and various events in Savitri's life. When the interviewer does not ask questions, Savitri simply moves from topic to topic by free association. Although religion is mentioned frequently, nothing Savitri or the interviewer says indicates that she was asked to give an overview of her religious thinking.

The subsequent tapes have a very different tone. Savitri seems to have decided that, since the interviewer was not guiding her according to his (or Zündel's) agenda, she would impose her own. Savitri evidently decided to use the interviews as an opportunity to tell the story of her life, probably to provide material for future biographers. All of tape two is devoted to a narrative of her life from her birth on 30 September 1905 until her arrest in Cologne on 20 February 1949 for distributing Nazi propaganda. Tape three continues the narrative until her trial and conviction in Düsseldorf on 5 April 1949. The rest of the tape is devoted to her memories of George Lincoln Rockwell, Colin Jordan, John Tyndall, Françoise Dior, Matt Koehl, and the Cotswolds Camp of 4–7 August 1962, where the World Union of National Socialists was formed. Savitri allows herself a number of digressions but never loses the thread of her narrative. Tape four begins with more recollections of National Socialist comrades, but the bulk is devoted to lengthy discourses on Christianity and Hinduism and a brief discussion of Judaism. The first side of tape five is somewhat disorganized, but deals mostly with the philosophy of history and life in the present Dark Age. Side two underscores Savitri's biographical aims. She retells the story of her life up to 1978, filling in some, but alas not all, of the gaps in her earlier narrative. She then concludes with a reading of her poem "1953," the opening words of which are "And Time Rolls On."[19]

When I first heard these interviews, I recognized immediately that they should be published as a book. Savitri's autobiographical narrative is far from perfect. She spends a good deal of time retelling stories she already told at great length in *Defiance* and *Gold in the Furnace*, while long stretches of her life remain undocumented. Nevertheless, these interviews not only contain much that is unavailable in Savitri's other writings, they constitute an ideal introduction to her life and thought.

There are radical differences between written and spoken discourse. A transcript of a perfectly adequate, even eloquent, interview seldom reads well on the printed page. Thus the spoken word always requires editing to become the written word. What is remarkable about the Savitri Devi interviews, however, is how little editing they required. Savitri was a remarkably eloquent speaker. She could speak at length on complex and difficult topics without reference to notes. She could digress at length from the main line of her argument, then pick up where she left off. She had a prodigious memory from which she could pull obscure names and dates and remarkably accurate quotes with ease. Yes, she occasionally repeats herself, but she repeats herself in her books as well. Yes, she sometimes loses the thread of her argument. Yes, she occasionally gets a name or date wrong. But in ten hours of extemporaneous speaking, it is not remarkable how many mistakes she makes, but how few.

By far the greatest labor was the transcription of the original tapes. Savitri is sometimes very hard to understand: she speaks rapidly and with the odd accent one would expect of a woman fluent in eight languages[20] and familiar with some twenty others. She is usually too far from or too close to the microphone.

---

[19] The poem is the last of 16 in a volume of prose poems written in 1952-53: Savitri Devi, *Forever and Ever: Devotional Poems*, ed. R. G. Fowler (San Francisco: Counter-Currents, 2012).

[20] English, French, Greek, Italian, German, Icelandic, Hindi, and Bengali.

She is frequently drowned out by the street din of New Delhi. Sometimes it is possible to transcribe particular words only because English is my native tongue, and I can recognize them even in garbled form. Unfortunately, Savitri uses many unfamiliar names picked up in her world travels and her reading of world history. She also throws in phrases in French, German, Greek, Sanskrit, and Bengali. The French and German phrases were usually recognizable, but the other languages caused great difficulty.

Thus I had to check, and frequently correct, my conjectural transcriptions using a number of sources. In some cases, I could check my transcriptions against Savitri's published writings and her unpublished correspondence. I also made use of internet search engines. Sometimes I used contextual information furnished by Savitri to find the word or phrase in question. Other times I simply resorted to typing in different possible transcriptions until I stumbled upon the correct one. When the internet was exhausted, I resorted to contacting specialist scholars. And as my last resort, I browsed through the indexes of books in several college libraries. Where my transcription remains conjectural, I have indicated this with a footnote. I found it impossible to transcribe three phrases in Greek, one in Bengali, one in an unknown Indian tongue, and one in French. Fortunately, Savitri provided English translations for all of them, so I did not need to include the foreign phrases. Perhaps sharper ears can fill these *lacunae* for future printings.

Once I was satisfied with the accuracy of the transcripts, I had to transform them into the book before you. To this end, I made the following editorial interventions, in order of increasing invasiveness. First, I corrected all errors of grammar and diction. Second, when Savitri edits or corrects her own speech, I follow her lead and present only the corrected statement. Third, out of considerations of clarity, I completed some sentence fragments where the missing words are clear from the context. Other fragments I left standing to preserve the occasionally telegraphic style of Savitri's speech. Fourth, I occasionally divided an impossibly tangled sentence into two or three more readable sentences. Fifth, occasionally words are cut off at the beginnings and the ends of the tapes. Where it is possible to infer the gist of the missing words, I inserted them in square brackets to preserve continuity. Sixth, I removed all the words of the interviewer, but to preserve continuity I inserted in two places the gist of his questions in square brackets. Seventh, I deleted needless repetitions. Eighth, Savitri sometimes offers two or three accounts of the same events. Since these repetitions often contain some new information, they cannot simply be deleted. Therefore, I have combined the various accounts of the same events into single accounts. Ninth, I have repositioned texts to form four thematically unified chapters. Where I could not integrate a point into the flow of the text, I placed it in a footnote. I always indicate when the words in the footnotes are Savitri's. My basic editorial principle throughout was to make only the minimum changes necessary for clarity and readability. I did not edit to improve Savitri's style.

In the case of the poem "1953," I transcribed it exactly as recited, then consulted a number of manuscript and typescript versions to determine the line and stanza breaks, punctuation, capitalization, and emphasis. Unfortunately, the manuscripts and typescripts were not entirely consistent in these matters, so I chose to follow the versions that sounded best to me. When reciting the poem, Savitri made several small word changes that I decided to preserve in the final edited version, simply because these changes may have been deliberate on her part, not mere slips of the tongue.

Having reviewed my labors one last time, I am satisfied that nothing extraneous has been added and nothing essential has been deleted.

In my use of punctuation, I have tried throughout to preserve the quality of Savitri's speech: her pauses, her emphases, the little dialogues she narrates. I wish I could have captured other qualities of Savitri's voice: wonder as she recounts her night on the flanks of an erupting volcano; aesthetic pleasure tinged with eroticism when she describes Hindu and Buddhist ceremonies; boiling indignation when she speaks of injustice and cruelty, especially to animals; love and longing when she speaks of her cats; respect and affection when she tells of her husband A. K. Mukherji; similar warmth and respect when she speaks of Sven Hedin, Hertha Ehlert, Marianne Meinecke, Gerda Strasdat, Muriel Gantry, and George Lincoln Rockwell; mischievous glee when she recounts her childhood insolence and naughtiness; girlish naïveté when she shifts suddenly from discussing Hitler's grand strategy to describing the sari she bought to wear to the victory celebrations; hushed, choked tones when she recounts how that sari and many others were later stolen in a Paris train station; and finally the drollness of some of her stories, such as her account of the one time she was slightly drunk or her reflections on whether she would like to be reincarnated as a German ("Suppose my father was an anti-Nazi. It can happen in Germany, you know."). All these nuances remain on the tapes.

When Savitri quotes from a book, I have used quotation marks, but it must be borne in mind that she is quoting from memory, not from the printed page.

With one exception, which is noted, I use a last initial followed by a dash to conceal the names of people who may be alive and who might not wish to be mentioned in these pages.

My editorial notes perform six functions. First, as indicated above, when I found it impossible to smoothly integrate some of Savitri's words into the text, I placed them in notes. Second, where Savitri is obscure, I try to provide clarification. Third, where appropriate, I furnish additional information from or citations to Savitri's other books and unpublished correspondence. Fourth, where Savitri refers to or quotes from books, I try to provide citations. Fifth, where she refers to historical figures, I provide their names, dates, and other relevant information. I deemed some figures in no need of introduction: Hitler and other leading National Socialists, Lenin, Stalin, Churchill, Roosevelt, Gandhi, Oliver Cromwell, Louis XIV, Henry VIII, Alexander the Great, Julius Caesar, etc. Even though most people would be hard-pressed to provide their dates, it would seem pedantic for me to provide them. Finally, I note gaps and conjectures in my transcription.

I chose the title *And Time Rolls On* because I wanted the title to be Savitri's creation, not my own, and it was the best candidate in the interview tapes. It is, however, a perfect title, given the centrality of the Indo-European cyclical view of history to Savitri's thought.[21]

If you find any errors, please contact me through the Savitri Devi Archive at archivist@savitridevi.org, so that I can correct them in future printings.

R. G. Fowler
Berkeley
22 October 2002
(The 20th anniversary
of Savitri Devi's death)

After nearly three years of delays in publication it gives me great pleasure finally to see this book through the press in time to commemorate Savitri Devi's centennial year.

Atlanta
30 September 2005
(The 100th anniversary
of Savitri Devi's birth)

In the second edition of *And Time Rolls On*, I have corrected several transcription and formatting errors, reset the type for easier reading, and omitted the Appendix (a German translation of the poem "And Time Rolls On") and the Bibliography. Both texts are available online at the Savitri Devi Archive (http://www.savitridevi.org). I omitted the Appendix because it turns out not to have been translated by Savitri Devi. As for the Bibliography, it is constantly growing, so any print version will rapidly become obsolete. Thus it is best to check the online version.

San Francisco
14 November 2012

---

[21] See *The Lightning and the Sun*, ch. 1, "The Cyclic View of History."

ACKNOWLEDGEMENTS

I wish to thank all the people who made this book possible: chief among them are Ernst Zündel, for providing a copy of the interview tapes and giving his permission to publish these edited transcripts, and Ryan Schuster, for paying to have them transcribed; Ingrid Rimland for her support and assistance; Joe Pryce, for the arduous but invaluable labor of checking the original transcripts against the tapes; Beryl Cheetham for providing the photograph that appears on the front jacket flap, for pointing out errors in the edited transcripts, and for giving me her correspondence with Savitri and with Muriel Gantry, which proved a treasure trove of useful information; D. A. R. Sokoll and John Morgan for their eagle-eyed editing; Miriam Hirn for providing information for the notes and bibliography and pointing out errors in the edited transcripts; M. L. for giving me Savitri's correspondence with O. L. and for pointing out errors in the transcripts; Georg and Magdlen Schrader for providing their correspondence with Savitri and their recollections of her stay with them; Colin Jordan for the gift of a copy of *Gold in the Furnace* that Savitri originally gave to Françoise Dior; William Pierce for supplying materials for the bibliography and notes; Kevin Alfred Strom for Savitri's correspondence with Revilo P. Oliver and information for the bibliography; Christian Bouchet and Alexander Baron for information for the bibliography; Matt Koehl for copies of Savitri's correspondence with him and with George Lincoln Rockwell, another treasure trove of information; Miguel Serrano, Martin Kerr, and S. G. D. for copies of their correspondence with Savitri, which proved extremely useful for identifying a number of proper names; and Terry Cooper, Diana Hughes, Nefertiti Saleh, Mark Weber, and others who wish to remain anonymous for providing information for the notes.

Georg and Magdlen Schrader took Savitri into their home for six weeks in 1982. It was one of her happiest times during her last, sad, nomadic year. In an undated letter to Beryl Cheetham from July or August 1982, Savitri writes, "I have been *very* happy — in spite of my declining eyesight and stiffening body — among these extraordinarily kind, *understanding*, and extremely well-informed friends. Many a time I have felt ashamed of my own poor knowledge — especially concerning German medieval *and* later history — when compared to theirs. Frau Schrader is all the more praiseworthy that during her school days, there was in Germany *no* teaching of history *at all* for children or adolescents. She learnt the lot *by herself*, in well-chosen books (far *better* than the amount of *falsehood* that one learns nowadays in schools not only in Germany but everywhere in Europe!). As for *Herr* Schrader, he is a real *scholar*, whose talk is for me a delectation." Because of their help to Savitri, and to me, I dedicate this book to them.

R. G. Fowler
Atlanta
30 September 2005

For this second edition, I wish to thank D. A. R. Sokoll, Arjuna, and everyone else who pointed out errors in the first edition, and Matthew Peters for his meticulous proofreading.

San Francisco
21 January 2013

Chapter 1

AUTOBIOGRAPHY

1. EARLY RECOLLECTIONS

I was born in France on the 30th of September, 1905. Not of French parents, completely. I was a French citizen automatically because all children born in France are automatically French citizens. But my mother was English. My father was, I would say, a Mediterranean man. His mother was from Lombardy. Now he is Greek by his father, but his father had taken French nationality long ago. So: Greek, Italian, and English.[1]

And I was born of already aged parents. My mother was 40, my father 45 or 46.[2] And I don't know if this detail is interesting or not, but it seems I weighed 900 grams, not even a kilo, at birth. As a young person, I was always an admirer of ancient Sparta in Greece, and my mother used to tell me, "If you had been born in Sparta you would've been thrown in the chasm at birth." The chasm is a cleft between two mountains, and babies who were not fit to be either warriors or mothers of warriors were just dropped into that at birth, at the order of the Spartan magistrate.[3] In antiquity they brought up only the fit ones. And of course I would've been considered as good for nothing. I was 900 grams, not even a kilo: into the chasm. But I was born in France, in democratic France, so I was allowed to grow up.

I was the only child, and very early I liked the conversation of grownup people. I never really liked to play with other children. I found their games silly. I liked discussions. I liked asking questions, queer questions like this one, for instance: "What is fire made of?" or things like that.

---

[1] Savitri Devi's given name was Maximine Julia Portaz. Portas/Portaz is short for Portassi. Savitri's mother was born Julia Nash. Her father's name was Maxim Portassi/Portas/Portaz.

[2] According to Savitri's letter to H. J. of 1 October 1980, her father was born on 14 February 1861, thus he was 44 when she was born.

[3] The chasm of Apothetae is on the slopes of Mount Taygetos. See Plutarch's *Lycurgus* in his *Lives*.

I can remember very far back. I can remember my perambulator. My mother told me that she sold it when I was two. I remember it very well, very well. I remember being sick of peaches. Sick in my perambulator. I remember the bed cloth, white and blue with tassels. I used to pull the tassels and say, "You come, you come, you come," and throw them away. And I remember once we were in the park, and I put my hand outside my perambulator, and it was all wet. I said, "Mummy, what's that?" I only spoke English because my mother was English. She was Cornish. So I put my hand out, and I said, "What's that?" She said, "That's the dew." Well, that was a new word! Until we came home, I repeated it: "dew, dew, dew, dew." I remember that as though it was yesterday. I was about one-and-a-half. I have a good memory for things. And things that impress me, I remember them always. Always.

Well, for instance, I remember snails. In my neighborhood, you put live snails in vinegar to force them out, to eat them. I said, "The poor snails." I always loved animals. I was always indignant at any kind of action of humans against them. I refused to eat meat. My mother and father didn't eat meat very often. They ate meat on festival days. Sometimes Sundays, and Christmas, Easter, days like that. But I didn't want to even on those days. And for Christmas I had peas in butter, boiled peas in butter. That was my Christmas dinner. And a slice of plum pudding made with butter. She didn't make it with suet, because she knew I wouldn't have eaten it otherwise. I had very strong ideas. And nothing could've made me change.

And one thing that upset me from my childhood when I was five is experiments on animals, circuses, the fur industry, all things where animals are the victims. Experiments on animals, never! I said, "As long as that exists, I'm not going to say a word against things that happen to human beings." And to this day when I hear of things that go on in Africa, in Uganda — Idi Amin Dada is supposed to be a monster, a tyrant, whatever you like — I couldn't care less. As long as they put up with experiments on animals in their laboratories, I'm not going to criticize Idi Amin Dada. He's a Negro. Let him do what he likes. After all, his victims are also Negroes. I couldn't care less. Negroes among Negroes. Let them do it.

They used to give missionary literature to me. The little girl brought up in cannibal surroundings. The mission school comes to the village. And she's indignant at the idea of eating people, people of the enemy tribes. And she ends up by becoming a Christian. I used to tell people openly, "If you call that superior, and if you must admire this little girl, why don't you admire me? I have standards." I didn't say it in those words, of course. I meant, "My standards of behavior are higher than yours. You don't respect animals. I do. So why don't you admire me if I have to admire this little girl?" That was insolent. I was as insolent as possible. I never was afraid of being insolent unless I was severely punished, like in school.

Another thing that I remember that was in 1912 is my first film. My mother wanted to see *Quo Vadis*. It was playing at the cinema in Lyons. And she wanted to put me in somebody else's house. She wanted to go alone. Nobody wanted me because I was too naughty. So she had to take me with her, and she took me. And I saw *Quo Vadis*. Of course I didn't understand the intrigues of the film. But I saw marble staircases, Roman ladies draped in pleated material, going up and down with their Roman hairdress, everything beautiful and harmonious. Of course there were the lions in the arena and the blessed Christians. But I admired the lions. I loved them. Great big cats. I didn't find any objection to them eating people. They're great big cats. I thought that if I had been in the arena I would have caressed them. And when I came out I told my mother, "When I grow up I want to be a Roman." She said, "Why do you want to be a Roman?" "Because they are beautiful. You see, mummy, they are beautiful. I like their dress." And now, after so many decades, when I see myself draped in a sari, I find it something like the dream of a child of six realized.

Another thing that struck me in this film was the newsreel. The newsreel was about the sinking of the *Titanic*. The *Titanic* sunk I think on the 12th of April, 1912, and I saw the sinking in the newsreel. And somebody told us, the speaker, that there was an English lady who was not allowed to get into the lifeboat because she had a dog, a little dog. They said, "You can come in but not your dog." She said, "I would rather go and be drowned with my dog than come in without it." And I remembered that. And when I came home I said to my mother, "Now look how illogical, look how stupid! The lady might weigh 50 kilos, say the dog, 10 kilos. They refused the lady with the dog, 60 kilos. And if a human being comes along weighing 95 kilos, they'll take him. Look at the illogical thing! If they want to save many, many people, they should save only the children and let the grownups die in the sea. That's their logic. They are against their own logic. I don't like that, mummy. I don't like that." That was one of the things I said when I was six.

I went to school for the first time, on the 1st of October, 1911. I was exactly six. I knew reading and writing already and could multiply, add, subtract, and divide by one figure. My mother taught me that. In the Catholic school I knew that I had to keep my mouth shut according to good Christianity. And in the council school where I went afterwards, I had to keep my mouth shut about the French Revolution, which I hated. I never liked the Declaration of the Rights of Man and the idea of equality. I didn't like it. I found that something beautiful is not the equal of the same kind of thing ugly. I thought that the strong cannot be the equal of the weak, etc. There were some natural values above all.

They had the *Déclaration des droits de l'homme* on a panel in the corridor, and one day I asked permission to go to the WC (excuse me).[4] And they said, "All right, you go." I didn't go. I went to the corridor, stood in front of the panel, and did this awful gesture.[5] It's very rude to do that in French. I did that at it. And the headmistress caught me and said, "Why are you doing that?" I said, "Because that's all lies." "Who told you that, your father?" I said, "No, no, my father is for it. He likes that stuff, but I don't." "Why don't you like it? Why do you think it's lies?" "Well, because equality is a lie." "How do you think equality is a lie?" I said, "Because a beautiful girl is not equal to an ugly girl. An ugly girl is inferior." And I named two girls in my class. I said, "So-and-so, I like so-and-so. She's a good girl, of course, but she's inferior to this one. This one's a beauty." A blonde, blue-eyed, beautiful girl named Aimée Villon. And the headmistress could say nothing.

---

[4] WC = water closet, i.e., toilet.

[5] In *Defiance* (Calcutta: A. K. Mukherji, 1951), Savitri states that she also stuck out her tongue at a bust representing the French Republic (*Defiance*, 334).

She said, "Well, you'll be punished." I said, "Punish me if you like. I don't mind. I'm not for the French Revolution." "You'd rather be a serf under the kings?" I said, "As a serf under the kings, I'd have something to love. The majesty of the king is something that can dazzle me. But there's no majesty in a republic, in an aggregate of so many hundreds of men who give out decisions. What is there to love in them? What is there to love in them? They are not a person. I can love a person. I can't love an assembly." I said that. They didn't say anything else to me. But I was quite young.

Just before the First World War, I began my weekly visits to the Musée Guimet. It was an Asiatic museum. Or rather, it was the Lyons branch of the big Asiatic museum of Paris. I was playing, making mud pies, in the public garden not far from there. It started raining. "Mother," I said, "it's raining now. We have no umbrellas. Where must we go?" My mother told me, "We must go and take shelter somewhere. We can take shelter in the museum." So we went into the museum, took shelter from the rain.

And my mother asked me, "Would you like to see antiquity or animals?" I said, "I'd rather see antiquity because the animals are stuffed. I don't like to see stuffed animals. I like to see live ones." "All right." The first hall was Assyrian sculptures. There was a mummy there. We saw Egyptian antiquities, Assyrian antiquities, and then we went upstairs. It smelt of sandalwood and incense. And I inhaled it deeply. I liked it. And there were Tibetan pictures, and there were Siamese pictures. I liked the style too. It was a very good place. I was in the Orient at once. Straight into the Orient. I liked it. I saw the Indian room, and I saw the Chinese room, and I saw the Japanese room and everything. And I was very interested.

And I asked, "Mummy, can I come here every Sunday?" And my mother said, "Yes, every Sunday from 2:00 to 5:00 it's open. You can come here. We'll be quiet." Because I used to make enough noise for ten at home. And I went there every Sunday for ten years or nearly. And that was my Asiatic formation. I learnt the history of Asia, the little I knew of it in those days, from the museum. I had a book, *The Musée Guimet*, covering all the history, mythology, and popular religions of Japan and China—old China, before Mao, of course.[6] I was very interested. I liked it. Asia never felt foreign to me. I don't feel foreign here. Any more than I do in Europe.

2. GREEK NATIONALISM

Of course I was brought up in the Christian religion. I was christened. My parents were married in the Anglican Church. I was christened there and went over to the Greek Church in Lyons. I wouldn't say I was re-christened because there is no re-christening, but I was given the option of joining the Greek Church. Anyhow, I grew up between the English friends of my mother and the increasing Greek community of Lyons, mostly Greeks from Asia Minor, especially from 1922 onwards.

I was much more inclined to think myself Greek than anything else. Even England didn't attract me as much as Greece. I didn't like my mother's English friends very much. I found them dull. Their conversation was dull. They always spoke of people who were sick. "So-and-so had an operation, so-and-so is 'poorly.'" It was boring. And then the church, the church: "What did the Cardinal say in his speech?" It was boring.

But I had the Greek colony, and those Greeks were mostly Greeks of Asia Minor. And they had an idea, all the Greeks had that idea. They called it the *Megali Idea*, the Great Idea. The dream of all Greeks in one state. Those of Greece, of course, those of Thrace, those of the coast of Asia Minor on the Black Sea, those of the coast of Asia Minor on the Aegean Sea. Capitol: Constantinople. The reconstruction of the Byzantine Empire, to the profit of

---

[6] I find no record of a book with this title, but Joseph Hackin wrote a number of books associated with the Musée Guimet, including *Guide-catalogue du Musées Guimet. Les collections bouddhiques. Inde centrale et Gandhâra, Turkestan, Chine septentrionale, Tibet* (Paris: Librairie Nationale d'art et d'histoire, 1923); *La sculpture indienne et tibétaine au Musée Guimet* (Paris: Librairie Ernest Leroux, 1931); and with Thcang Yi-Tchou, *La peinture chinoise et l'art bouddhique Tibetan au Musée Guimet* (Paris: Geuthner, 1910). The volume that best fits Savitri's description is Joseph Hackin, et al., *Mythologie asiatique illustrée* (Paris: Librairie de France, 1928). In English: *Asiatic Mythology, a Detailed Description and Explanation of the Mythologies of All the Great Nations of Asia* (New York: Crescent, 1963).

the modern Greeks. That was the dream of everybody. Even when they had a marriage festival or some ceremony, the last toast embodied that idea: "And let us go to Constantinople, children." I grew up with that.

I loved Greece not because of ancient Greece, and I would put stress on that. Of course, I loved ancient Greece. I loved Sparta, especially. But it is not so much ancient Greece as modern Greece of my times and modern Greece of the Independence War, 1821–1830, that attracted me. What I liked in contemporary Greece was this. They replied to those who told them that they should join the First World War on the Allied side to become big, to become great in territory, "We are small, but honorable." "Greece, small and honorable." I liked that expression very much.

And then I liked some episodes of recent Greek history like the Suli episode of 1799. These Greek women of the village of Suli were fighting the Turks. And when they saw the Turks had surrounded the rock on top of which they were, and the men fighting below were practically all killed, their alternative was the Turkish harem or death. They started a dance. They took each other's hands, and they went and danced around on top of the rock. They also sang a song that is popular in Greece today. I could sing it. And each time one neared the cliff, she threw herself below — with her child if she had a child, or with her children if she had more than one. And all 250 of them died like that. I found that piece of modern Greek history quite uplifting. And I liked it. I liked to feel myself the compatriot of these women.

3. FOUR WARS

Now I have remembrances of four wars. The Balkan War, 1912–1913: I remember the news we had of it, I remember the part I took in it, how glad I was when the Greeks took Salonika on the 26th of October 1912. It was the name day of Saint Dimitri, who was the patron of the town. And I remember all the kind of things like that, all the facts of the Balkan War. I resented my mother wearing a ribbon on a hat, Bulgarian colors. They were the fashion in France. I said, "Why do you wear Bulgarian colors? Bulgarians are our enemies." And they were in the Balkan War. Anyhow, then the First World War, 1914. And then the one that influenced me the most, the Greco-Turkish War in 1920–22. And then the Second World War.

The First World War, I remember it. I remember the school. I went to a Catholic school. I was sent to a Catholic school. And they would tell us, "Now you must put money into the box in front of the Holy Virgin Mary for her to bless the Allies." I didn't like that. Why should she bless the Allies? She wasn't French. She wasn't English. What had she to do with this war? I told my mother, "Mother, she was from Palestine. Why should she bless the Allies and make them win the war?" I said, "Don't put any money in." "Of course, that's nonsense." "Don't put any money in the box." "All right."

And then I had many answers that didn't quite satisfy me in any way. I was always questioning and always wanting to think for myself. Something happened in 1914. They told us, "The Germans, you see, are real barbarians. They went through Belgium, never asking permission of the Belgian government." I said, "All right, if you don't ask permission and you go through a country without it, then you are a barbarian. Quite right."

But in 1915, the French landed in Salonika in Greece without the permission of the Greek government. And they started not only doing that, but they started deepening the cleft between the Prime Minister Venizelos and the king of Greece, Constantine I, who was the brother-in-law of the German Kaiser.[7] I said, "Why did they do that? They are barbarians if they did that. If the Germans are barbarians for marching through Belgium, the French must be barbarians for landing in Greece. And the English must be barbarians for blockading the coast of Greece in 1916 for ten months and not allowing anything in. If you don't allow goods to come into Greece, Greece will starve. It only produces olive oil, raisins, tobacco, and that's about all. You can't live on that. So what is this hypocrisy?"

And when the brawl started in early December 1916 between

---

[7] Eleutherios Venizelos (1864–1936), several times elected Prime Minister of Greece, was the chief foe of the Greek Monarchy during his political career. In her letter to H. J. of 1 October 1980, Savitri claimed that Venizelos was a Freemason, a fact that she regarded as quite significant. Constantine I, King of the Hellenes (1868–1923), ruled Greece twice, from 1913–17 and again from 1920–22. His wife, Queen Sophia, lived from 1870–1932.

Greeks and French sailors that had landed there, and there was a big row in France—54 of the sailors were killed in the brawl with the Greeks—I was indignant. And then the French and English bombarded Athens in December '16. They call that the "November days" in Greece, because the calendar is 13 days different.

That put me absolutely against the Allies in the First World War. I took some chalk from the school, and in the evening when nobody could see me, I went behind the newly-built railway station and wrote on the wall, *"A bas les Alliés! Vive l'Allemagne!"* — "Down with the Allies! Long live Germany!"[8] I didn't know what Germany was in those days. Germany was just a patch of color on the map. But still I thought Germany would never be so hypocritical as to tell tales to me that some people are barbarians for doing a thing, and the people who do the same thing on the other side are not barbarians. They are fighting for liberty, and they are fighting for all the highest values.

Anyhow, time passed. The First World War came to an end. I was on the German side because of the hypocrisy of the Allies, because of what they told me: "These were barbarians, and these were not. These were fighting for themselves, and these were fighting for democracy." I said, "I don't like that kind of *deux poids, deux mesures*—two weights and two measures." The war came to an end, and I remember something awful, the screams of the crowd in the streets: *"L'Allemagne paiera! L'Allemagne paiera!"* "Germany will pay! Germany must pay!" Poor Germany, she was crushed completely, Austria too, and still they were screaming against her, "She must pay! She must pay! She must pay!" I hated that kind of insistence on the enemy's defeat. It was not chivalrous. It hurt my feeling of chivalrousness.

Another thing that shocked me very much after the First World War was the fact that they sent to Germany all the dark troops of Senegal. The occupiers of Germany were not French. They were Senegalese. And I knew there was a resistance, and I was admiring the resistance. I didn't know much about it. But I knew what was told in the papers. And always this idea of hu-

---

[8] According to Savitri's letter to H. J. of 1 October 1980, the station was the *Gare des Brotteaux* and the slogan was written in meter-high letters.

miliating the country that had been defeated. Well, it should just have been finished. Do like the Ancients did. I used to compare the Allies and the Germans to the heroes of the Trojan War. I knew of the Trojan War, of course. I felt as though it was a contemporary war although it was 3,200 years before our times. After the battles, the heroes would mix together. They did not have any grudge against each other. I would've liked the Allies to show that kind of spirit. But they were anything but chivalrous.

4. EDUCATION

Now I passed my first examination in my life in 1917 and the second and third ones in 1921. In 1922 and '23 I had more examinations. I landed in Greece for the first time on the 9th of August 1923 and left Greece on the 5th of December 1923. I entered the university in Lyons, where my parents were living, in January of 1924. I passed my first examination, in psychology, on the 25th of June, 1924. On the 2nd of March, 1925, I passed my second examination in logics,[9] with Mr. Goblot as a master.[10] I passed my third examination, in ethics and sociology, on June the 25th, 1925. In that examination I questioned the idea of progress and answered just as I would answer today. It was a brilliant examination. I had 18 out of 20. Nobody ever gets an 18 in the university for the arts. You get it in science, of course. In mathematics it's all right. But in arts you never get it. My other exams I passed with 14, 15 but never 18. That was a very good one. I had another examination, in 1928, my last examination in the university to get the M.A. There are four exams for the M.A., *license ès lettre*.

Then I began work on my doctorate. To have a doctorate—what they call a state doctorate, a doctorate that, if you are a French subject, gives you the right to teach in a French university—you have to write two books, and quite thick ones. In 1928, I went to Greece to prepare my *thèse complementaire*, my complementary thesis. That is to say, I began with the second one, which was the easiest. Well, I wouldn't say the easiest. But the shortest.

---

[9] The French sometimes use the plural "logics" to refer to the whole range of subjects in philosophy.

[10] Edmond Goblot (1858–1935) is still known for his work in logic (in the narrow sense of the term).

I wrote an essay on Theophilos Kaïris[11] of 300 or so pages. Theophilos Kaïris was a Greek who was born in 1784 and died in prison in 1853 for not being in accordance with the Orthodox Church. The real object of my thesis was not the person of Kaïris so much as the mentality of the modern Greek. The modern Greeks condemned Kaïris for repudiating the Orthodox Church, which was the national church. The ancient Greeks condemned Socrates because he did not believe in those gods in which the city believed. "He's an Athenian. He should believe in the gods of Athens. He doesn't? Well, out with him. He must drink poison, hemlock." I said, "It's the same mentality." And to show the similarity of that mentality of modern Greeks and ancient Greeks, making religion purely a national affair, I wrote that thesis.

I traveled extensively in Greece. I went all around Peloponnesus on foot and on horseback, alone. And I came back in November '29, having already finished my second thesis. But it was not printed yet. I had to have the first one. The subject of the first one was: What is simplicity in mathematics? Or in science in general? I started writing on simplicity in science in general, and I thought that in order to write something like that, I had to get a smattering of scientific training, otherwise I couldn't do anything. That subject had been given to me by the university teacher, Mr. Goblot, Edmond Goblot, one of the greatest teachers in France, greatest logicians anyhow. So I came back to France in '29 and went to the science university. And there I took an examination in physics-chemistry in July '30; general chemistry, in November '30; mineralogy, in July '31; and biological chemistry, in July '31. If you like, it is a whole L.Sc., *license ès sciences*, in physics-chemistry. I got that in '30–'31. And then I sat down to write my greater thesis.

But in the meantime, Mr. Goblot died. Mr. Étienne Souriau[12] was now teaching at the Sorbonne. And he said, "Don't write on *simplicité des sciences*, simplicity in sciences. It will be much too long. Confine yourself to *simplicité mathématique*, mathematical

---

[11] Maximine Portaz, *Essai-critique sur Théophile Kaïris* (Lyons: Maximine Portaz, 1935).

[12] Étienne Souriau (1892–1979) was known primarily for his work in aesthetics.

simplicity, what is the essence of it, analyze that." And that took me 500 pages or more. And he told me that I should write part of my thesis on the mathematical theories of Mr. Brunschvicg.[13] I didn't intend to write about Mr. Brunschvicg at all, but my teacher insisted on it, so I had to do it. It was about mathematics anyhow. It was not about anything else.

My principal thesis was finished in 1934 and printed, along with the other thesis, at my parents' expense.[14] In the meantime I went to India in 1932. The theses were printed in my absence and the proofs sent to me. And then I came back just for the *soutenance de thèse*.[15] That is to say, to have a discussion about the subject with six professors. There was one professor of mathematics, one professor of Greek, and four professors of logics, different subjects in philosophy, and the *soutenance de thèse* took place in Lyons on the 1st of April 1935.

5. THE DISCOVERY OF NATIONAL SOCIALISM, 1923–32

And then slowly the Hitler movement took place. I didn't know much about it in those days. I was 14 in 1920. On the 24th of February, 1920, the party was founded in Munich. All right. Slowly, slowly I started finding out that there was a German patriot fighting for his country, fighting against the Versailles Treaty. That is to say, he was the opponent of these frenzied people whom I had seen in the streets saying, *"L'Allemagne paiera! L'Allemagne paiera!"* – "Germany must pay! Germany will pay!" I liked him. I liked him as a foreign leader, but that was about all. And then I heard of his aim. His aim was all Germans in one state. I liked that. I liked that for the very reason that found it was my own idea transposed on the German plane.

I had been brought up and had lived with the idea they call in Greek the *Megali Idea,* the Great Idea of all Greeks, those of Greece who have already been freed, those of the Greeks in Thrace, those

---

[13] Léon Brunschvicg (1869–1944) was a Jewish philosopher noted for his scholarly works on Descartes and Pascal. Savitri evidently did not relish discussing his theories, probably because he was a Jew.

[14] Maximine Portaz, *La simplicité mathématique* (Lyons: Maximine Portaz, 1935).

[15] Thesis defense.

of the Greeks on the coast of Asia Minor, on the Aegean coast, the coast of the Black Sea, Constantinople. Well, in those days Constantinople had more than half a million Greeks. It was a Greek town practically. All those would be in one state. The reconstruction of the Byzantine Empire with Constantinople as the capital. I wanted that. And I said to myself, "Well, if there's a German who wants the same for his country, good luck to him. I'm all for it." And especially I didn't like the Allies. I never liked them. I never liked the victors of the First World War. So, so much the better.

And I used to follow whatever I heard of him, and the first great thing I heard of him was the *Putsch* of the 9th of November, 1923. I was in Athens at that time. I spent the afternoon of the 9th of November on the Acropolis. I remember that. And the next day it was in the papers. The next day I heard of it. And my reaction was: "Pity he didn't succeed. That would've been a fine lesson for these swine." (Excuse me.) And the lady in whose house I said that, a Swiss lady called Mademoiselle Mauron, said to me, "And who, if you please, do you call 'these swine'?" I said, "The Allies, Madame. I don't like them. I wish he had won. Really I wish he had won." Anyhow that passed. Mademoiselle Mauron didn't like me, of course. But I couldn't care less.[16]

Before this had been the Greek-Turkish War, '20–'22, and I knew that those former Allies of the First World War had helped the Turks, or more or less showed indifference, and they had told the Greeks to go on and on and on and conquer Asia Minor. But they never helped them, not even the British. As far as the French were concerned, Mr. Franklin-Bouillon signed a treaty of alliance with the Turks in March 1921 during one of the Greek offensives in Asia Minor.[17] And I said to myself, "They tore up our Treaty of Sèvres, that was just, that gave back at least some Greek territory to Greece. They tore it to pieces, and they started saying, in 1920 already, after the return of King Constantine to Greece, after the Greek elections against Venizelos, they started saying, 'All right, we'll tear the Treaty of Sèvres into pieces.' Why shouldn't that Treaty of Versailles and why shouldn't that Treaty of Saint Ger-

---

[16] Cf. *Pilgrimage* (Calcutta: Savitri Devi Mukherji, 1958), 105–6.

[17] Henry Franklin-Bouillon (1870–1939) signed his agreement in Ankara with Atatürk on 20 October 1921.

main be torn into pieces to do business also? If they don't respect our Treaty of Sèvres, why should I respect their Treaty of Versailles? Good for Hitler."

I was all on his side because he was against the Treaty of Versailles. I considered the Treaty of Versailles an infamy, especially compared to the Treaty of Sèvres that was not anything bad. It was quite just. The Treaty of Versailles separated people who shouldn't be separated. It put together people who were not to be put together. Czechoslovakia is the Pakistan of Europe. They put together Czechs and Slovaks who hate each other. And some Ruthenians and some Ukrainians and three-and-a-half million Germans who didn't want to be there, who wanted that to be Germany. I can understand that. And I thought, "If he wants all Germans in one state, well I want all Greeks in one state. Good for him." But I did not yet call him my Führer. He was the Führer of the Germans. And I liked the Germans. Although I had never met any.

I met one. The first German I met, I will speak of him. He was one Geißler. I wonder if he's alive still. That was just after the First World War, 1918. For months and months, in 1918, 1919, there were German prisoners in France. And a man called Mr. Lagrillon was the head of the camp near Lyons. They were building the foundations of the hospital. It still exists. It is called the *grange blanche*.[18] And this Mr. Lagrillon invited my father and my mother and myself to visit the camp one day on Sunday. And when we were in the camp, he said to my father, "Your wife is English, isn't she? And your daughter speaks English? Well, we have a German prisoner who speaks English too. Would you like to meet him?" My mother said, "Yes, of course, I'd like to meet him."

So in came one of the prisoners, a tall man, red hair, red-blonde with a very aristocratic bearing and gold-rimmed spectacles, and he presented himself. I don't know if it was Geißler or Geßler or something like that. And my mother spoke to him, and she was a pacifist, my mother. She said, "I am so sorry that our two countries fought for so many years. We should never fight again. There should be peace on earth and blah, blah, blah; blah, blah, blah" — a lot of peace talk.

---

[18] White barn.

My father didn't understand English at all. And then my father said to me, "Now would you like to say something? You speak English too." I said, "Yes, why not?" And I said, "I am glad you are the first German I met. Well, do you know, during the First World War I was on your side, not on the side of the Allies, not for any other reason but because they are hypocrites. They say one thing and they do another thing. I don't like that. And I really like you. And I wish, one day, that you'll be the first nation, that you conquer the whole of Europe and be the dominant people in Europe. I wish that. That would give a lesson to these people. The Allies, I don't like them." I repeated it two or three times. And he smiled, and he didn't say a word.

I wonder whether during the *Kampfzeit*, during the struggle for power of Hitler, he thought of me sometimes, that thirteen-year-old girl who told him, "I wish your country to be the leader of Europe." Anyhow, whether he did or whether he didn't, I don't know. But I would like to know whether he is alive still. He would be now — of course I was 13, he might have been 20, 22 — he must be more than 80 now if he's alive, because I'm in my 74th year.

And I followed the movement of Hitler with great sympathy, as the movement of a foreign leader, working for his country, nothing more. But at the same time, under the influence of the Musée Guimet, I was in touch with all the religions of Asia, and I liked to study them, and I liked them. I liked many of them. I liked Shinto, the national religion of Japan. I liked the idea of hierarchy that you find in the Hindu religion: the idea of all the races in the world represented in India with the Aryan at the top. It's the only religion in the world that tells you that the Aryan is to be at the top of all other races.

And that, combined with Bible study, put me against the Jews. My mother sent me to a sort of Sunday school, and I learnt a lot. I had an aunt also, a very pious aunt, an admirer of the Jews as God's own people.[19] And she told me I must read in front of her every Sunday afternoon a chapter of the Old and a chapter of the New Testament. And I did so. And the reading of the Bible just put me against the Jews. I did not learn opposition to the Jews in

---

[19] Nora Nash.

Mein Kampf. I didn't read it till it was published. It was not published in those days. I learnt opposition to the Jews in the Bible. Nowhere else. In the Old Testament, especially. I told my aunt, "Why should I admire these people who say they are God's chosen? What bad taste to choose these people. I would've had better taste than that. I would have chosen the Greeks or the British or the Germans or something else, or the Indians perhaps, but not these." "Why?" "Well, they have ways of living that I don't like."

For instance, there's a woman named Jael. She's in the fifth chapter of Judges, I think. In the Song of Deborah in Judges, she is called "blessed woman, blessed among all women who live in tents."[20] And she's the only one in the Bible called blessed among all women except the Blessed Virgin Mary, mother of Christ. Why is she called blessed among all women? Because after the battle of Mount Tabor, when the Amalekites were fleeing in front of the Jews and the head of the Amalekites, the general Sisera went to her tent in the desert, the tent of Jael, wife of Heber the Canaanite, and told her, "I'm thirsty; give me water." (I know what it means now to be thirsty in the desert. I've crossed the desert. In those days, of course, I didn't know it, but still I knew what it was to be thirsty.) And she said, "All right, come in my tent, and I'll give you water, not only water, I'll give you milk, and you can sleep here." And in he came. She gave him milk. She put him to sleep on something, on a cot, let's say, and while he was asleep — it says in the Bible, I didn't invent it — she took one of those nails by which you fix the tent and hammered it through his head, and then she went out and called the Jews and said, "Come along, come along. I killed your enemy Sisera. Come and see him." And for that act of cowardice, she's called blessed among all women. I didn't like that. I said, "If that's Jewish courage, well thank you very much."

And I also didn't like the episode of Agag, king of the Amalekites, handed over to Samuel the so-called prophet and cut up alive into pieces on an altar of stone.[21] Why? Because Samuel, on the part of God, had told Saul the king of the Jews to spare no prisoners. Kill them all, and the women and the babies and the cattle.

---

[20] The story of Jael is in Judges 4, the Song of Deborah in Judges 5.
[21] 1 Samuel 15.

Kill every one of the Amalekites. And he didn't do it. He kept them as slaves. He kept the animals in order to eat them later on. And he kept Agag. And Samuel said, "Because you didn't listen to the command of God you are no longer king of Israel from this minute. And where is Agag?" "Here he is." "All right." And he cut him to pieces all alive. I found that very nasty for a prophet.

And I didn't like also the episode of David, the very good king, in 2 Samuel 12, verses 30 and following, in which it is said after the conquest of Rabbah, the capital of the Ammonites, he just put a sword into some of the prisoners, had them sawed in two, and others were put alive in brick kilns, thank you very much. And, moreover, these Ammonites were people of the same race as the Jews, more or less. They were the children of Ben Ami, the son of one of Lot's daughters who married her own father, just like the Moabites, the sons of Moab, the son of another daughter of Lot with her own father.[22] But they were Semites, and they were very close to the Jews, but they did not worship the Jewish God. That was the only difference. The Ammonites worshipped Milcom, and Moabites worshipped Chemosh. What's the difference? Why should people quarrel over their gods? I didn't understand that at all, and I didn't like the "chosen people." I said, "Why should they be chosen?"

And why should Christianity, that comes from that, be the international religion? We had religions before. We had our own national religions. We were Hellenes. We had the religion of the Romans. We had our Nordic religions in Germany, in Russia, in France with the Celts, the Druids, and all that. I liked those old religions, and I wanted to go back to them.

But I said, "To be honest, I like something of the Byzantine church. I like the chanting, and I like the ceremonies. I don't like the Christian values, but I do like the Orthodox Church. I must *see* the cradle of Christianity before I do anything." I had the old Aryan Great Idea. I said, "Why did we change our gods, really? But I'm going to see what Palestine looks like. What does the cradle of this foreign religion look like?" And I went there.

So in Greece in April '29 I joined a Greek pilgrimage to Palestine, third class. It was cheap, and we were to stay 40 days in

---

[22] Genesis 19:37–38.

Palestine. We stayed till the end of May. Visited the place thoroughly. I was shocked. I saw these old ladies and some young ones, flat on their bellies, kissing the Holy Land whenever they saw some relic of the days of Christ. And they are all faked, mind you. You know the cloth with Christ's figure on it?[23] There are 39 of them in the whole world, not one. And I don't know how many foreskins. There's one foreskin of little Jesus at the Vatican. I think there are about 19 or 20 dispersed in all the world. He didn't have 19 foreskins. He had one, naturally. Everybody has one, all males. The contortions, the signs of exaltation in front of the slightest thing, and behaving really in what I call a servile manner because it was the Holy Land.

I was also shocked by the foreign atmosphere of the land. I felt myself in quite different surroundings from those of Greece. Of Europe, of course, but even of Greece, which is an Oriental country. In Greece we say, "I'm going to Europe" when we go to Italy. Europe is considered as something different. Whatever was under western Roman domination is Europe. What was influenced by the Byzantine Empire—that is to say, Greece, the Balkans, Russia—that's not Europe. That's something else. Well, in fact, if not geographically, at least ideologically, they are right. Greece is not Europe. Nor is Russia. Nor are the Balkans. Whatever was under the Byzantine Empire is not Europe to this day in the Greek speech.

So I looked at that, and I said, "Well, Holy Land? What is the Holy Land? Holy Land for the Greek is Greece. Holy Land for a German is Germany. Why should Palestine be the Holy Land of the Greeks? Why should we call, in Greek schools, the history of the Jews 'holy history'? What is holy about it?" And it dawned on me that the whole of Europe has been for centuries under the grip, the spiritual grip, of foreign people. We go to the cathedrals, these beautiful cathedrals, and we see the Jewish prophets— Moses and all the others—along with the saints, and the saints are Jews, most of them. Some, of course, are not. But most of them are. All the first ones are. The apostles are. Well, Jesus is supposed to have been one. And why should we bow down to these? Why don't we bow down to our own people? We have philosophers.

---

[23] Probably the Shroud of Turin.

We don't need the fathers of the church. Well, in fact the fathers of the church put a lot of Aryan philosophy into their Jewish tradition. That's another question. I said, "Goodness me, what an influence of Jewry, what a great grip of Jewry on our race. Why should we be under that grip? Who is going to free us of that grip? Who is going to give us our own self again?"

And it suddenly dawned on me, sometime in April 1929 — I don't know if it was the 20th; I hope it was the 20th — and in Palestine of all places, that this foreign German leader who wanted all Germans in one state and wanted the abolition of the treaties of Versailles and Saint Germain, really wanted more than that, much more. And "much more" meaning: the freedom of Europe, the freedom of the Aryan race, from any kind of Jewish spiritual overlordship. He's the one who's going to free us from that. Well, if he's that, then he's not only the Germans' leader, he's my leader too. *Mein Führer.* And from that day, I felt, not that I was becoming a National Socialist — I never became one — but that I had always been one, without knowing it. That's what I felt. And I started thinking of going to Germany and joining the movement. It was the movement of liberation.

But then something else came into consideration. I had just taken Greek nationality officially when I was 21. I didn't believe that I should keep French nationality when I was more attached to Greece than I was to France. At the Greek Home Ministry, the Ministry of the Interior as they call it, they said, "Miss Portassi, why are you doing that? You will have no advantage at all in taking Greek nationality because your diplomas are French. You did all your education in France. In France you would have a career. In Greece you'd have none." I said, "I don't care. I shall not be the compatriot of Mr. Franklin-Bouillon who signed the secret — well, more or less secret — treaty with the Turks in 1921, nor with General Sarrail who landed in Salonika without permission of the Greek government in 1915.[24] And that's all I want." "What will you live on?" "I'll give lessons." "But anybody does that without diplomas. You have diplomas." I said, "I don't care. I don't care." He said, "When you are old and with no pension, no work, you

---

[24] General Maurice Sarrail (1865–1929), commanding French troops from Gallipoli, landed in Salonika on 5 October 1915.

will regret it." Well, I am old now, and I'm sorry to say to those who told me the contrary, I do not regret it. I do not regret any act of sincerity.

People told me all sorts of things: "You will regret not knowing this. You will regret not knowing that, not trying this or trying that." I said, "There are so many things I can't try." "To be in love, to never fall in love. You'll regret it one day." I don't regret it at all. I regret I couldn't see Peru. Yes, that I regret. And I regret I never went to Germany during the great days. I couldn't go.

Anyhow, I thought in those days, "Now if I go to Germany they will say, 'This woman was a French national at birth. She took Greek nationality when she was 21. What does she want now in Germany? Is she a kind of spy or something like that?'" There would be mistrust. So I thought to myself, "No, I will start working in Greece itself for the old ideology, the old pagan ideology.[25] And if I cannot there, I must go somewhere else. But I must only go to Germany when I have something to show, some achievement that I have had elsewhere. I'll not go to Germany before. Especially not now, during the struggle." So I kept out of it.

In Greece I met with the opposition of the people who loved the church: "You are going against the religion of our fathers." I told them, "Dear me, what do you mean by the religion of your fathers? If nobody in your family had ever gone against the religion of *his* fathers—that is to say, the Olympian gods—you wouldn't be now a Christian. So why do you blame me?" Anyhow, I found after a year or two that I could do nothing. I went back to France. I took my L.Sc. in chemistry, physics-chemistry. And then I began my doctoral thesis, my first thesis, *La simplicité mathématique,* what is mathematical simplicity?

6. INDIA, 1932–39

And then, while writing my thesis, I felt I should go somewhere and start something else: a collaboration of something of today with the eternal spirit that Germany represented. And I thought of India. I said, "India, it's a country of many races. But

---

[25] In *Defiance,* Savitri describes her pagan missionary work in Greece (*Defiance,* 292).

it's the only country in the world whose religion proclaims the Aryan race as the most excellent of all and would give the leadership to Aryans only, according to tradition." I don't mean to say that in India today the leadership is in the hands of Aryans. Anything but. India was in those days under the British.[26]

And then I heard that there was an outlook in India, not man-centered, but life-centered. Man was not everything. Animals were respected. I thought so. When I came here, I heard that there were experiments done upon them. I said, "That would be the British rule. When the British went away, it would stop." But it didn't stop. On the contrary, it went on and on. The British infected the minds of Indians with democratic ideas and humanitarian ideas, and now it's not Aryan.

I didn't know a single Indian, but one fine day, after the death of my father in February 1932, I had a part of his inheritance, although a small part, just a quarter.[27] My father was not really rich. It was in reality the money of my mother that belonged to my father because she was married, what they call in French, without a contract, that is to say without a money arrangement. The money was mine anyhow.

I went to the British Consulate. I got a permit for India and sailed off to India. I would sail to Colombo[28] without knowing where I was going and what I would do there. I just had the money. The British Consul told me, "It will last three months." "Why?" "Because you have to travel first class. You are a European." I said, "All right, those who want to keep up Europe's prestige by traveling first class, they can do so. I shall travel cheap to make my money last," and I went all the way to India fourth class. There were four classes then. I didn't care. No ventilation, smelly. I didn't care as long as I could see the country and see the temples.

In Ceylon was my first experience with Buddhism. I went to a Buddhist temple in Kandi and put an offering in front of the

---

[26] Savitri is not saying that the British were not Aryans, but that they prevented the Aryan castes in India from exercising leadership.

[27] According to Savitri's letter to H.J. (1 October 1980), her father died of a stroke on 24 February 1932.

[28] In Ceylon/Sri Lanka.

Buddha along with other women. I felt the beating of drums in
my body. It was an exotic experience. It was something new. And
some of these women were quite fair. "After all," I said, "Buddhism is really an Aryan religion. Originally it was founded by
an Aryan. It's something better than Christianity anyhow." And
from there, after several days in Ceylon, about a fortnight, I went
to Talaimannar and Dhanushkodi, India. Talaimannar is the Ceylon station. Dhanushkodi is the Indian station.

And there I went to the Rameshwaram temple. I went there on
a festive day, and I saw in the Rameshwaram temple the festival
of Vaishakha Purnima, in the month of May.[29] This series of seven
elephants, one behind the other, with purple draperies. Beautiful
dark young men, like bronze statues, holding them in the darkness. With this queer music — very, very peculiar music I had never heard. And then suddenly the procession all around the sacred
tank, following the chariot of Rama and Sita, Rama and Sita being
the king and queen of Ayodhya years and millennia ago. They
were both Aryans, Rama and Sita. They were Kshatriya Aryans.
And they conquered the South. They conquered the South, says
the Indian legend, with the help of the monkeys. In reality it
means they conquered Dravidian strongholds, Dravidian power.
The Dravidians were much more advanced than the Aryans,
technically speaking. The Aryans conquered them with the help
of the aborigines. The aborigines are pictured as monkeys. The
king of the monkeys, Hanuman, gave his alliance to Rama. They
conquered the South. And they took back Sita. Sita had been tak-
en away by the king of the South, that is to say, Ravana.[30]

And I saw this crowd all around the sacred tank, under the full
moon, with one palm tree in the background, a violet sky, beautiful. And this crowd throwing flowers of jasmine and other flowers on the chariot of Rama and Sita. The crowd of dark people,
Dravidians. Dark people honoring the Aryan conqueror, represented white, as well as his wife, in the chariot. Honoring him

---

[29] In *Defiance* Savitri gives the date of the festival as 17 May 1935
(*Defiance*, 69). Cf. Savitri's description in *A Warning to the Hindus*
(Calcutta: Hindu Mission, 1939), ch. 3; paperback edition (New Delhi:
Promilla Paperbacks, 1993), 59.

[30] The story of Rama and Sita is told in the *Ramayana*.

with praise, with flowers, with a whole ceremony, thousands of years after the conquest.

And I stood against the pillar, and I thought of the song the Germans sung in those days, *"Deutschland gehört uns heute, und morgen, die ganze Welt"* —"Germany belongs to us today and to-morrow the whole world."[31] And I thought, *"Today* the whole world." Here you are: non-Aryans in crowds come and worship as a god an Aryan king of old. That's lovely. I was proud of my race, proud of myself, proud of being a National Socialist. And I said to myself, "One day I'd preach National Socialism to these people. To the élite of them, at least, to the Aryans, and see what happens. They might be our allies." At least their religion *is* our ally. It is the only religion in the world that is perfectly compatible with National Socialism. I mean to say, of the living religions. I'm not speaking of ancient pagan ones. Of the living religions, it's compatible with our *Weltanschauung* absolutely.

And I went further north, from temple to temple. I visited quite a lot of Indians. I remained in Pondicherry for one time or two. I gave a lecture in Pondicherry. I don't know how much it was appreciated.

---

[31] The song is "Es zittern die morschen Knochen" ("The Rotten Bones Tremble") a.k.a. "Wir werden weiter marschieren" by Hans Baumann. In addition to a harmless change of word order, Savitri substitutes "gehört" (belongs to) in place of "hört" ("hears"), which gives the song an imperialistic tone:

> Wir werden weiter marschieren,
> Wenn alles in Scherben fällt,
> Denn heute da hört uns Deutschland
> Und morgen die ganze Welt.

> We will march on,
> Though everything falls to pieces,
> For Germany hears us today,
> And tomorrow the whole world.

This alteration of the song appears quite frequently in literature on National Socialism. It would be interesting to determine whether the song was first altered by National Socialists themselves or by anti-Nazi propagandists.

Now in the South I had an experience. In Trichinopoli, I was looking at the town, looking from a distance at the magnificent temple nearby, the temple of Sri Rangam, bursting out of the tropical vegetation. And there was a boy chanting in Sanskrit on the platform. It was the platform of the hill. The temple is on a hill. It's called the golden temple because it's covered in gold.

And I looked the other way, and I saw a kind of box, an enormous building full of windows. Ugly as anything can be. So I asked the people who were there, "What's that thing?" "Oh, that's the Jesuit hospital." I said, "Good, they came to destroy this Sri Rangam temple. It's such a beautiful thing. And to build that. If I can possibly fight this importation of Christianity in India, I shall do it."[32]

And I went all over South India with a magnifying glass, figuratively of course, trying to find an organization standing up for the Hindu, that is to say, Aryan tradition. Against *all* philosophies of equality and all religions of equality. I found none. Anyhow, I went up North, and I reached Bengal, and I stayed in Bengal some time.

And I went back to Europe, but just for a very, very short time, in 1935. Why? Just to do my *soutenance de thèse*, that is to say, to take my doctoral degree. And a job was waiting for me on my return after I would learn Hindi. The job was in Jallundhar College, not very far from Delhi, to teach the history of England and the history of India. But that was to be in '36.[33] Before that, I had to learn Hindi thoroughly. So I came back from Europe, and I went to Shantiniketan, the open-air university near Bolpur in Bengal, to learn Hindi and to perfect my Bengali.[34] I used to speak Bengali and write Bengali already. I started learning Bengali in France. I didn't know a single Bengali or a single Indian, but I had

---

[32] Cf. *Pilgrimage*, 127–28.

[33] In the fifth tape, Savitri confuses the chronology a bit by adding, after mentioning the Jallundhar position, "Oh, I went to Mathura. I worked in Mathura for one year, 1936. '37 I went into Jallundhar, and I left. '36 I came to Calcutta. End of '36. I can't remember exactly when it was. I get mixed up in all this."

[34] Savitri records her impressions of Shantiniketan in her *L'Etang aux lotus* [*The Lotus Pond*] (Calcutta: Savitri Devi Mukherji, 1940), ch. 9, "Demeures de paix" ("Abodes of Peace").

read in French translation a novel of Saratchandra Chatterji, *Srikanta*,[35] and I liked it very much, and I said, "If I have to begin with one Indian language, I'll begin with this one." All right. So I wanted to perfect my Bengali and to learn Hindi. I went to Shantiniketan.

So in Shantiniketan what happened? I knew the great poet Rabindranath Tagore.[36] I didn't know that he was surrounded by all sorts of people, some of them former missionaries and some of them Jews. I didn't know that his teacher of German was called Margaret Spiegel, a Berlin Jewess with 13 languages. Not stupid at all. She had been two years at Gandhi's ashram, telling Gandhi, of course, that there is nothing more opposed to his non-violence than National Socialism, trying to drive him away from all these kinds of things. And the secretary of Rabindranath Tagore, Amiya Chakravarty,[37] a Bengali Brahmin, thought it good to introduce me to Margaret Spiegel. He thought to himself, "Now this one is a white woman, *mem-saheb*, and this one too" — he didn't see any difference between the Jewess and me; she didn't look Jewish, in fact — "I'm going to bring them together, the two *mem-sahebs*." I was introduced.

You can imagine what I was in 1935. I was 29 years old. And I was arrogant. I felt that whatever happens to me in one part of the world, I always have Germany to go to. I have a place to go

---

[35] Saratchandra Chatterji, *Srikanta*, trans. J.-G. Delamain (Paris: Stock "Le Cabinet Cosmopolite" No. 39, 1930). The novel is available in English translation under the author's full surname (Chatterji is a contraction): Saratchandra Chattopadhyaya, *Srikanta*, trans. Aruna Chakravarti (New York: Penguin, 1993). Chatterji/Chattopadhyaya lived from 1876–1938. He was a fervent Indian nationalist and poured these sentiments into his novels. *Srikanta*, however, deals more with sexual politics and is an attack on hypocritical social norms, including the caste system.

[36] Rabindranath Tagore (1861–1941) was born in Calcutta to a wealthy and powerful Brahmin family. The author of some 50 volumes of poetry, plus novels, short stories, essays, dramas, travelogues, and two autobiographies, he was awarded the 1913 Nobel Prize in Literature. Tagore founded Shantiniketan in 1901.

[37] Amiya Chakravarty (1901–1986) was a well-known poet, critic, and translator. He was secretary to Rabrindranath Tagore from 1924–1933. He later held professorships at Boston University's Smith College and the State University of New York at New Paltz.

to. I couldn't care less. So I talked very frankly. So she at once found out who I was, and I didn't mind telling her. And she said to me, "I left Germany of my own free will—I wasn't turned out—because I didn't want to see the shadow of a Nazi anymore, not the shadow of one. And I come here, in a place of Indian culture, and I meet you, and you are worse than the whole pack rolled in one."

I said, "Why am I worse than the whole pack rolled in one? That's a great honor." She said, "Well, over there they goosestep along the streets and they sing, '*Deutschland gehört uns heute, und morgen die ganze Welt.*' But they don't think of the *ganze Welt* at all. They think only of their blessed Germany." I said, "That's natural." "But you," she said, "you think of the world. You are not a Nazi because Hitler saved Germany. On the contrary, you like Germany, because it's Hitler's country." I said, "Yes, exactly, exactly."

So I said, "What do you think I came to do?" "You came to make the élite of India your allies." I said, "Exactly." She said, "There you are. You're worse than the whole pack rolled in one. They never thought of that." I said, "If I had spoken to the Führer, we would've done something like that." I think it was the best thing to do. Well, in fact, the German Counsel-General of Calcutta in those days, and long before those days, did that.[38] She said, "You want to conquer India." I said, "I want to conquer *Aryan* India." There are Indians who are perfectly White and Aryan, and there are some a little bit darker. They're still Aryan. They're not any darker than southern Europeans and lighter than some southern Europeans.

---

[38] In *Souvenirs et réflexions*, Savitri mentions that during his term of service, Dr. Eduard von Selzam (1897–1980), German Counsel-General in Calcutta since 1931, collaborated closely with Savitri's future husband, A. K. Mukherji in the publication of his periodical *The New Mercury* (*Souvenirs et réflexions*, 275). For more on A. K. Mukherji, see §7 below. Nicholas Goodrick-Clarke also names two other German Counsels, Baron Wernher von Ow-Wachendorf and his successor Count von Podewils-Durniz, who may also have collaborated with Mukherji. (See Nicholas Goodrick-Clarke, *Hitler's Priestess: Savitri Devi, the Hindu-Aryan Myth, and Neo-Nazism* [New York: New York University Press, 1998], 67.)

And then I joined the Hindu Mission. The Hindu Mission in Calcutta was an organization headed by Satyananda Swami in order to bring back to Hinduism Indians who had severed themselves from it and to make the greatest number of Indians possible call themselves Hindus whether they were or not. Because according to Hindu tradition, the aborigines are not considered Hindus nor are the untouchables, but the British had introduced democracy into India. One man, one vote. And they were all voting.

And they introduced the Communal Award, voting by religion. Bengal having 55% Mohammedans, the Bengal assembly had to have 55% representative Mohammedans. So you could only change that by making a few Mohammedans convert to Hinduism. And that's what the Hindu Mission did, in spite of the tradition that doesn't want any form of Hindu converted to Islam or Christianity or anything else to come back into his caste. Even today, I think, in the South you cannot come back to it. The Hindu Mission took them back into their castes. Only for that.

I worked for the Hindu Mission for years and had to travel all over Bengal, Bihar, and Assam, lecturing in Bengali mostly in Bengal and Assam, lecturing in Hindi in Bihar.[39] I was allowed to sprinkle my lectures with other things, especially with quotations from Mein Kampf, as much as I liked. And when I had met the head of the Hindu Mission, the founder, Satyananda Swami, I told him, "Look here, I'm a European pagan. I'm a disciple of Hitler. Can I talk my own talk in my lectures?" He wanted to employ me as a lecturer. He said, "You can say whatever you like. I consider your Hitler as an incarnation of the gods, at least of the god Vishnu, who is the god that keeps the world in place against destruction, against decadence. I honor him. You can talk about him as much as you like. Only you must talk about him from the Indian point of view. You must interest the Indians in him." I said, "All right." And I did that.

In my speeches in the name of the Hindu Mission, I used to quote Mein Kampf. I used to quote The Myth of the Twentieth Century by Alfred Rosenberg. I used to quote quite a number of things.

---

[39] In Defiance Savitri describes her lectures as "violent, eloquent speeches" (Defiance, 292).

And I used to tell them that there was a movement in Europe in favor of the original Aryan values, just as there are in India people who stick up for the Aryan values. And I was quite pleased. I remained in the service of the Hindu Mission all these years. Of course staying in Calcutta now and then and mostly traveling in Bengal, Bihar and Assam. I learnt a lot of knowledge through these travels, a lot about the people of India and the different castes.[40]

7. ASIT KRISHNA MUKHERJI[41]

In those days I didn't know Mr. Mukherji yet. I was far from suspecting his existence. But I knew a paper called *The New Mercury*. It was published in Calcutta by A. K. Mukherji. And that paper was the only Hitler paper in India. It was a cultural and somewhat political magazine, but more cultural than anything else. There were articles in it like the history of the swastika, like an article from the Führer himself, recopied, "Nation and Architecture." More of the articles showing the homeland of the Aryans, and this and that. I used to read it with delight.

And the ordinary newspapers were more and more anti-German. That is to say, from the landing of Jews in India in 1933, the money that they gave to the papers made the press, slowly, slowly turn. And from 1937 onwards, it was completely on the other side. There were stories of Nazi atrocities or oppression, tyranny and whatnot, and the "poor Jews." And people talked of it. And I used to say, "Well, the poor Jews did so many things in the Old Testament that I have no time for them. Their atrocities in the Old Testament are much worse." "Oh that was a thousand years ago, thousands of years ago!" "It doesn't matter to me. It's all the same. Time doesn't count for me."

Anyhow, I used to read this paper with delight. And one day I asked some Greeks whom I knew, "Could I not meet that gentleman who edits this paper?" They said, "Yes, well, he was a

---

[40] For an account of Savitri's travels in India up to the end of 1936, see *The Lotus Pond*.

[41] Asit Krishna Mukherji (Mukherji is a contraction of Mukhopadhyaya), was born on 13 April 1904 and died in New Delhi on 21 March 1977.

neighbor of ours once. We can introduce you." And I was introduced to Mr. Mukherji, on the 9th of January 1938. And when I
told him I was in Shantiniketan once, he said, "Oh, you are the
person whom I refused to meet in 1935." I said, "You refused to
meet me?" He said, "Yes. I didn't know you. Somebody just told
me that there was a Greek woman in Shantiniketan who had
more or less my ideas. And I said, 'She cannot be. She cannot
have my ideas, and in that case, why did she come to that Jewish
nest Shantiniketan? Why didn't she go somewhere else? She must
really be a Jewess out of the ghetto of Salonika.'" I said, "Of
course I wasn't that." He said, "I know it now. I can see it now.
But why did you go to that place, Shantiniketan?" I said, "Because it was cheap. One pound and a half, and you were living
there with all expenses for six months. And I had not much money. I went there to learn Hindi." "All right, I know it now. I'm
very sorry I couldn't get to meet you then." Like that. That was
Mukherji.

Anyhow, we had a talk. We had a long talk. One of his first
questions was, "What do you think of Dietrich Eckart?"[42] I was
amazed to see an Indian talking of Dietrich Eckart. I said, "Well, I
know he died on the 23rd of December, 1923, just after the *Putsch*.
He was a poet. '*Deutschland, erwache,*'[43] I remember his poem.
'*Sturm, Sturm, Sturm. Deutschland, erwache!*'" He didn't say anything. In fact, Eckart was much more than that. He was initiated
into the *Thule-Gesellschaft*,[44] the secret initiatic society that was behind National Socialism. Probably Mukherji knew that. And I
didn't know it in those days.

And then we talked of all sorts of things. We talked of history.
I was amazed at the quantity of Byzantine history he knew. I said,
"Where did you ever come to learn Byzantine history?" He said,
"You see, my thesis was on imperial Russia, the connection be-
tween imperial Russia and Britain in the 19th century, their deal-

[42] Dietrich Eckart (1868–1923) was a poet, playwright, and journal-
ist as well as an early member of the NSDAP. Hitler dedicated *Mein
Kampf* (1925) to him.

[43] "Germany, Awake!"

[44] On the Thule Society, see Nicholas Goodrick-Clarke, *The Occult
Roots of Nazism: Secret Aryan Cults and their Influence on Nazi Ideology*
(New York: New York University Press, 1992), 135–52.

ings especially in connection with India and Afghanistan." It was
the thesis of his doctorate at the University of London.[45] "And
imperial Russia is the continuation of Byzantium. You cannot understand the history of Russia and the mentality of the Czarist
people unless you have a knowledge of Byzantine history. So I
learnt about Byzantine history." I said, "Congratulations, you do
things thoroughly. I like that." And we became friends. I saw in
him a person who really had our ideas, not because he was directly Hitlerian, but he was Hitlerian because he was an orthodox
Brahmin. And he saw in our *Weltanschauung* the Western edition,
if you like, of his own philosophy, his philosophy putting the Aryan race above others and the idea of hierarchy of all races under
the Aryan.

He had just given up *The New Mercury*. That is to say, *The
New Mercury* was confiscated. He had no copies of it. It was
forbidden by the British, according to the change of their policy
of 1937. And I said, "What are you doing now?" He said,
"Now *The New Mercury* is suppressed, and I am doing something else. I'm connected with the Japanese." He was, in fact,
the right hand of the Japanese Consul-General.[46] He said, "I'm
giving out a new paper, *The Eastern Economist,* for Japanese interests. Would you like to write in it?"

So I wrote an article on Shinto in it. I wrote an article on the
14th of August, 1281, in it.[47] It was the day in which the fleet of
Kublai Khan attacked Japan—or wanted to attack Japan. It was
dispersed by the storm. Like the invincible Armada of 1588 in
England. And the Japanese emperor, Meiji, wrote a poem about
it: "Up to the end of your capacity, do whatever you can, and
then when that is done, and you can do no more, kneel down and
thank the Divine Wind of Ise for dispersing the Tartar fleet."

---

[45] A. K. Mukherji's dissertation was entitled, "A Study of British
Diplomacy in Central Asia."

[46] According to Goodrick-Clarke, K. Yonezawa and his successor
T. Yoshida (*Hitler's Priestess*, 72).

[47] See Savitri's essay, "Shinto: La via degli dei," ("Shinto: The Way
of the Gods"), *Arya* 4 (1980). This is an Italian translation by Vittorio
de Cecco from the English original, the fate of which is unknown.
This essay probably contains the substance of Savitri's essays for *The
Eastern Economist*.

The Divine Wind of Ise is the most sacred temple of Japan. It's at Ise that the government of Japan sends a delegation if they want to do something important. In 1940 or '41, they sent a delegation asking the gods, "Shall we attack the United States?" The gods said, "Yes." So they attacked the United States. In '45, after the Hiroshima bomb, they said, "Are we to surrender and save the country, or are we to die, all of us?" The gods said, "No, don't die. Japan must live." It was a good time to surrender, and they surrendered.

They gave great politeness to the Americans, and when the Americans said, "Democracy is the best thing." They said. "Oh yes, yes, yes." "Your emperor is no god." "All right, he's a man." "And you mustn't teach such nonsense as the *Kojiki* in the schools." The *Kojiki* is the history of the gods. "You mustn't teach that in the schools. That's nonsense." "All right, we won't teach it." And this and that, and smiles up to here, and salutations. Until the Americans gave a good peace treaty and went away. And when they were away, the next day they taught the *Kojiki* in the schools. They said, "Now you're off. We can do what we like now." I wish the Germans had the same attitude. I wish the Germans had the same attitude.

And not only that, but the thing they did—and it's the first thing I'd see if I ever went to Japan—they erected a temple to Tojo, to the prime minister of Japan in the great days, the ally of Adolf Hitler, and to his co-war criminals who were hanged by the Americans the same time as him. They have a temple. And where is the temple? A few footsteps away from Hiroshima, at Gamagore. The children of the schools go to see Hiroshima. They kept a part of it as the Americans left it, and they told the children, "This is American handiwork. This is the destruction of the atom bomb. Now we are going to pay our respects to the great minister Tojo. Now we are going to Tojo's temple. We are going to burn a stick of incense in front of Tojo's picture and the picture of other so-called war criminals," and that's that.

Why doesn't Germany do that? Imagine German school children going to see the ruins of Dresden or the ruins of some other place, left as they were, and told what destruction the Allies had wrought on Germany and then going to a temple, a place where pictures of Adolf Hitler, pictures of Göring, pictures of Himmler and other people would be honored, and getting a speech there and getting some uplifting talk. Imagine that. That will come one day. Not tomorrow.

[Before founding *The New Mercury*, Mr. Mukherji traveled in Soviet Russia for two years.] Without knowing who he was, and thinking he was just an Indian student, they wanted to make him into an Indian propagandist of Communism. So they caressed him. They were nice to him. He traveled first class, that is to say, soft instead of hard, all through Russia. But he knew Russian. He had learnt Russian from the White Russians in London, and he spoke Russian, and he wrote Russian, and he was a very good Russian scholar.

And he looked at everything. They took him to the Pavlov place, where Pavlov had tortured these poor dogs. He was disgusted. He hated it. They took him to factories. He was not interested. They said, "What would you like to see?" "I'd like to see old churches." Anyhow, they took him to see old churches. They took him to see whatever he liked. And in the end they said, "Would you like to be a Communist agent for us in India?" He said, "Not exactly. You see, I'd rather stay with my family. I don't want to put my nose in politics," and this and that.

He wanted to come back through Central Asia. That the British didn't allow. He had to come back through London. He came back. Landed in India. The Indian Communists opened their arms to him: "Mukherji, you were two years in the Soviet paradise, how lovely! You're going to write for us now." He said, "Not a bit." "Not a bit?" "I like the Russian people. They are people, some good, some bad, like everybody, but I don't like the régime." "You don't like the régime? Funny." "I don't like it. That's all. I'm not going to write for you."

And then the anti-Communists, Western-style, also took him into their confidence: "Well, Mukherji, that's wonderful. You were two years in Russia and you don't like the Communist people. You don't like Communism. You write for us. We are anti-Communists." He said, "You are not anti-Communists. I put you in the same bag as the Communists. I'm not going to write for you either. You're just the same thing. What is the difference? Personal capitalism, struggle for money, and there is state capitalism. What's the difference? You are *not* what I want."

And after a month or two out he comes with the only Nazi paper in India, *The New Mercury*. The Communists took the first edition and came to him: "Mukherji, A. K. Mukherji, is that you? It can't be you, because you spent two years in Russia. You can't write this kind of stuff." He said, "Well, you see, I leave it to you. A. K. Mukherji can be many people. A. K. is a common initial." Anyhow, they found out it was him. They were absolutely against him after that. In fact, he has a sister whose eldest son was a Communist. He never spoke to his sister or to his nephew. To this day he did not want me to go to her house for an interview. The second son is also a Communist.[48] Anyhow, quite a number of Communists are among the high caste Indians. I don't know why. It's like that.

[Mr. Mukherji] was sent to Europe by his brother. His brother was the head of the family because his father was dead when he was five years old. It was a large family, eight children. Two sisters married. They are both living still. Older than he. There were six brothers in all, six brothers and two sisters. And they belonged to a very old Brahmin family. His brother, Ashoka—I don't know if he's living still; if he is living he must be over 80—is perfectly, well, you would take him for a European if you see him. And Mr. Mukherji himself—if you see Sophia W—, who is Greek, that is to say, European—he was fairer than her in complexion.[49] He had dark eyes, and he was a Mediterranean type, but he was fairer than Sophia who was a European. And one brother is a little darker than he. His sister is darker than he. He was one of the fairest. And he felt Aryan.

You know the Brahmins of Bengal are not really Bengalis. Bengal, in the early Middle Ages up to the beginning of the 12th century, was a Buddhist country. Buddhists have no caste. That is to say, there was a mixture. There was a mixture of aborigines,

---

[48] The two Communist nephews are the well-known writers Subrata Banerjee and Sumanta Banerjee. According to Subrata Banerjee, Savitri informed him of A. K. Mukherji's death and Banerjee's "younger brother" (whom I am assuming is Sumanta Banerjee) performed the funeral rites at the request, or at least with the acquiescence, of Savitri Devi (Subrata Banerjee, "Note on Ashit Krishna Mukherjee," unpublished ms.).

[49] Sophia W— was one of Savitri's friends in New Delhi.

Dravidians, all sorts of people, but no Brahmins. Then came a
dynasty after the Palas called the Sena dynasty. And the second
king of that dynasty, Vallaala Sena, wanted to introduce the caste
system into Bengal. So he had to import Brahmins. There were
none! He imported them from North India.

He imported several families, and those families married only
among themselves, because there are very strict rules for marriage
in India. You have to marry within your *sreni*. A *sreni* is a subdivision of a caste. And outside your *gotra*. A *gotra* is a subdivision of
a *sreni*. For instance, a Mukherji is what they call in Bengal a *Rari*
Brahmin. He should marry the daughter of a *Rari* Brahmin. But
not a Mukherji. Somebody outside his *gotra*. All the Mukherjis are
one *gotra*. He has to marry a Banerjee or a Chatterji or a Gongody.
But not one of a different *sreni*. Not a Laieri, not a Maitra, not
what they call the *Barendra* Brahmins. He has to marry within the
Rari Brahmins.

Now how did he marry me? Well, he married me for me not
to be interned at the beginning of the war. If he had not married
me, I would've been in a concentration camp. All people who
were known to be against the British, known to have subversive
ideas, were put into camps immediately after the war began. So
we married at the outbreak of the war on the 29th of September
1939.[50] We had a religious ceremony according to Hindu rites as
well as a civil ceremony because I had embraced Hinduism long
before I met him. The religious ceremony was made by the Brahmin of the Hindu Mission, the priest Girija Kanta Goswami who
knew me very well, and he married us in front of the sacred fire
as was done in the old Aryan days. It's a beautiful ceremony. We
were taking as the witnesses the stars, moon, and sun. Although it
was, of course, 10:00 at night. Marriages are done at night in Bengal. I wore a bright purple sari and he was in white with garlands
of flowers around our necks.[51]

And we married, and we went, he to his house and I to my
house. In the end, after several months, we took a flat: four rooms,
two for me and two for him. And we had no kind of marital life
at all. We were ideological co-fighters, friends, and that's all. We

[50] This is the date of the civil marriage ceremony.
[51] The date of the religious ceremony was 9 June 1940 (*Defiance*, 497).

used to meet now and then to discuss things, to read books together, and that was all.

The rules of orthodox Hinduism are very strict concerning marriage. According to the Aryan tradition in India, a Hindu Brahmin is not allowed to marry even a Brahmin of his province if that Brahmin is not of the same sub-caste, *sreni*, as himself. He is to marry outside his *gotra* and inside his *sreni*. If the *Rari* Brahmin is not allowed to marry even a *Barendra* Brahmin of Bengal, how can he be allowed to marry someone else outside? He's not allowed to marry a Kashmiri Brahmin. He's not allowed to marry a Madrasi Brahmin. Even if the Kashmiri Brahmin is perfectly White. And if he marries somebody else, he should not have any children. He should not found a family like that. You don't found a family in India. You enter a family that is already existing, existing for centuries. You continue a family, and you cannot continue a family if you are not of the proper caste.

So we decided not to have any family at all, and not to have any family at all means no intimacy at all. If you don't want a family, you have no business having anything else but Platonic relations with your fellow beings. Ceasing Platonic relations is only when you want a family. We kept up to it. We kept up to it to the very end. Because we believe in that. We believe that the forces that God has given us for the sacred purpose of continuing our families, for giving children of our race to the world, are not meant for a pastime. They are not an entertainment. They are not, as you say, superfluous forces that should be wasted. Either they should be used for the divine purpose or not used at all. So we became friends. We became friends, and we remained friends. It was perfectly all right. I was quite happy, most happy. We had the Führer. Our link between us was the Führer.

8. WORLD WAR II, 1939–45

One of the first things Mr. Mukherji told me was, "You go back to Europe. There will soon be war, and you'll be much more useful over there than you are here. Go back to him who is in reality life and resurrection, the only one there is today, and he is the one man in the world who will appreciate you and understand you." What a damn fool I was. I thought myself useful in India. I was working for the Hindu Mission fighting Christian missionaries, fighting Islamic missionaries, fighting Communism, fighting anything that was against Hindu tradition, Aryan tradition. And I thought I was useful. I was a damn fool. I thought, "Who is going to make quotations out of *Mein Kampf* if I go away?" As if this was important, making quotations of *Mein Kampf* in Bengali or in Hindi, in Bihar, in Bengal, in Assam. I had the three provinces under my jurisdiction. I used to travel among these three provinces. Who is going to do that if I go away? I thought that important. I was—I repeat for the third time—I was a damn fool. And I didn't go to Germany. I said I'd go later on, and I'd show the Führer the few things I'm trying to do in India. I wanted to tell the Führer, "I'm bringing you an alliance of the élite of India." I wanted to tell him that. If the war had turned out differently, perhaps I could've been able to tell him that. I don't know.

Anyhow, I didn't go, and the war came, the declaration of war. And one day Mr. Mukherji came to me with a poster: War, W-A-R. He said, "What are you going to do now?" I said, "I would so much like to go to Europe now." He said, "I'll try to arrange with the Italian Consul"—he was his best friend—"to send you to Europe—send you first to Italy and then to Germany.[52] And we'll arrange for you to speak in Bengali. We have somebody for Hindi, but you know Bengali even better than Hindi. In Bengali and in modern Greek, you'll speak on the German radio war propaganda." I said, "I'd be delighted. Under Goebbels. I'd be delighted. And Goebbels would probably introduce me to the Führer one day or another." I was delighted.

Of course I'd have to renew my passport. My passport was exhausted. And, for convenience of course, it would be better if I had an Indian passport. And not only for this convenience, but they were interning in those days all the people who were against the British war effort. And Mr. Mukherji told me, "Everybody knows in the secret places"—he was in touch with the secret police himself through some Bengalis who were working for it—"Everybody knows that you are against the British war effort. You are for Hitler. You will be interned automatically. They are interning so many people. The only way not to be interned is to

[52] The Italian Consul is probably Camillo Giuriati. See *Pilgrimage*, 11.

take an Indian name and an Indian nationality. If you like, I'll give you my name." And that's how we married.[53]

Now we had to do something during the war. We couldn't really stay like that. We wanted to help Germany. We wanted to help Hitler. It was very difficult to help Adolf Hitler during the war. It was far away. All the Germans were gone. But there were some who were there. And there were the allies of Adolf Hitler, the Japanese, who were on the spot.[54] And Mr. Mukherji was the right hand of the Japanese Consul in Calcutta. He was very, very friendly with them. He was, in fact, the only foreign advisor, the only non-Japanese, that they ever met in whom the Japanese had full confidence.

They didn't have any confidence in me. Oh, no. I was a White woman. I was nothing. I happened to be his wife, all right, all right. We have no objection to that. Women aren't much in Japan. But at least a woman like me, not a Japanese woman. There are some very celebrated Japanese women in Japanese history. But they had no confidence in me, till 1945. In fact, till 1949, till I proved that I was on their side and on Hitler's side.

For the time being, they just were friendly with him, and he knew that they were going to attack Burma. They were going to come nearer to India, and our dream was they would enter India, go east, and the Germans after the attack on Russia would enter it from the northwest, and then meet in Delhi, and in the Red Fort the Führer would be proclaimed *Weltführer*.[55] That was my dream. That was his dream too.

The war rolled on. Burma was the first target. The Japanese were in Burma from 1941. In 1942 they conquered Burma. The Americans and British fought against them.

Now, during the whole war, we brought Americans to our

[53] As explained in §12 below, Savitri's new passport came too late, and she was unable to return to Europe. It was impossible for her to go to Italy after it entered the war on the German side on 10 June 1940, and it was impossible for her to go to France unless she was a supporter of de Gaulle.

[54] On the fifth tape, Savitri relates an interesting fact: "He could not go with me to Japan. We were supposed to go to Japan in '42. We couldn't go."

[55] World leader.

house. We got in touch with Americans. I used to bring them from some club for them and for the British. The club had a name: [The East and West Club.[56] Its purpose was to help them to] understand Indian ways. To eat with their fingers, curry and other Indian dishes. To know something about astrology, something about yoga, something like that. So I used to go to the club with a nice sari and my big swastika earrings. The swastika is also an Indian symbol. It's an Aryan symbol, in fact a neolithic symbol, for all Aryans of that time period. And the Americans would look at me queerly and say, "Why are you wearing that?" "But that's an Indian religious symbol. My husband's an Indian." "Why doesn't he come to the club?" I said, "Because, you see, he's very orthodox. He won't eat things that are cooked differently from what he's accustomed to eat. He won't eat cakes that have eggs in them and this and that. He doesn't come." "Can we see him?" I said, "Well, what do you want to see him for?" "He must be an interesting man." I said, "Yes, a very interesting man. He does yoga, and he's a very good astrologer." "Oh! A good astrologer! Let's go to see him." Every week I had a jeep or two jeeps full of Americans to our house.

Now my brother-in-law Ashoka gave us whiskey. I never touched it, of course. I never touched alcohol in my life. I don't like it. I don't like the smell of it. Mr. Mukherji would distribute whiskey to them and talk. I was never present at the talks. At most I would tell them, "You can see my cats." I had a number of cats in my room. I loved all felines, cats and leopards and tigers and lions, whatever you like. They would say, "Oh, so many cats, good, good, good. And are you interested in anything? What are you interested in? Are you interested in the war?" I said, "Not at all. I am interested in antiquity and cats," and in fact I was writing a book on Akhnaton of Egypt in those days — antiquity.[57]

---

[56] *Defiance*, 37.

[57] Savitri completed her book *Joy of the Sun: The Beautiful Life of Akhnaton, King of Egypt Told to Young People* (Calcutta: Thacker, Spink & Co., 1942) on 14 February 1942. In May of 1942 she began writing her major book on Akhnaton, *A Son of God: The Life and Philosophy of Akhnaton, King of Egypt* (London: Philosophical Publishing House, 1946) (later retitled *Son of the Sun*). Savitri also published two other works on Akhnaton while in India, a pamphlet entitled *Akhnaton's*

So he talked with them. I was never once present at the talks. But I know the Americans were delighted with his talk. They thought he was the best democrat in the world. They presumed without asking—they never asked him—that he must be anti-Nazi, and they started talking. And when they had eaten and drank, they talked a lot, some of them. The most talkative—funny enough—some of the best ones for giving information, were top-ranked Jewish officers in the American army. I remember one who gave us very good information.

And the information would go to four Indians who used to cross the Burmese frontier every fortnight or so and go straight to Yamagata's headquarters the next morning and give the information to Yamagata, the head of the Japanese in Burma.[58] And like that quite a number of things happened in Burma that were unexpected. At least three top-secret aerodromes were blown to pieces. Some units of the Allies were encircled and had to surrender. Anyhow, Burma was conquered. And the Japanese entered India in Imphal, and when they were in Imphal we thought, "Now they are going up to Delhi." They didn't go as far as Delhi.

Anyhow, I'll always remember Mr. Mukherji coming one day to my room at midnight and telling me, "So-and-so, American Jew, has just told me that such-and-such aerodrome was exploded the other day. It was bombed, bombed to pieces." I said, "Very good." He said, "Yes, and you told me that I was wrong in calling Göring that 'Fettsack,' 'fat bag' in front of that Jew. If I had not showed him that kind of disposition, he never would have told me anything about the aerodrome. So I suppose Göring wouldn't mind to be called, in a joking manner, to an American Jew, 'fat bag,' if that's the result. What do you think?" I said, "I think you are a diplomat." I said, "And you must be a diplomat. If you cannot use force of arms, you must use force of diplomacy. What can you do in the wartime? We can't support the Führer

---

Eternal Message: A Scientific Religion 3,300 Years Old (Calcutta: A. K. Mukherji, 1940), which was completed in Calcutta in December, 1940, and another work, *A Perfect Man: Akhnaton, King of Egypt*, now apparently lost, which was published after *Akhnaton's Eternal Message* and before *Joy of the Sun*.

58 Probably Vice-Admiral Yamagata Seigo, d. 1945.

directly. We must support him through his allies." And so that's what we did.[59]

Anyhow, the war turned out badly. We expected it to turn out well. It turned out badly. We expected Stalingrad to fall, and while the battle of Stalingrad was on, I remember Mr. Mukherji sipping Greek coffee that I had prepared for him in our house, sitting near next to me and telling me, "Look here, you have seen the Khyber Pass, the way of conquerors, these great blood-red rocks and ochre rocks and white rocks, all sorts of rocks. There's not a blade of grass. It goes from Afghanistan to India." "Yes, in 1936 I went through the Khyber Pass myself. It's a beautiful place, a wild place."[60] "Imagine then, now, the German army coming right through there. Imagine the echoing of the tanks, and imagine the song:

Wir werden weiter marschieren,
Wenn alles in Scherben fällt,
Denn heute gehört uns Deutschland
Und morgen die ganze Welt.

"That song in the Khyber Pass. We are the third wave," he told me. "The first wave: the first Aryans who came to India—although there were several waves, they were not one—they came from the northwest. And second: the troops of Alexander. And third, this is the third wave." I said, "Yes, wonderful, wonderful. And they'll meet with the Japanese, with our allies. They'll meet in Delhi, and in Delhi there will be a big ceremony at the Red Fort, and our Führer will be their Führer. I'm going to buy a sari to wear on that day."[61]

---

[59] In *Defiance*, Savitri reveals that by 1949 at least, the British were aware of Mukherji's espionage activities. They asked Savitri specifically if she had ever taken part in Mukherji's conversations with the Americans. See *Defiance*, 102–3.

[60] For Savitri's experiences in Afghanistan, see *The Lotus Pond*, ch. 8, "La terre sans maître" ("Land without a Master").

[61] In another telling of this story in the interviews, Savitri mentions that the Red Fort is, "the ancient stronghold of the Moguls in Delhi. The treasures are lost. They are all in Persia. They were taken in 1739 by the Persian king Nadir Shah who looted India, looted Del-

And I went and bought a beautiful silk sari with a border of silhouette swastikas as big as that, ten centimeters, all around the bottom, and I didn't wear it yet. I was going to wear it at the Red Fort only for the Führer. But I showed it to my mother-in-law. And my mother-in-law, an orthodox Hindu, knowing more than I do about the right spirit of things, said, "You are not ashamed of yourself, you a disciple of Adolf Hitler, to buy such a thing?" I said, "Why?" She said, "But a sari will drag on your feet. The border will touch your feet. Isn't it a shame the holy sign, the swastika, will touch your feet? That shouldn't be done. It's an insult to the holy sign." And she was right from the Hindu point of view. You should never have a holy sign on a sari border because the sari border touches one's feet. It's not right. So I said, "All right, I won't wear it. I'll buy something else." She said, "Buy something else with a different pattern. The swastika, the holy swastika must not touch your feet." Anyhow, that sari I took back to Europe. It was stolen from me on the 16th of August 1946, with many other saris, in my suitcase, in the Saint-Lazare station in Paris.

In the meantime, things went on. The war went worse and worse, worse and worse. Whatever we did was useless. We felt it was useless. So in October '44, I had enough of it. I didn't want to know when the capitulation would come. So I left my cats in the charge of Mr. Mukherji and of the servant we had, a very reliable good servant, and I took the train for the South.[62] I left Calcutta, and I traveled all through the sacred places and temples and places where I had no risk of meeting anybody. I didn't want to know when the capitulation would come. I saw on my way an awful thing. At this point I was in a train, between I don't remember what place and Tiruchchendur in the South. There was a gentleman in the same compartment, and he was holding a

---

hi, and took them off; and they are in the Museum of Teheran now. Still the Red Fort is there, and it is beautiful."

[62] Savitri did not spend all of her time in the South. She took the manuscript of *A Son of God* (a.k.a. *Son of the Sun*) on her journey, and recorded that the book was finished in New Delhi (in the North of India) on 24 January 1945. See Savitri Devi, *Son of the Sun: The Life and Philosophy of Akhnaton, King of Egypt*, 2nd ed. (San Jose, California: Supreme Grand Lodge of AMORC, 1956), 303.

newspaper in English. And I read upside down the headline of the paper, "Berlin is an Inferno." I felt cold. And anyhow, I went to small towns, and I kept to temples, and I kept to the Hindus not concerned with politics. I avoided newspapers, and I didn't know when the capitulation came.

I knew it three weeks later. I was in a place called Sringeri, on the western coast, or rather on the ghats overlooking the western coast. It's a very celebrated place. It's the birthplace of one of the greatest Indians of all time, Shankara Acharya[63] of the 8th century, the one who wiped out Buddhism from India and restored the old Aryan values of Hinduism. Buddhism was casteless, you see. Hinduism is not. And I went in a café there to have a cup of coffee. I was staying at a place for tourists. And in the café there were two men from Hyderabad, two Mohammedans. Mohammedans or not, I don't know. Anyhow, they were speaking Urdu. I don't know Talibu, the language of Sringeri, or any of the languages of the South, in fact, any of the Dravidian languages. But I can understand Urdu, and they were saying, "It's three weeks already since in Europe the fighting is finished." So I knew it was finished, and I felt very cold. I didn't even finish my coffee. I felt very depressed.

And on my way back, in one of the stations of South India, there was no place at any place for tourists. There were no rooms. I was tired. I went and slept in the grass outside the station. And a policeman came. He said, "Old mother, you get up." He gave me a kick to get me up, and I got up, but I was angry. I looked at his number, and I went and reported him. "This man has mishandled me. He gave me a kick and won't allow me to sleep in the grass. I didn't know where to sleep. There was of course a kind of place for women. But with women and children and babies crying and the radio playing on. I couldn't sleep there. I told him."

His chief came and said to me, in front of him, "Is it this man?" I said, "Yes, it is this man." "Shall I dismiss him? He has eight children." I said, "No. Don't dismiss him, not because he has

---

[63] Shankara Acharya (late eighth to early 9th century AD) was born at Kalady in Kerala, but he did establish a number of *maths* or monasteries, the chief of which is at Sringeri.

eight children. I couldn't care less how many children he has. But because I cannot be responsible for this catastrophe. Why should I? Why should I bear a grudge? He's just a small man. He's not responsible for anything except for kicking me. Let him kick me. It doesn't matter. I deserve it. I deserve it because I'm on the defeated side. We shouldn't be defeated. And please don't dismiss him at all. There is one I would like to dismiss, Roosevelt." He was dead already. "Roosevelt, Churchill, Stalin—these people. I can do nothing against them. Why should I do anything against this poor man?" That's how I answered, and the man was so grateful to me. He said, "I'm so grateful to you. I have a big family depending on me." I said, "All right, all right, all right. You are just one man among millions."

And I went back to Calcutta in July '45. All the end of '44, all the beginning of '45, till July I was traveling in different parts of India, all alone, trying not to know what was coming, what was happening. So I entered the house, and knocked. Mr. Mukherji opened the door, and the first thing I said in Bengali was, "What is the news?" And he said, "What is the news? Four. Four zones. That's all. Germany cut in four." And we both felt very depressed.

He said to me, "Don't feel so depressed, because it has to go on. Things have to turn. This is the Dark Age. This is the Kali Yuga, the Dark Age, what they call the worst age in the succession of four ages. You can't expect anything better. But after the Kali Yuga, Kalki the redeemer, the one who is to put an end to this succession of ages, Kalki, he must come. He couldn't come until his forerunner came. His forerunner is Adolf Hitler. He couldn't win the war because he was nothing but the forerunner. He wasn't the one. He said so himself." Actually he did. He told that to Hans Grimm, "I'm not the one who is to come. I'm only his forerunner. I'm preparing the most urgent work, that's all. He's still to come."[64] Mr. Mukherji said, "And you live and see." I said, "I wish I had been in Europe, and I would've died." He said, "Probably you were destined to live. Everybody mustn't die. If every-

---

[64] Hans Grimm, *Warum? Woher? aber Wohin?* [*Why? Whence? and Whither?*] (Lippoldsberg: Klosterhaus Verlag, 1954), 14. For the complete quote, see ch. 4, §2, below.

body in the movement dies, there's no more movement." "All
right. All right."

Then what happened? July, August, September, October came.
There was the yearly festival, the Durga festival and the Kali festival. Kali is the dark goddess, the dark blue goddess. We call her
"*Usu Shyama*," the dark blue one. She's supposed to represent the
strength behind the Shiva entity, that is to say, the destroyer. Destroyer and creator. He's destroyer and creator. But all the gods
have a *shakti*, a female entity next to them, we call the consort of
the god. And she is the energetic side. So Kali, dark blue with four
arms, two arms holding a sword and a cut-off head, and the two
other arms bless them. She is the author of earthquakes, the author of volcanoes—the author of all that's destructive. And at the
same time she makes the corn grow. She is the universal mother.
There's a great festival for her in October, first the Durga festival,
then her festival. I went to both festivals. And she's the avenger.

And I remember myself. I took part in the festival like a frantic
person. The women smeared their hands and faces with red and
purple on that occasion. I smeared myself too. I did what they
did, and I can see myself still in the Kali temple in Calcutta in
front of the statue with the drums beating and resounding in me.
The Nuremberg trial was on at that time. It must've been in November. It had just begun or it was going to begin.[65] "Mother,
dark blue mother, avenge them, avenge them, avenge them, the
martyrs of Nuremberg." I knew they were going to be killed.
"Avenge all those they are going to nullify. A terrible time is coming, but help us to come out of it." And that idea of the dark blue
mother followed me all through my years in Europe. I'll explain
that just now.

9. RETURN TO EUROPE, 1945–46

Anyhow, end of '45 I went back to Europe. I gave my cats in
the charge of some friend I knew, a very good man who was living at a barracks.[66] He told me, "I'll distribute them in the kitch-

---

[65] The Nuremberg Tribunal began on 20 November 1945. The Kali
Puja is celebrated in October or November, on the night of the new
moon in the Bengali month of Kartik.

[66] The name of the barracks is unintelligible.

ens of the barracks. They'll have more than enough to eat and drink." Two of them, out of the 20 or 30 I had, Mr. Mukherji kept. And I left. Why did I leave? It was heartbreaking for me to leave my cats, and to leave Mr. Mukherji also. But I wanted to see Europe again, and I wanted to take part in whatever resistance there could be. I wanted to show my defiance against the victors at any cost. I'd scribble on the walls. I'd distribute papers. I'd do what I can. But I must go. But I couldn't go to Germany. I could've gone to Germany if I had been one of the followers of de Gaulle, for instance, or something like that. I could've worked with the Allies. But being what I am, I couldn't go. Directly anyhow. I said, "All right, I'll go to England, and from England I'll go. Or I'll go to France, and from there I'll go. I'll manage."

So I went to England. The first episode after my landing in England I told in my cat book, *Long-Whiskers and the Two-Legged Goddess*. It's a story. It's a true story. It's 15 years of my life in connection with cats. It's called *The True Story of a "Most Objectionable Nazi" . . . and Half-a-Dozen Cats*. Anyhow, that episode I related in that book.[67] So I'll let it alone now. The second episode: I saw a streamer across Oxford Street: "Nazi Atrocities, 1½ shillings Entrance." They were showing photographs, so-called photographs, propaganda. I didn't go in, naturally. I wasn't going to spend 1½ shillings for nothing, to see nonsense. And even if it were true, I couldn't care less.

I lived in England. Wherever I went, the radio. I didn't listen to the radio. I never listened to it. I never had a radio or a television set. I don't want one. But when I went to people's houses I had to listen to the radio. I had to hear it, the same old stuff all the time, all the time. And on my way back, on my way home, on the ship

---

[67] Savitri Devi, *Long-Whiskers and the Two-Legged Goddess: The True Story of a "Most Objectionable Nazi" . . . and Half-a-Dozen Cats* (Calcutta: Savitri Devi Mukherji, n.d.), ch. 7, "The Cat's Teaching." The episode in question is the encounter on a London street with a ginger-colored cat named Sandy. This encounter was very important to Savitri, for she apparently thought Sandy was the reincarnation of her cat Long-Whiskers, and she imagined their encounter was pivotal in the life of Sandy as well. See ch. 8, "Dreary Years" and ch. 9, "Sandy's Choice." It is very difficult to separate fact from fiction in *Long-Whiskers*, which is surely Savitri's strangest book, but also her best-written one.

already, the "de-Nazification, the re-education of Germany, the re-integration of the German people into the community of Christian nations," and all that. I hated it. If I had not felt that perhaps one day the victors would be in even a worse plight than I saw my comrades in, I would've thrown myself into the sea from the top deck. I couldn't do it. Because I thought to myself, "One day you might see better. You might see the revenge."[68] And ever since the end of the war, wherever I went, my two main occupations were feeding stray animals, especially cats, and gloating over any nasty thing that happened to any of the victors of 1945.

So I landed in England. And I got disgusted, and after a very short time, in February '46, I said, "I must go to Europe, to France, at least to see my mother again." I didn't know anything about her, just a card, a word now and then. I went to France, only to learn my mother had been in the French resistance.[69] And that separated us. I loved her deeply, until then. But that separated us forever. That separated us completely. Although, I said to myself, "She has given me my Viking blood. She is a descendant of the Vikings of Jutland, North Denmark." The first of our family came to England in the 10th century, according to her. They were not even Christians when they first came over. They were worshippers of Odin and Thor. And I have their blood. Why did she go into that nasty organization, the French resistance? Why did she allow herself to take pity on the poor Jews? And that put me against them even more.

---

[68] See *Long-Whiskers*, ch. 6, "Heliodora's Homeward Journey."

[69] Savitri's mother was 75 in 1940, so it is unlikely that her role in the resistance went beyond complaining, in private, about the German occupation. According to Terry Cooper, who knew Savitri from 1966 to 1971, Savitri told him that her mother's resistance activity consisted of a weekly tea party (Terry Cooper interview, 12 April 2002). According to Savitri's nephew Sumanta Banerjee, "She [Savitri] once told me about her mother, who lived in France, and who, when in her 80s [sic] during the Nazi occupation of France, joined the Resistance movement. By then she had disowned her daughter. I asked Savitri-*maami* how she would have received her mother. Without batting an eyelid, she said: 'I would have shot her dead'" (Sumanta Banerjee, "Memories of My Nazi *Maami* [aunt]," *Times of India*, 19 April 1999).

It was always the same thing: "The poor Jews." I said, "I couldn't care less for the poor Jews." She said, "Yes, but I do. They are human beings. They are living creatures." I said, "I don't care for all living creatures. I only care for the four-legged ones, the four-legged ones and the élite of the two-legged ones. The other two-legged ones, I don't care for. They are not the élite." In the works of a great painter, I will take the masterpieces. I don't care for the small stuff, you see. When you make an anthology of poems or works of art, you take the best and leave the rest. And if God is a great artist, I'll take the best of what he did. And I'd rather have a small picture, without any pretension, just a little *aquarelle*, a watercolor picture, done perfectly, than a big fresco with mistakes in it, that is to say, worth nothing. An animal is a small picture, God's masterpiece on a smaller scale.

I'd rather have that. I'd rather have a perfect police dog — say, an Alsatian — than a man who's not worth it. It's much nearer the spirit of selection, of perfection. It's perfect as a dog. A tiger is perfect as a feline. The best of the Aryans, say, Rudolf Hess.[70] Rudolf Hess is the top of the Aryans, to me. Top, absolutely. You have to look at his face, especially when he was young, and you see his career, to see him saying at Nuremberg, "I would follow him, as the greatest son of my country, even if there was a stake awaiting me at the end of the road." He said that. And Otto Ohlendorf.[71] To somebody I wanted to show my theory, I took the picture of

---

[70] On the first tape, Savitri is asked why the Allies continue to hold Rudolf Hess in solitary confinement: "He must know things that if he came out he would say. They couldn't keep him from saying them. He must know things. And another thing is the *rancune*, the resentment of the Russians. If he had succeeded, there would be no Communism today. Russia would've been finished. Suppose he had succeeded: England and Germany together against Russia. America wouldn't have had time to come in. It would've been finished. The Russians cannot put up with that: the idea that, if that man had succeeded, they would have been finished, and well-deserved."

[71] Otto Ohlendorf (1907–1951) held a Ph.D. in sociology and was a professor at the University of Berlin. He rose to the rank of SS-*Standartenführer* and was the commander of *Einsatzgruppe D*. He was executed as a war criminal. For more on Olendorf, see ch. 3, §9 and ch. 4, §7 below and *Pilgrimage*, 251–58.

Otto Ohlendorf and a picture of a tiger and said, "Look at this: the top of the feline race, the top of our Aryan race."

Anyhow, I didn't stay long, until August '46. I went back to England. All my luggage was stolen in Paris, on the 16th of August '46, in the *Gare Saint-Lazare*. I came back to England thinking the manuscript of my book *Impeachment of Man* was lost. I had another manuscript of it. It was printed in India 14 years later because I couldn't afford to print it before that.[72] I printed five or six hundred.

In October '46, I was staying at 104 Grosvenor Road, in a very quiet room. It was a building for nurses, a kind of hostel for nurses. They used to sleep in the daytime. At night they were on duty. So it was perfectly quiet in the daytime and at night. And that's what I wanted. I liked physical peace. So I was there on the night of the 15th to 16th of October '46. And I never read the papers. I didn't want to read them. I didn't want to see the evolution of the trial at Nuremberg. I hated it. But I couldn't sleep. I couldn't. I couldn't detach my mind from the fact that I knew, without reading the papers — everybody knew it — that the 11 were to be killed on that night.

I was thinking about it. I was thinking about it. And then suddenly, I was not asleep, but I felt exactly as I used to feel after my exercises at Hatha yoga ten years before.[73] I was no longer in that room. I don't know how I went through the walls. I was in Göring's cell. And I saw Göring just as I see you. He was seated with his hands like this.[74] And suddenly he did like that. As though he saw me and was rather astonished. I had something in my right hand, a tiny little piece of I don't know what, something I held. And I said to him, "No fear" — "*keine Angst.*" "No fear. I'm not an

---

[72] Savitri Devi, *Impeachment of Man* (Calcutta: Savitri Devi Mukherji, 1959). *Impeachment* was begun in Calcutta in July, 1945, shortly after Savitri's return from her travels around India to avoid news of the Axis defeat. It was finished in Lyons on 29 March, 1946. The Preface was written in Calcutta on 22 June 1959.

[73] See ch. 3, §9 below.

[74] According to Sven Hedin (1865–1952), diary entry of 6 June 1948, Savitri told him that, "Han satt med huvudet i händerna" ("He [Göring] sat with his head in his hands") (The papers of Sven Hedin, box 41, National Archives of Sweden).

enemy. I'm one of your people. I wish I could save you all from this ignominy, but unfortunately the heavenly powers gave me permission to save one, and one only, up to my choice, and I chose you because of your kindness to creatures. Because of your solicitude to animals."

Göring had been a hunter in his youth. He had given it up. And he liked animals, that's true. But some hunters do at the same time they're hunters. He had a leopard for a pet. The leopard used to lie at his feet and purr, like a big cat. I knew that. What I knew also was that he contributed with the Führer to the setting up of the *Reichsjagdgesetz*,[75] a book thick like that. It is much more than a regulation of hunting. It's a protection of nature. Traps are forbidden. One man hunting by himself is forbidden. It must be two. If an animal is wounded the other one will shoot it. Mustn't kill females. Mustn't, mustn't, mustn't, mustn't. The Führer could not forbid hunting altogether. He did what he could to lessen the effect, and Göring had a part of that.

That I knew before I got into this kind of queer state. I said to him, "Take this," and gave him what I had in my right hand. I said, "Take this, and don't allow these people to kill you as a criminal. You are not one. Anything but. Now I must go. Goodbye. Heil Hitler!" And I vanished. And I didn't see anything of the kind. I fell completely unconscious after that. I saw Göring, and I was unconscious. I gave him whatever I had to give him. I was unconscious.

I woke up. It was 10:00 in the morning. I never wake up at 10:00. I wake up at 6:00. I never sleep like that. I opened my eyes. I said, "What a queer experience I had. Where did I go last night?" Anyhow, I bathed quickly, and I went downstairs. It was a rainy day, drizzly. I never bought a paper as I told you. I wasn't going to buy the paper on the 16th of October, anything but. But I couldn't help seeing the headlines on the papers. There was a newspaper kiosk just opposite. Headlines like that. Eight centimeters high. "Göring found dead in his cell, half past two in the morning. Nobody knows who gave him the poison. Potassium cyanide."

I'll never forget it. And I felt cold all over my body. It seemed

---

[75] Reich Hunting Law.

to me that I saw the Nataraja, the dancing Shiva, as he is presented in Hindu temples, dancing in the clouds. And I said, "If this
has been done through me, use me in greater things still. If it's
me, that's the best thing I did in my life." I don't know what really happened, to this day. I know what experience I had. I know
what I felt. I know what I saw. I don't know anything more. Is it a
genuine experience? What is it? I just don't know. I don't pretend
to know, and I don't like to speak of what I don't know.

Less than two years later, on June 6th, 1948, I met Sven Hedin,
who is a scholar of Tibetology and has roamed all over Central
Asia and seen things in Ladakh and Tibet. I asked him, "What
would people in Ladakh or Tibet think of this?" He said, "My
dear, they would find that the most natural thing in the world.
That is no problem for a Tibetan or for a Ladakhi, for a Buddhist
Lama. No problem at all. You went into the astral plane. You
gave Göring some astral potassium cyanide, and it materialized
in his hand. He took it and died, instead of being hanged." I said,
"I wish I could've done it for the 11." "Well, you could for one. Be
thankful that you could for one." That's what Sven Hedin told
me. I don't know any more than that. I never had a psychic experience in my life. That's the only one.

10. ICELAND, 1946–47

I thought that in going to a place that had been neutral during
the war, I would get rid of all this atmosphere. It was an atmosphere of suspicion. It was an atmosphere of hatred for anything
that was National Socialism. I thought to myself, "I'll go to Iceland. Iceland is a far away place. I won't hear anything of Nazis
there." And on the 8th of November '46, I sailed to Iceland from
Hull. I had no money except £25. The boat cost £20. I landed in
Reykjavik with £5 after a very, very stormy journey.[76] The room
at the hotel cost £5. I could stay one night even without the breakfast.

So I went to the Salvation Army. Where should I go? And I

---

[76] In *Gold in the Furnace* (Calcutta: A. K. Mukherji, 1952), Savitri
describes being on a ship in a storm on the North Sea and makes it
clear that she found the experience thrillingly sublime (*Gold in the
Furnace*, 178).

told the Salvation Army that I came to learn Icelandic. "I'm interested in the language, and I'd like to get a job." And they said,
"We have no job, unfortunately for you, not with your doctorate
and your L.Sc. and M.A. degrees. The only job we have is the job
of a maidservant in a farm some miles from Reykjavik, to wash
the plates." I said, "Give me that job." They said, "You'll have
your afternoons free. You can learn Icelandic in the afternoons."
So I worked. So I washed plates for a month on an Icelandic farm.
I picked up a little Icelandic, not much of course, and I continued
picking it up. I continued learning the grammar and improving it
as much as I could. I admired the Nordic type of Iceland. Beautiful people. Beautiful people. And to think that so many of them
were on the other side. Against all I stand for. That put me out.
But they were beautiful.

And one day I had a call. The Icelandic farmer had a telephone. Iceland is an extremely modern land—very modern. And
the phone call came from an Icelander of Reykjavik telling me he
had an Austrian wife. He would like me to live in a room he
would give me for nothing. The only condition was that I would
speak French with his Austrian wife. I said, "All right." I came to
his home. The dog of the farm followed me for ten miles all
through the snow. I caressed the dog, and he even came to the
home of this Icelander. And he had something to eat and went
back. I stayed there. I stayed there nearly a year.

I saw the eruption of Mount Hekla. On the 29th of March '47 it
started, and it lasted practically the whole year. I went to see it on
the 4th of April, and I spent the night of the 5th of April on the
slopes of the erupting volcano. I wanted to spend the first night
there, but the people who were with me took my cloak, and I had
to go down again too. I couldn't stay the whole night—snowy
night too—with no cloak, no overcoat.

The second night I went up by myself, 11:00 at night, after
work. I went up to one kilometer from the big crater. There were
five small craters and two big ones. And I admired it. Imagine a
snowy landscape, a landscape of silver. The full moon over that in
a violet sky, and in front of the full moon a pennant of volcanic
ash, volcanic smoke, black, as black as can be. And hanging in the
sky, beautiful Northern Lights—green and purple, greenish-
yellow, moving like that, and purple fringe. It was beautiful.

I was in front of the lava stream. The lava of Mount Hekla is an acid lava. It contains 60–65% silica. It is thick. It doesn't run like water, like the Vesuvius lava or like the Stromboli lava. It takes time to walk, walks a few meters per day. And the top of it is with a crust as thick as five centimeters, or perhaps more. And when that breaks under the pressure of boulders from inside it makes a queer noise like broken crockery. I was there going up and down, up and down along the stream for the whole night.

And I wanted to go around the stream and go nearer to the crater. But some scientists who were there told me, "Don't do that, because the two lava streams might merge into one and you'll be in an island surrounded with lava, and you won't be able to come out." So I couldn't do that.

Suddenly flames came out—two, three places, new tiny little craters. I fled, of course. But all the time what impressed me was the roaring of the volcano, like the original sound in the Hindu tradition. The original sound of creation is "Aum."[77] The volcano says every two or three seconds, "AUM! AUM! AUM!" And the earth is trembling under your feet all the time.

Anyhow, I waited. I saw the sunrise over that. It was a beautiful landscape. And I tried to come down. Instead of coming down, I got myself lost. And I had in my hand a big slice of lava. I had some small ones too, but I had a big one as well, 10 or 15 kilos. There was a boulder there, that flung itself out of the lava stream in front of me, and it came rushing in front of my face. It was 15 or 10 centimeters in front of my face. If that had hit me I wouldn't be here to speak. And then it went cold, and when it became cold I took a slice. I took a big piece and carried it about. I thought I would give that to some friends when I got back. But it was heavy, and I was getting exhausted, and at one time I couldn't find my way back. I absolutely couldn't find my way back. I started weeping out of desperation. I said, "I crossed the river to come here. Where's the river?"

Then I found the river. I went down, and I left the big boulder alone. I couldn't carry it any longer, and then I saw somebody on the bank of the river. I saw two children. I called them. They ran away at my sight. And I saw a man, and I asked him. I said, "The

---

[77] On "Aum," see the 12 verses of the Mandukya Upanishad.

so-and-so farm, the farm from which I had started, where is it?" "It is right here. It's around the corner. You go down. You turn left. It's around the corner."

I got back to the farm, and I looked at myself in the looking glass. When I saw myself in the looking glass, I understood why the children fled. My face was black with volcanic ash and smoke, absolutely black, and my eyes were red with volcanic ash in them, and they were aching, and there were white tears in the black. I looked awful. I quite understood. Anyhow I washed my face, and I sat down and had a nice cup of coffee and had a piece of bread and butter, and the day passed on, and I went back to the place where I was staying a few miles away from the volcano. But that was a unique experience.[78]

I love volcanoes. I would like, if I had money and opportunity, to see all the volcanoes of the earth. I'd like to hear Chimborazo and Cotopaxi on the equator.[79] I'd like to hear their roaring, see their lava streams. I love them. I remember an expression that was familiar to us in school about the Pacific Ocean, "*la ceinture de feu de Pacific*" — "the fire belt of the Pacific" — Japan, Alaska, South America, all around, all around. I'd love to see them. But I only saw three in my life.[80] I don't know if I will live long enough to see another one.

Anyhow, in the summer of that year, I had a few pupils. I lived in Iceland. I got to learn Icelandic. I used to speak fluently. It's a language very akin to German, and when I knew Icelandic and could hear the radio and could hear people speak, I thought it was no better than England. Only the landscape was different.

---

[78] Cf. *Defiance*, 72–73, 203, and 456–57; cf. *Gold in the Furnace*, 258.

[79] Chimborazo and Cotopaxi are located in Ecuador. At 20,700 feet (6,310 meters), Chimborazo is the tallest mountain in Ecuador. The peak has the distinction of being the point on the Earth's surface furthest from its center. Chimborazo has not erupted during human history. At 19,374 feet (5,897 meters) Cotopaxi is the second tallest mountain in Ecuador and the tallest active volcano in the world.

[80] Presumably the aforementioned Vesuvius and Stromboli, which implies that Savitri's travels also included the Bay of Naples and Sicily. Savitri visited Italy at least four times, in 1923, 1926, 1950, and 1953. Although she did not consider herself fluent in Italian, she knew the language well enough to read it and give lectures in it.

But the mentality of the people was just the same. The same stupid anti-Nazi mentality. Fed on propaganda and fed on reaction to anything that hurts human beings.[81]

11. PROPAGANDA MISSIONS IN GERMANY, 1948–49

And then I came back to England from Iceland at the end of '47, and there I had to struggle a long time too. Until it was possible for Mr. Mukherji to send me a little money. He was himself in difficulty at the time. He had no job after the war. His past injured him a lot from the point of view of jobs. In fact, he couldn't send me anything until '48. But I already had a job. I got a job in the dancing company of Ram Gopal as a dresser.[82] I had to take care of the costumes of the girls and all that. It was not badly paid: £5 a week in England, £10 a week abroad. I was taken to France. I was taken to Norway. I was taken to Sweden. We stayed two-and-a-half months in Sweden, and that took me to June '48.

Of course, I didn't like the surroundings very much, and I don't mean the surroundings in Sweden. I mean the surroundings in the company. The stage manager, Mr. Ben Topf, was a Jew. A Jew who said in the train he would like to see the larders full and the arsenals empty in Germany, naturally. And I hated him for it. And then the impresario was another Jew, Mr. Braunschweig. A fat little man, with tiny little legs, very small bones. He looked like two threads and a fat body on that. He was very ugly. Anyhow, even if he had not been ugly, he was a damned Jew.

In Sweden on the 6th of June, 1948 I met somebody extraordinary. I met Sven Hedin.[83] I wanted to meet him. I knew he was one of our people. But they told me, "Sven Hedin meets nobody

---

[81] Savitri finished her *Akhnaton: A Play* (London: The Philosophical Publishing House, 1948) in Reykjavik on 16 April 1947. For accounts of her worship of the Midnight Sun and her visit to the Godafoss (Waterfall of the Gods) during her journey to Iceland, see *Defiance*, 80 and 335–36.

[82] Ram Gopal (1912–2003) was one of the leaders of the revival of classical Indian dance and one of the most celebrated and widely traveled dancers of the 20th century. See his *Rhythm in the Heavens: The Autobiography of Ram Gopal* (London: Secker and Warburg, 1957).

[83] On Hedin and Savitri's first propaganda trip through occupied Germany, see *Gold in the Furnace*, ch. 4, "The Unforgettable Night."

after '45. He doesn't want to meet anybody. You can try." So I wrote a letter to him, and he said, "Yes, you can come on Sunday. You can come at 2:00." I came there at 2:00, and I told him, "You see, we are going to Germany on the 14th." I had been spending two or three nights, up all night, writing papers.[84] I had intended to spend all my salary in Sweden buying chocolate, sardines, butter, cigarettes, putting a paper in each box and throwing them from the windows of the Nord Express. We were going to pass through Germany. "And I'd like to know, can we have any hope?"

He said, "Why do you say, 'Can we have any hope?' Do you have *no* hope?" I said, "Well, I'm doing this just as an act of defiance, but what to do? Those of Nuremberg, they have killed them." Sven Hedin said, "Don't fear. Germany has more such men." I said, "Yes, but when will they appear?" "They'll appear in time." And I said to him, "What about the Führer? Is he dead or alive?" He said, "Whether he's dead or alive, he's eternal. What does it matter to you?" I said, "I'll never see him if he's really not alive." "Well, even if you do see him, what difference would it make? The war is lost anyhow. And his ideas are true anyhow, even with a lost war." I said, "You are right. You are right."

And with this sort of talk and with the encouragement he gave me, he said, "You can distribute your papers if you like, all through Germany. If you get into trouble . . ." I said, "I don't care. I don't care if I spend my life in an Allied concentration camp." "In that case, carry on." I felt my wings, my old wings were growing again. He wanted to give me supper, if you please. I never expected it. "It is 7:00 now, you can have supper with me." I said, "At 7:00 I must be at the theater. It's a night show. I have to be there. It's my job." He said, "All right." So I went.

---

[84] Savitri supplies a translation of the flyer in *Gold in the Furnace*: "In the midst of untold hardships and suffering, hold fast to our glorious National Socialist faith, and resist! Defy our persecutors! Defy the people, defy the forces that are working to 'de-Nazify' the German nation and the world at large! Nothing can destroy that which is built in truth. We are the pure gold put to test in the furnace. Let the furnace blaze and roar! Nothing can destroy us. One day we shall rise and triumph again. Hope and wait! Heil Hitler!" (*Gold in the Furnace*, 34).

The first person I met in the theater was Ben Topf. He looked at me and said, "Mrs. Mukherji, what happened to you?" I said, "Nothing happened to me." "You look 20 years younger." I said, "Do I?" I said, "I met a great man." "What kind of great man?" I said, "Sven Hedin, the great explorer of Central Asia. The one who found out the real way that Lop Nor and other Central Asian lakes go around and round and round. They follow the same route." He said, "For that you are so pleased to meet that man?" And I said, "Yes I am. I am interested in archeology and explorations. What can you expect?" He didn't believe me, of course. He found it queer. He wouldn't have found it queer for long.

We went through Germany on the night of the 15th. We were in Flensburg, and on the 15th at night we left Flensburg. We had gone, of course, through Denmark. I saw the Baltic Sea in the sunshine in the morning. I said, "It's probably the last time I'll see anything beautiful like this if they put me in a camp. Well, it doesn't matter, doesn't matter a bit." And at Flensburg I started doing what I wanted to do, what I describe, or tried to describe, in *Gold in the Furnace*.

I stood at the window, in the corridor of the Nord Express. I refused to eat anything. I refused to drink anything as long as we would be on German territory. I knew Germans in those days were starving. I said, "I'd do like them: neither sleep nor eat nor drink." I was standing there, with my leaflets in packets, packets of cigars, packets of cigarettes, packets of this, packets of that. The whole way, along the railway, I could distribute as many as I liked. I saw a young couple pick up a packet of cigarettes. "Cigarettes," they said, "*Zigaretten.*" All right. They picked it up. I thought to myself, "They're going to open it and find my leaflets inside. Good." And it went on like that. All night. All night.

In the night, the middle of the night, at Duisburg—I'll never forget this—I had no more packets to distribute, except one packet of butter I was keeping for Aachen. I put leaflets, as many as I could, in my Icelandic cloak and threw that cloak on the platform. Some railway employee took it. Two railway employees, in fact. They came into the compartment. It was pitch dark. Everybody was sleeping. I was alone in the corridor.

They asked me, "Do you speak German?" I said, "Yes." "You

sent us that cloak?" I said, "Yes. It's a good cloak; it's an Icelandic cloak." "Yes," they said, "But there are dangerous papers in there. Do you know about these papers?" I said, "Yes, of course I know. I wrote them." "So you know what you are doing?" I said, "Yes, I know what I'm doing." "And why do you do it in that case?" I said, "I'm doing it because for the last 20 years at least I've been revering Adolf Hitler and loving his people because they are his people."

And I expected them to say, "All right, you're under arrest. Come along." That was my expectation. Instead of that, one of them with tears in his eyes put out his hand to me and said, "*Wir danken Ihnen im Namen ganz Deutschlands*."[85] And I felt so moved. It's one of the greatest days or the greatest nights in my life, along with the night on Hekla. It was equal to the night on Hekla. I was so pleased. He said, "But next time don't throw your cloak out where there are many people. Throw it out in the station where nobody's waiting and the train is going on." I did that.

We reached Aachen. There I gave out my last packet, some butter. A man took it and went away on a bicycle. In the distance I saw a house that was no longer a house, nothing but a cellar. In front of the cellar entrance there were two plates and two cats, each one eating from a plate. I said, "Good for you, German people. You are yourselves starving, and still you think about the poor cats." I blessed them.

And then I thought of something else. I thought, "Dear me, 500 people from Flensburg to Aachen have taken leaflets of mine. They could've had a good salary or some money. They could've had milk for their children for eight days if they had gone to the police and said, 'These things are falling from the windows of the Nord Express.' And I would be arrested. And not one of them did it. Not one of them did it. "*Heil dir, meines Führers Volk!* I'll come back."

And then we reached England again on the 16th of June. And I managed to come back. But how to come back? How to come back? I had no military permit, and it took six months to have one, and they wouldn't give one to me. England wouldn't give one to me. I tried to get a military permit. I never got one.

---

[85] We thank you in the name of all Germany.

So one day I prepared some leaflets, had them printed in England by an Eastern European who was on our side, more or less.[86] And I came to Paris. And in Paris I telephoned Georgette Soustelle, the wife of Mr. Soustelle,[87] the right hand of de Gaulle. She had been in school with me.

She was quite astonished, "You are in Europe? I thought you were in India." I said, "Yes, I was in India. I'm in Europe now." "And what do you want?" I said, "I'd like to go to Germany." "What do you want to go to Germany for?" "Just to write a book, a sort of *reportage*. I'm tired of writing about antiquity. I want to write something else. Can your husband give me a permit? I can't get one from England." She said, "All right. We'll get you a permit, all right. What's wrong with that? What were you doing, by the way, during the war?"

I said, "During the war I was feeding cats in Calcutta. I always did love cats." "All right," she said, "You always were a lover of cats. I know that. So you were feeding cats in Calcutta." I said, "Yes." I said, "What else do you expect me to do? I couldn't do anything. I couldn't do any resistance like you, because first of all I was far away." "Oh, I see, good, good, good." So in two days I had my permit.

The next day, the 11th of September 1948, I was on the train: Saarbrücken and then Germany. And I reentered Germany via Saarbrücken with this time 11,000 leaflets and posters to post up. I passed with great luck through the customs in Saarbrücken, but

[86] This Eastern European sympathizer is Count Geoffrey Potocki de Montalk (1903–1997), poet, printer, and pretender to the throne of Poland. According to Diana Hughes (interviewed 10 and 17 November 2001) and Terry Cooper (interviewed 12 April 2002), Savitri met Potocki in London in late 1945 or in 1946. On Potocki, see Stephanie de Montalk, *Unquiet World: The Life of Count Geoffrey Potocki de Montalk* (Wellington, New Zealand: Victoria University Press, 2001).

[87] Jacques Émile Soustelle (1912–1990) was before the Second World War a widely published academic specialist in Mexican and Central American anthropology and history. During the war he worked for de Gaulle, and after the war he had a long and prominent political career. He later became director of the École pratique des hautes Études. Throughout his career, he continued to publish in anthropology. Soustelle's wife Georgette was also an anthropologist.

they were hidden in books or hidden in fashion magazines, and I continued this job. I had no money, except my jewelry. I would sell some jewelry, get some money, and continue sleeping preferably in waiting rooms in the stations in order not to have the expense of hotels.

12. ARREST AND INTERROGATION, 1949[88]

I distributed in all 11,500 leaflets or posters.[89] I put them on the wall. I would've been quite left alone. Nobody would've interfered because I used to do it cleverly, until I met a collaborator. This was in the station of Köln, Cologne, on the 13th of February 1949. I saw a young man, very tall, a former SS man. He just came out of prison. He was a prisoner of war of the French. And he told me his story.

They sent him to the Congo under Negro supervision, after telling the Negroes that they, the whole lot of them, 18,000 SS, were all enemies of their race and whatnot, and they could do what they liked to them. There was not a single Frenchman in the camp, he told me. The head of the camp was a Negro. A French citizen of course, but that's all. And they had a very hard time. It was a lead mine. They had water up to their waist and hardly anything to eat. And 4,800 out of the 18,000 saw the coast of Europe again. The others all died. That's what he told me. And that impressed me, of course.

I was writing *Gold in the Furnace* in those days. I had written three chapters. I gave him the three chapters and translated them to him. I translated part anyhow, and he liked it. And he said, "Where are you going?" I said, "Taking the train to Hamburg. I want to see some people in Hamburg, and then I'm coming back, in a week." All right. He said, "I'll take you to the train."

So he came to the train with me. I gave him a leaflet on the way. I said, "You go to the WC and read that in the WC where nobody can see you, and tell me what you think of it." He read the leaflet, came out again. It was 2:00 in the morning and very

---

[88] *Defiance* is a much fuller telling of the story recounted here in §§12–14.

[89] Presumably the 500 leaflets of the first journey plus the 11,000 leaflets and posters of the second.

cold. He came out and put his two hands on my shoulders and said, "Who wrote that?" I said, "I." "You wrote that? But you are not a German." I said, "No, but I'm an Aryan still. Without being German I'm still an Aryan, and I owe allegiance to Germany as the country that tried to save the race from decay and all the consequences of Judeo-democratic domination." He said, "Give me as many of these leaflets as you like, as many as you can. I'll stick them up for you." They were posters, not leaflets, with a great big swastika like that, ten centimeters long, ten centimeters wide. I gave him a good hundred, and out he went.

And my train went, and I came back after eight days, as I said. I came back, and he had told me, "When you come back, you go to the Catholic Mission" — there was a Catholic Mission and a Protestant Mission in every station in Germany in those days — "and you ask for the address of Gerhard Waßner. That's my name. I've found a room until then. I'm staying in Köln. So they'll tell you where I live, and you can see me." That's exactly what I did, eight days later. On the 20th of February, the night between the 20th and the 21st. It was about midnight. I went to the Catholic Mission. I said, "Could you give me please the address of Gerhard Waßner?" As soon as I said that, a policeman who was nearby said to me, "May I see your passport?" I said, "Of course." I showed him my passport. He said, "Come along. Leave your things here. Come along. We have something to talk about." I didn't like that idea. I followed him, left my things there. I followed him.

And he told me, "What's the business of the *Flugblätter, Plakate und Flugblätter?*" — that is to say, posters and flyers, leaflets. So I made myself as innocent looking as I could. And I said, "What are posters and what are leaflets? I don't know what . . ." He said, "They are papers with propaganda." I said, "I don't know anything about this. What is it you mean?" I did not know that Waßner was under arrest already. That I couldn't guess. So he said, "Look here, we are going to show you." And he put one of my posters on the table. He said, "Do you know about that? Has Waßner given you those?" And then I understood him. Then only I understood that Waßner was under arrest. How did they find the poster?

I said, "Yes. But you're making a mistake. Waßner didn't give me any of those. I gave about a hundred to Waßner." I said, "Waßner is completely innocent in this affair. He probably didn't know what he was doing. He took them and put them in his pocket, and I doubt whether he read them or not. I don't know. But I gave him about 100." He said, "What did you intend to do?" I said, "I intended him to stick them up. And of course I have no money to pay him, but I have a few pieces of jewelry. I could've given him some of my jewelry." And they said to me, "Who pays you?" I was indignant. I said, "What do you mean who pays me? Nobody pays me. I do this because I love the National Socialist idea."

"You'll find nine boxes that were once full of jewelry, and they're now empty. That jewelry I sold bit by bit in order to pay for my journey into Germany from Saarland six or seven times, in order to stay in Germany, and in order to finance also the printing of my leaflets." He said, "They were printed in Germany?" I said, "No, they were printed abroad." "Who printed them and where?" I said, "I can't tell you that." He said, "We have methods to make people like you speak."

And I really thought, when they said that, I really thought they had the authorization to do what they liked with me. And as I had heard many horror stories of how my comrades fared in the hands of the German police after the war, I thought my turn had come. And I really was afraid. I really was afraid. I looked at my hands, and I said, "If they pull out my nails, what will I do?" Anyhow, I prayed. I prayed to the heavenly powers to give me strength, and I felt really that I was getting less afraid, and I had the courage to tell them, "Well, you can do what you like to me, but there's one thing you cannot do, and that is to kill the idea which I represent. So you can have me. You can do what you like with me."

I didn't tell them, "I won't speak." I was not at all sure that I wouldn't say anything under torture. And I thought that was what was awaiting me. But as I said these words—"You can do what you like, but you cannot kill the idea that I represent"—as I was saying these words, something in me told me I had been telling this to different people, under different forms, for the last several thousands of years. And I felt that I, my real I, was above my body. My body was something different from my self. I felt that.

It was a queer experience. Anyhow that passed away, and they said to me, "You are under arrest, Madam." It was half past two in the morning. I said, "I'm so glad to be under arrest. This puts me not quite so far away from my comrades. I'm nearer to them now. I'm very happy."

And then a man came. I don't know what he was. But he looked like a Jew. He said, "Now come along. We'll take you to your cell." And they took me to a cell, down the stairs, down the stairs. It must've been 20 or 30 yards or meters underground. He opened the dark cell and pushed me in. The inside was full of mud. It was black, black, black on my feet. And there was one bed. I couldn't see what was on the bed. I just banged against it. That's how I knew it was a bed. I couldn't see a thing. And they shut the door. And I banged at the door. I said, "This is full of mud. Couldn't you give me at least something to sit on? I can't lie down in this, but I can sit at least and not have my legs, my feet all muddy." He said, "You can take that." And he gave me a stinking piece of . . . I don't know what, bedclothes or something. A stinking piece of cloth. I said, "You can keep it for yourself. It stinks. I don't want it. I'd rather have the mud."

And then a voice came from the darkness and said, "A new one." I said, "Yes, a new one." "Oh, dear, where did they get you?" I said, "At the station." "What have you been doing? Stealing something?" I said, "No, I've been distributing leaflets and putting up posters against the occupation." "Oh," she said, "That is something good. That is something honorable. You won't get out of it very easily. I'll get out of it. I've been stealing the ration card of somebody for my children. I have six children. They'll let me off, but they won't let you off." I said, "It doesn't matter if they don't. I'm here for that. I'm here to testify to my idea, to our idea—I don't know if it is yours also or not." Anyhow she said, "We were all right under Hitler, but I can tell you, now these swine came, and everything is wrong. We have rationing, rationing. We have hardly anything to eat. We have 25 grams of fat every month. I mean to say, you are quite right to fight them." I said, "I'm glad to hear it, from you, a German." She said, "Would you like to sleep on my bed?" I said, "No, the bed is too small, and I'm not sleepy at all."

I said, "May I sing? If you're not going to sleep, may I sing?"

She said, "You can sing as much as you'd like. I'm not sleepy. I've slept all day." I said, "All right." I started singing every one of the National Socialist songs I knew. With all my enthusiasm. I was very happy in this place. And in the morning, as it dawned—it dawned late of course; it was in February—I saw four feet at the very, very high window as though two people were listening. They listened to a message from underground. I was actually in the physical sense underground as well as in the moral sense. And then they came in. They opened the door. They took out this woman, who was called Hildegard, I don't remember what. And they left me in.

And time was passing, and time was passing. I had had nothing to eat all day and all night. That doesn't matter. When are they going to come? Are they going to leave me here the rest of my life? I was feeling anxious. And about 5:00 in the afternoon—it must've been that late; it was dark, anyhow—they took me in a black car, what they call in English, I think, the Black Mariah, and off we went to some place. And there interrogation started.

One Mr. Hatch asked me questions, and there were Germans. There was an *Oberinspektor* and some other Germans. They were police. And I wanted to speak German because the Germans were there. He said, "No, no, no. Your trial will be in English. You will be tried by a military tribunal under the laws of occupation, the statute of occupation, and you are to speak English only." I said, "All right. Ask me questions about my name, career, my life history, and whatnot."

And he said to me, "Queer, you have a [British] passport [from India. And you have a French military permit with] a stamp that you are French. And we find in your things a certificate of nationality from the Greek Consulate of Lyons, dated 1928, stating that you are Greek. How is it?" I said, "It's just nothing. It's just that I forgot to tell the people that gave me the French military permit that I was of Greek nationality. The French military permit was given to me, and they were kind enough to give me a recommendation to the French authorities, the French and Allied authorities. The recommendation was of Mr. Soustelle himself, the right hand man of Mr. de Gaulle. I forgot to tell him I was of Greek nationality." I said that in an ironical manner, and they couldn't help smiling.

The recommendation that the French people gave me was not a French passport. I had a British passport from India, given out in India in 1940. I never could use it because they gave it to me too late. I had to renew my passport anyhow, and I wanted to come to Europe. I wanted to come to Germany in 1940 and give out war propaganda in Greek and in Bengali. But for that I had to renew my passport. I was now Mrs. Mukherji, so I went to the Indian authorities, that is to say, the British authorities, and asked them for a passport for France. Not for Germany, of course, for France. I would've gone to Germany very easily from France.

And they said, "All right, we'll give you one." And the passport was dated the 30th of April, but they never gave it to me in April. They gave it to me at the end of June when there were no communications left, and one could not leave India unless, of course, one was known as an Allied friend and one was going to join the resistance of Mr. de Gaulle or something like that. Then you had every plane facilities. But everybody knew what I was. Nobody gave me any plane facilities. You understand. And when I went to France, when I got the military permit from Soustelle they put a stamp on my passport, "French born." I was French born if you like, since every child born in France is French.

Then they asked me a few questions, and one of the questions was, "You certainly have letters." By the way, while I was in that police room before they told me that I was under arrest, I had a few addresses. I took them out of my bag very slowly on my lap and tore them in bits, and taking them in my hand, as though I was coughing behind a pocket handkerchief, I swallowed them. When they asked me if I had any addresses, I said, "No, I have no addresses." "You don't know any National Socialists in Germany? Do you mean to say that you know nobody?"

I said, "I know nobody. In fact I know only two National Socialists in the world." They said, "Two?" I said, "Yes, two." "And who are these? Can you tell us their names?" I said, "Very gladly. One is the Führer, and one is myself. I don't know any others because, you see, when they tell you that they are very good democrats, you have no means of knowing whether they tell the truth or are telling lies. And if they tell me, 'I'm a good National Socialist,' how do I know if it's true or not? But of these two I'm perfectly sure. That's all I can say."

And they said, "You say in your leaflets that he's alive, your Führer. Do you believe it?" Well, in those days I really did. I said, "Yes, I do." And he said, "How did you know it? Did any one of his disciples tell you?" I said, "No, an Indian astrologer told me. And I believe in astrology, because I'm a Mediterranean person, or one half Mediterranean at least, and we are all superstitious on the Mediterranean shore." And that was that.

And then Hatch told me, "You are going to pass the night in my house." I said, "Why? If I were a German you would put me in that dark cell. Why don't you put me in that dark cell as I am? I don't want any special treatment." "Well, you are a British subject. An Indian passport, you are a British subject." I said, "Well, no longer now." But still they said, "You have a British passport dated 1940. The passport is good until 1950. We are in 1949. Therefore, you have to come."[90]

And I went there. I saw a beautiful house, well-furnished, spacious, and a lovely Scotch woman with red hair and two lovely children, and that was Hatch's family. And I said, "Some poor German family has been expelled to make place for them. A German family as beautiful as these people. Some German woman looking exactly like Mrs. Hatch and some German children looking exactly like the little Hatches." I said, "Isn't it a shame that people of the same race looking exactly like each other have such a fight, such a war, and then expel each other from their homes?" I said that to Mrs. Hatch. And she said, "What do you wish? This is war. What can you expect? We can't do otherwise."

Anyhow, she said, "Would you like to have something to eat?" It was about 7:00 at night. I said, "Yes, as long as it's vegetarian." She said, "You are vegetarian for health reasons? Or for other reasons?" I said, "I always was from my childhood. I always had a revulsion at the sight of quarters of meat hanging in

---

[90] The possession of an unexpired British passport was the legal pretext upon which the British established their jurisdiction to try and hang William Joyce, a.k.a. Lord Haw-Haw (1906–1946) for treason. Savitri's British passport, plus the fact that the British were aware of her husband's espionage activities during the war, could have led her to a similar fate.

front of the butcher's shops. I never took any meat, in fact. I love animals, and I don't approve of killing them for food. We can eat other things." And she said, "You love animals, but you don't mind the thousands of people that your comrades killed?" I said, "Why should I mind? They weren't animals. Animals aren't anti-Nazis." And she was shocked. But I was perfectly sincere. And I would say it again.

You see, in those days, I used to believe in all these atrocity tales. But they didn't shock me. And they didn't shock me—I repeat it—for this very reason: that I thought to myself that as long as people tolerated all these atrocities on animals, there's no reason why any country should not commit atrocities on its own enemies. Enemies are not as lovable as animals. They are not lovable at all, in fact, and animals are. And that was that. And the woman was shocked. Anyhow, she said to me, "What would you like to eat? I have an omelet." I said, "You can give me an omelet if you like, an omelet with perhaps something in it, onions or whatever you have to put in it, but absolutely no meat." All right, she gave me an omelet. I enjoyed it.

And then the interrogation started. Hatch was present again. He brought a typewriter and a typist and the same old interrogation, the same old questions, the same old questions: "What prompted you to be a National Socialist? What made you a National Socialist?" I said, "I always was one. I became conscious of it once long ago, 1929, but I always was one in fact." And he said, "What do you like in it?" I said, "The idea of perfection. The idea that man should be perfect. There is a perfect type of each race. Every race should strive to its own perfect type."

In fact, National Socialism is an Aryan racialism, but you could transpose it. I can very well imagine a non-Aryan, say a Japanese, having the same ideas as ours. In fact, I said, "In 1940 I met a Japanese in India, one of the members of the Japanese Consulate, and he told me, 'Your National Socialism, we Japanese consider it a Western brand of Shinto. It's the same spirit as our Shinto religion, that is to say, the cult of the sun, the cult of heroes, and the cult of ancestry. It's nothing else.' I said, 'Yes, you are right.'" And recently, that is to say 1978, I had a letter from a Japanese teacher in Nara, and he told me point blank, "We Japanese are all National Socialists in our own way. We are not Aryan racialists because we are not Aryans, of course. But we believe in blood and soil. What's more, this can be said of any race in the world, any conscious race." And that's why if to be a religion, the basic principles of the doctrine have to be universal, I can say National Socialism is a religion.[91]

In fact, higher animals are racialist and lower animals too. They won't mate with anyone except creatures of their own race. Certain spiders will go miles and miles to get to the female spider of the same kind as himself. They have that instinct. The highest of the beings on Earth have that instinct and the lowest. And the intermediate ones haven't got it. An average dog, especially what they call in India a pariah dog, will mate with any bitch. Spiders don't. Insects don't. Plants don't. Minerals don't. There are strict laws of combinations between minerals in chemistry. And higher human beings don't. The intermediate human being is just like the dog: mates with anybody. We want to be the highest. National Socialism is for teaching the Aryans to become real Aryans, that is to say, the top of the race and to be able to guide others, to bring the whole race up. We don't want any kind of people in our Aryan race who behave like dogs, like pariah dogs. That's what we want.

He said, "All right. And have you any examples of this in the world? This is not the voice of the majority." I said, "Not now. Not now, since Christianity and since some other international religions have brainwashed the world, but it was so in antiquity."

---

[91] In the last sentence of this paragraph, Savitri actually says that National Socialism is "universal," not that it is "a religion." But this is a slip of the tongue. Savitri is offering an argument, and the claim that National Socialism is universal is one of the premises (established by the Japanese teacher), not the conclusion. The conclusion is that National Socialism is a religion. Thus the argument runs as follows: If National Socialism is universal, then it is a religion. National Socialism is universal. Therefore, National Socialism is a religion. The first premise of this argument appears false, for although universality may be a necessary condition for being a religion, it is not a sufficient condition. Other conditions must also be satisfied before National Socialism can be considered a religion. It seems certain, however, that Savitri knew there were other conditions for being a religion and believed that National Socialism met all of them as well.

I said it was so in antiquity. He said, "It was so among the Jews."
I said, "Not so much among the Jews as among other people. The
Jews were racialists, provided the people of their own race had
the same religion as themselves. They were of the same race as the
Moabites and as the Ammonites, but these two didn't worship
Yahweh. The Moabites worshipped Chemosh, and the Ammo-
nites worshipped Milcom. They were other gods. Therefore the
Jews hated them.

But among the races of the world in general, religion didn't
count. Religion was a matter of personal affairs. They used to
worship each other's gods. The Jews themselves were always
worshipping the gods of the Canaanites. The Bible is full of their
infidelities to Yahweh. They didn't think twice about it. They
didn't think twice about sacrificing to other gods. It was the fashion. Nobody cared for this religious fanaticism. And Adolf Hitler
says that himself on page 507 of his *Mein Kampf*, edition of 1935:
'In the world of antiquity it was much freer than ours. There was
no such thing as religious intolerance. Religious intolerance, religious terror entered the world with Christianity,' and he's perfectly right. Perfectly right." So that's what I said to him.

And they said, "Well, what is your model state in antiquity?" I
said "Sparta." They said, "We like Sparta too, but we don't like
National Socialism." I said, "What you are saying now is really a
contradiction. You can't really like Sparta and the Spartan way if
you are against National Socialism. It was nothing else. It was
nothing else." They said, "But it was awful. You see, what they
did in Sparta was awful. Babies who were not either fit to be warriors or mothers of warriors, who were badly formed or didn't
weigh enough, they used to just kill them on the spot, throw them
into the depths, the chasm."

I said, "Yes. My mother always told me I would've been in the
chasm myself because I only weighed 900 grams at birth. But it
wouldn't make any difference to the world, of course. But why do
you criticize the Spartans for doing that under command of the
state when in all Greece they did worse, just for the whims of the
fathers? The fathers didn't want another girl, it would mean another dowry to give at the time of marriage, and they said, 'Well,
if the next baby is a girl, you just expose her,' and they put her in
an earthen pot on the street corner, and she was left there either to

be taken by the first kind-hearted person who wanted her, or left to die. It was done all over the ancient world. Why do you criticize Sparta only?"

And there was a discussion like that between Mr. Hatch and another gentleman who came, and myself. It was very interesting. I was delighted to talk of antiquity. It was one of my subjects. And in the end it was after 2:00 or 3:00 in the morning, and then was told I could go to sleep.

The next day I was taken from Köln to Düsseldorf, and all along the way, along the *Autobahn*, I couldn't help saying, "You see these beautiful *Autobahnen*? This is the work of Adolf Hitler. You will use them. You can't help admitting that these are things that he did." And the occupation people answered me, "Yes, all right. And Germany was easier to invade with these *Autobahnen*." I said, "I'm sorry for that anyhow." I think I had another interrogation. I'm not quite sure.

13. WERL AND HERTHA EHLERT, 1949

Anyhow, I landed in Werl. The very same day I was taken to Werl. And I told them, "I'm very glad to be in Werl where there are people of my own faith, quite a number of them." There were, in fact, 26 women in the women's department in the D wing, and about 800 or 1,000 men in the men's department. There had been 11,000 men in 1945, especially SS men. I was taken to the women's department and put in a cell—on remand. You see, I was not condemned yet. My trial lasted six weeks. I was only condemned on the 5th of April '49, not before. Before, I enjoyed certain privileges that people on remand have. I wasn't forced to work, for one, and I had quite a number of visits.

On the next day, the 23rd of February—which happens to be the anniversary of Horst Wessel's murder; he was murdered on the 23rd of February 1930, exactly 19 years after his murder—my cell opened in the morning and in came the head of the infirmary and a beautiful-looking woman, a blonde of about my age. In fact, just six months older than I. And I was introduced, "This is Hertha Ehlert, Hertha Ehlert of the Belsen camp.[92] She was a wardress in the Belsen camp. And she had been in several other

---

[92] Hertha Ehlert was born 26 March 1905.

camps before." All right. And she said, "You see, I'm a war criminal." And when she said that I put my arms around her and kissed her face and told her, "In my eyes there are no war criminals. There are only victims of democracy, and you are one." And she said, "I'm glad to hear that. Tell me, you who are a foreigner, they tell us all day long that we were monsters because we did this and that and the rest to the Jews. We persecuted the Jews, and it was wrong."

I said, "Those who tell you that, just ask them whether they belong to the Indian sect of the Jains or not." She said, "What is that?" I said, "There is a sect in India called the Jains. They don't kill anything. Not bugs, not fleas, not lice, nothing. It is their custom, and it is their religion. If a Jain tells me we were wrong to get rid of our enemies, people who were threatening the existence of the Aryan race, especially the existence of Germany, I would say, 'If you are Jains, all right.' But the people who are trying to brainwash you are not Jains. They kill bugs, and they kill fleas, and they kill flies, and they kill I don't know what else. So they have no right to tell us that we shouldn't kill enemies of our country and our race. A fly cannot do half the harm that an intelligent Jew can do. Certainly not. So if you can kill the fly, or if you can kill the bug, or if you can kill a louse, why can't you get rid of the intelligent Jew who is harming you? Or who threatens to harm you? Even the potential enemy. You kill a bug. The bug has perhaps not bitten you, but he *might* bite you. On that principle you go take his life. Well, if we did things like that to the Jews, we did it on the same principle. And the principle is admitted by everybody except the Jains."[93]

She was quite taken aback. She was delighted. She said, "I'm going to tell that to all the D wing." I said, "You can tell it to whomever you like. I'll tell it to the authorities if they come around and ask me tomorrow. I don't mind. It's logic. I am all for logic. I don't believe in things that are half one way and half the other. I have no time for the enemies of the Reich. None at all. Because the Reich represents to me the force that was doing its best to stem decay in the whole world, and therefore I feel myself personally responsible for whatever has been done in the name of the

---

[93] Cf. *The Lightning and the Sun*, 386.

Third Reich or whatever shall be done in the future if ever we get power again."

I told my mother that so many times. My mother was on the other side. I told her so many times, and I wrote it in letters. Well, in parentheses, the answer my mother had to that was the burning of my doctoral theses. I had left 500 copies of my doctoral theses in her keep, and she burnt them all, all except twelve, six of each thesis. And in 1946 when I saw her again and she told me they were burnt, she said, "Well, I could've burnt my own things. Of course I had heaps of ordinary books. I had heaps of papers. I had heaps of things. But as you feel responsible for all that was done in the name of the Third Reich, I burnt your things. Because of your Third Reich I was cold in 1942, so I burnt your things." I said, "That's logic." I didn't blame her for that. I'd much rather have her attitude than the attitude of these stupid people who would tell me, "Oh, you say so but you don't really believe it. You can't really believe it. You wouldn't really do it." Those fools I don't like. I prefer the one who takes steps against me on logical grounds.

Hertha was condemned to 15 years. She sat for nine years in a cell. They had condemned her to death. She was on the death list, to be hanged, when one of her keeps in Belsen, a Jewess who had become the mistress of a Britisher, told her lover, just like that, occasionally, on having a cup of coffee or tea, "Oh it's a pity for Hertha Ehlert. She was a good one. She used to give me even good coffee when I was sick in the camp. She made good coffee for me and gave it to me in spite of the restrictions." So for that, for that Jewess telling that to her English lover, she got 15 years instead of death. What are the reasons that make our destiny? It's a small thing. If that woman had not met that man, and if Hertha had not given her, once or twice, some good coffee, she would be dead now.

If you could see her, I will give you a word for her: She's a really beautiful Nordic. I don't know what she looks like now, but even when I met her she was over 40. I used to look at her like that. I told her, "As a two-legged mammal, you are much my superior. As a living creature, you're far my superior." She is the lady to whom I dedicated my *Defiance*.

Anyhow, she worked in the infirmary at Werl, and she used to come to my cell every day. I asked her, "What are you getting to eat?" And she said, "Oh, something that's just fit to eat for pigs." I said, "You know, I have British food because I have a British passport. Already this morning I had twelve slices of bread. I don't need twelve slices of bread. I take one in the morning, one at midday and one in the evening, and that's all. You can have the rest." I said, "You can have my coffee too. I take one cup, and I have a liter. Now, I have no meat because I told them I was vegetarian already, and they give me boiled vegetables at midday. I have boiled vegetables and nothing else, not even butter. But in the evening I get something nice. I get some macaroni or something nice, and I can eat that. There's generally very little of it, just enough for myself. But whatever I have in the morning, you come every morning and you take it for the D wing people, for the comrades." She was very pleased, and every morning she came, all the time I was in Werl. She had ten slices of bread. She had all my coffee except a cup for myself. And on Sundays I had a little bit of chocolate. I had some marmalade, and some butter. She had my chocolate, she had my marmalade, and she had my butter. I was very glad to give it to the comrades.

But that in course of time brought me into trouble. That is to say, there's a loophole on every cell. Now the women condemned to hard labor, who used to scrub the floor, could see through that loophole. And they could see me write after the time that was allotted to our work, and they wouldn't have reported that I wrote. I was not allowed to write. I was allowed only to do some sewing work for the prison. The director, Colonel Vickers, told me that I am not to write. But the *Oberwachtmeisterin*, the woman in charge of the work, told me I could write, provided I don't say that I'm doing it. I used to write after the time of work. That was after my condemnation, after the 5th of April, after I was no longer on remand. And that brought down on me the jealousy of these women who saw me in the morning because they suspected me of giving my white bread to the D wing women in the morning.

By the way, I had entreated the director of the prison to put me in the D wing, and he said, "No, you are to stay in the B wing," that is to say, with the women who are condemned for abortion, for murder, for theft, for breaking into houses, robberies, things like that. Mostly they were condemned for abortions. So I said,

"Why don't you put me in the D wing? I'm a political prisoner. I'm not a prisoner. I have not done anything." He said, "Yes, we put you in the D wing, and the next day the whole D wing will be singing the Horst Wessel Song. You are a firebrand. We don't want to put you in the D wing. You'll have to stay here." I didn't like it, not at all. I never forgave the authorities of Werl for keeping me purposely among the abortionists and the thieves and these people. I said to myself, "Thank goodness I was not forced to work in the workshop with the others." I was all alone. I blessed them for being alone. Rather alone than with these people. But I resented not being in the D wing and having to go around the courtyard for a quarter of an hour every day with these people. I met all sorts of types among these people. But their talk was boring. Their talk was men and food, nothing else. And their experiences in prison. Most of them had been in German concentration camps before the war. For the same offenses: for theft, for breaking in houses, things like that. The same offenses. One had been in different camps 18 times and was condemned for it by the Allies for the 19th time. These kinds of people. Putting me with these kinds of people. I'll never forget that.

14. TRIAL AND IMPRISONMENT, 1949

Anyhow, to come back to my trial, it took place on the 5th of April, '49. It was an ordinary military tribunal trial, occupation trial. The people judging me were military occupation. And there was an attorney-general who spoke, and he said that I was twice as guilty as anybody else because of my diplomas, my doctorate, my M.A., my L.Sc., my whatnot. And because I knew what I was doing. And he showed the ruins of Düsseldorf. We were in Düsseldorf in Mühlenstraße. And he said, "These ruins were brought about by National Socialists." I said, "No they weren't. They were brought about by Allied bombers against National Socialism." He said, "You keep quiet. You talk when you are told to talk."

And then they gave me a lawyer. I didn't want one. I said, "I can defend myself. I don't want a lawyer." They gave me one all the same. It was the rule. And the lawyer got a letter from Mr. Mukherji trying to make out that I was not a political person at all. I was much too simple to be a political person. That I liked National Socialism as a philosophy and a religion perhaps, but that really has no political meaning. And the lawyer said, "I'll use that letter, and by using that letter I can get you off several months." I said, "I don't want you to use that letter. Please don't use it, because it's not quite accurate. It tries to defend me, and I don't want to be defended. Whatever I have to say, I will say when they give me the right to speak. But I don't want my actions to be made smaller, less important on any account." He said, "All right."

The room was packed, and there two Jews in the first row. And they were grinning, and they were laughing. They were looking quite pleased. At the end, they told me that I could speak for a quarter of an hour or half an hour. So I spoke. And they asked me, "Why did you do this? Why did you stick up these posters?" I said, "I didn't stick up these posters and distribute these leaflets with the hope that by doing so I would resurrect National Socialism and make it the ruling force in Germany and in this world. Certainly not. That job is much too great for a single individual. It's the job of the gods. They'll do it in time, if it's their sweet pleasure.

"Personally I did it for three reasons. First, I obeyed my conscience. Didn't you tell the world in Nuremberg that a man has to follow his conscience? Of course, you said the 'world' conscience. My conscience is not the world conscience. It's a private conscience. But I follow that. I don't know what the 'world' conscience is. According to me it doesn't exist. So I followed my conscience. It told me to do this, and I did it.

"Second, I wanted to show the German people at the time of humiliation and martyrdom that at least there were some individuals on the surface of the Earth who were still for them.

"And third, I wanted to defy not only you, the occupation powers, but all those who were against us. I wanted to show them that drowning a whole continent in fire and phosphorus, killing millions of people—five million civilians were killed in Germany alone—was an easy task, and they did it. It was so easy. With ample Jewish money and technique put in service of a cause, that will work. But the difficult task, they couldn't do and cannot do, this difficult task being to de-Nazify, as they say, one person. Not many, one. And not a man at that. Nothing but a woman. And not a German woman at that. But a woman from the other end of the Earth. They cannot do that. They could kill me if they like. They didn't do it. That's their affair. But they could. They can't de-Nazify me. That's what I want to show. They can neither de-Nazify me nor can they de-Nazify the natural force. The principles of National Socialism, based on cosmic laws, will still be true wherever we are in the universe, on this planet or on other planets, whatever they do."

And that's what I wanted to say, that's all. And I started quoting something from *Mein Kampf,* and the judge stopped me. The quotation was, "The only thing that should prompt our action is neither the approval nor the reprobation of the people around us, but only our allegiance to the truth in which we believe."[94] I didn't say it in whole. I said it partly. And the judge interrupted me and said, "I don't want to know what your Führer wrote." I said, "I'm sorry. It's because he wrote things like that that I'm here. I acted according to his writings."

Anyhow, when the trial was over he said, "three years rigorous imprisonment." I thought to myself, "These people don't really love their blessed democracy." Because if I had been caught in the Russian zone it would not be three years rigorous imprisonment, it would have been 30 years in a Siberian camp, and I would be dead by now, long ago. But the Communists have a faith. A false one, but a faith. And they can understand people who have a different faith, and they know that any person who has a faith is dangerous, potentially at least, to all those who hate that faith.

These people don't feel the same. Their first concern is their bread and butter and their enjoyment. Democracy gives them that, all right. Long live democracy. If we came to power tomorrow and gave them the same thing, they'd say, "Heil Hitler!" So many did in Germany before the catastrophe. So many did, of that description. And they say the contrary now. Those are the democrats. Those are the Western anti-Communists, and they will be crushed by the Communists, because the Communists

---

[94] "But our views and our conduct will not be determined by the approbation or disapprobation of our contemporaries, but only by our duty to follow a truth which we have acknowledged." —*Mein Kampf*, vol. 2, ch. 2, "The State," trans. Murphy, 222.

have a faith, and they have none. Unless we crush the Communists. We are the only ones. We have seen that in Vietnam. Anyhow, that was long after these happenings.

I went out. I had taken with me my swastika earrings bought in India, great big silhouette earrings in gold. As soon as the sentence was given, and I feared no more—I mean to say, a next trial because of my earrings—I put them on. I stood up. I did the Hitler salute, looking at the people, and I walked off. Some people of the press wanted to interview me, but the authorities didn't allow it.

One thing I can say: the two Jews who were at the front were not laughing any longer. I don't suppose that I frightened them. I was not such a powerful person. But they felt the spirit. They felt that this can always begin again. As long as there are people who really are given to it, it can begin again. That's what they seemed to think. They didn't tell me so. I don't know what they thought. I can't read people's thoughts. But that's what seemed to me.

I walked off, and I was taken to Werl after that. That was my trial in Düsseldorf, Mühlenstraße, on the 5th of April 1949. Exactly two years after I watched the fire on the flanks of the burning Mount Hekla in Iceland, exactly two years.

On the 30th of May 1949, my cell was searched and my manuscript of *Gold in the Furnace* was taken. And I thought it was taken forever because Colonel Vickers, the head of the prison, told me, "If your book is subversive, it shall be destroyed." He told me that on the 10th of June 1949 when I came to ask if my book could be saved. He said, "You are not to ask anything. You are the most objectionable Nazi type I've ever met" —and he had been in Germany since 1945—"and I am not going to give any favors to you." Still, after I had prayed and prayed—not to him, but to the gods, repeating a certain Sanskrit mantra 21 times and that for 21 days (I didn't do it [for 21 days] on purpose)—the directress of the women's section in prison came in and told me "Muky"—they always used to call me Muky, the diminutive of Mukherji—"Your things have all come back, and Colonel Vickers is to give them to you. You go to his office. They are given back to you. Your book is given back to you."

I couldn't believe my ears. I didn't thank Colonel Vickers in my heart of hearts. I thanked the gods only. Colonel Vickers was an instrument, nothing more. Just as I am an instrument, nothing more. Anyhow, I got back my manuscript. It was put in a safe place until my release from Werl. At my release it was given back to me. Of course I kept it until I got it sent to India, and it was printed in India in '52. It was printed in India along with *Defiance*. Mr. Mukherji paid for the printing. And the proofs were sent to me. That's why there were so many mistakes in it. It was printed in India in my absence.

They had given me three years, but they kept me only a few months due to the intervention of the Indian government that Mr. Mukherji had set in motion.[95] I asked him, "Why did you do that?" He said, "Because you are more useful outside than inside. That's why I did it." I said, "Good." I said to my friend Hertha Ehlert, "I don't want to go out." She said, "Don't be a fool. You are of more use out than in. You can continue doing something. When you're in prison you can do nothing. Especially since they won't allow you to write any longer."

Some people had wanted my mother to intervene. My mother had been in the French resistance. She was not going to help a National Socialist and quite right. I admire her for that. I'm very grateful to her that she did not intervene. I didn't want to be freed by anybody, especially not the former French resistance. She wrote to me a letter, at least, that I liked very much. She said to me, "Now you are in prison. Think of the eagles that are in prison in the zoo, in your native town, in enormous cages. They are in cages still. An eagle doesn't want to be in a cage. They have done no Nazi propaganda, and still they are in prison for life. Think of them, and don't complain."[96] I was not in the mood to complain at all. I was very glad to be in prison for my ideas.

And then I was forbidden to go back to Germany for five years, but I went back all the same in '53. I stayed in the meantime in France,[97] and I gave lessons to live. Mr. Mukherji used to

---

[95] In *Defiance*, Savitri mentions that Mukherji went so far as to send a telegram to Jawaharlal Nehru (1899–1964), India's first Prime Minister, to intervene on her behalf (*Defiance*, 380 n11).

[96] Cf. *Pilgrimage*, 313.

[97] During her stay in France, Savitri lived in Lyons and completed *Defiance*. The Preface is dated Lyons, 29 August 1950. She also finished *Gold in the Furnace*. The Preface of *Gold* is dated Lyons, 21 Au-

send me some money now and then, but not much. I went to
Greece in '53, in January or February '53. And then I went back to
Germany via Rome. I took a plane to Italy, and in Rome I took a
train via the Brenner Pass to Germany.[98] And I came back to
Germany with a Greek passport in my maiden name, and nobody understood anything about it. I was condemned under an
Indian passport, as Mrs. Mukherji. I came back with a Greek
passport as Miss Maximine Portaz. And I was allowed to stay in
Germany. Mr. Mukherji sent me money. He could then. He sent
me 19 marks a month. I lived on my 19 marks a month. And I
started teaching. And I wrote *Pilgrimage*.[99] And after writing *Pilgrimage*, I started working again on *The Lightning and the Sun*. I
had already started writing it in '48, but I had not finished it. I
had written only one or two chapters. The three first chapters, I
think.[100] I continued, and then I took it to India in '57. I had a few
episodes that I described in *Long-Whiskers and the Two-Legged Goddess*. I had a cat.[101]

15. RETURN TO INDIA, 1957–60
And when I had to leave Germany in '57, I went back to India.
I went back to India in May, '57.[102] Why did I go back to India? I
went back to India for one sole reason. I could not publish *Pil-
grimage*. Mr. Mukherji had insufficient money. So I went back to
India to publish that and to publish also *The Lightning and the Sun*.

---

gust 1952.
   [98] According to *Pilgrimage*, Savitri flew from Phaleron to Campini,
then traveled to Rome, where she met Camillo Giuriati, former Italian Consul in Calcutta (*Pilgrimage*, 11).
   [99] *Pilgrimage* was finished on 6 February 1954 in Emsdetten in
Westphalia.
   [100] Savitri wrote ch. 1 of *The Lightning and the Sun* on 9 April 1948
in Edinburgh. She completed chapter 3 on 6 December 1948 in the
Karlsruhe railway station in Germany. She completed the book on 21
March 1956 (the Spring Equinox) in Hanover.
   [101] See *Long-Whiskers*, ch. 10, "Black Velvet" and ch. 11, "The
House in the Woods." Black Velvet (*Schwarzer Samt*) was the name of
Savitri's cat.
   [102] Savitri relates episodes from this journey in *Long-Whiskers*, chs.
13–15.

And I stayed there three years. I worked three years to finance these books. I financed them, and then I came back.

I went to Egypt first and was the guest of Johann von Leers.[103] Johann von Leers couldn't put me up directly so he gave me the address of Mr. Mahmoud Saleh,[104] a very enthusiastic admirer of the Führer, a Palestinian Arab, and his wife. And I lived with their family. They had two little girls. They gave ancient names to their children, Nefertiti and Tiy, instead of giving them Mohammedan names. When I left, the one thing, the one favor, Mahmoud Saleh wanted me to give him was a portrait of the Führer.[105] I gave him that, and he was very, very happy. Very proud of it. He had been in a Jewish concentration camp as an Arab for our cause in Palestine and suffered a lot but came out of it. And he was then the president of the anti-Zionist movement in Cairo.

From Cairo I went to Tell-el-Amarna, to the ruins of ancient Akhetaton, not far from Melawi in middle Egypt. I saw the ruins of Tell-el-Amarna. I came back to Maadhi, where I was living — Maadhi near Cairo.[106] Then I went to Alexandria. From Alexandria I sailed on a Greek ship to Beirut. In Beirut I was supposed to meet a National Socialist, and one in Baghdad also. Unfortunately it was June or July and they were both out. They were not living in these very hot places then, so I could not see any of them. So from Beirut I went to Damascus by car and from Damascus to Baghdad by the ordinary trans-desert bus. It was the second time I did this trip. I had done it already in '36. I forgot to say that in

---

[103] Johann von Leers (1902–1963) was a National Socialist university professor and a member of the SS who worked in Goebbels's Ministry of Propaganda. In 1954, he began working for the Nasser régime in Egypt as a specialist in anti-Zionist propaganda.

[104] Mahmoud Saleh (1903–1970) was actually Egyptian, although his wife was Palestinian. He was interned for five-and-a-half years by the British during World War II.

[105] According to Muriel Gantry, Savitri painted her own portrait of Hitler ("Curriculum Vitae of Muriel Gantry," unpublished ms., p. 22). It may be this portrait that she gave to Saleh.

[106] Savitri wrote her pamphlet *Paul de Tarse, ou Christianisme et juiverie* [*Paul of Tarsus, or Christianity and Jewry*] (Calcutta: Savitri Devi Mukherji, 1958) in Maadhi on 18 June 1957.

'37 I did a trip to the Near East by train and by ship. I visited Baghdad, I visited Syria, and I came back to India via the Persian Gulf in '37.[107] I forgot to tell that.

So this time I didn't come back through the Persian Gulf. I came back by bus, via Teheran. Stayed three weeks in Teheran to see the place, went to Pahlevi on the Caspian Sea, to see the Caspian Sea, and from Pahlevi back to Teheran, from there on to Mashid and from Mashid to Zahedan on the frontier between Pakistan and Persia. The train goes once a week to Lahore. I arrived on the day the train had left. Had to stay a week in Zahedan. I stayed in the Greek hotel. There are Greek hotels all over the world, and I was quite happy.

And then I took the train crossing Baluchistan. Baluchistan is one of the hottest places on earth, a desert of gravel crossed by the army of Alexander the Great, when he was coming back to Greece, or supposed to come back to Greece. He died on the way. Four-fifths of his army died of thirst in Baluchistan. Of course, I wasn't loaded with helmet and armor as they were. I was in a train in a third class compartment. There were third classes still in India in those days. There were in Pakistan at least. In the compartment were women, Mohammedan women, quite indifferent to me, and I thought to myself, as the train entered the desert of Baluchistan, "Now Europe is far away. Now I can do what I like. Now nobody's going to say a word to me if I sing the Horst Wessel Song," and I stretched my arm from the window, and I sang the Horst Wessel Song with all my enthusiasm over the burning desert. It was a sort of victory. The women didn't care a bit. They said, "You want to sing, well sing." I said, "All right." They even liked the song, some of them. And I reached Lahore. From Lahore I came to Delhi. I got on the train to Delhi on the 30th of July 1957, having come overland all the way from Europe and Egypt.

In the train I was assaulted. I was in the ladies' compartment, but five women who were with me all got off at Mathura, and the train was empty. A man came in and assaulted me, wanting money. I had a terrible experience. He nearly strangled me, and then I spoke gently to him. I gave him whatever I had. I had hard-

---

[107] Savitri also visited Egypt before World War II, perhaps at the same time (*Defiance*, 98).

ly any money, but I gave him what I had, and he got down. He jumped out of the train at the next station. I called the police but there was no way of finding out where he went.

I reached Calcutta two days later and went home, went to Mr. Mukherji's flat, and he received me very well. And I stayed there. I stayed there till August '57, and then I got a job in Joda near Barajamda in the province of Orissa.

There was an advertisement. Three German engineers from the East wanted someone, a German person or a person who knew German, to be a field interpreter between them and the Hindi-speaking or Oriya-speaking people. Well, I don't speak Oriya, but I understand some of it. It's very close to Bengali, and I speak and write Hindi. So I offered my services. Mr. Mukherji told me, "If you like to, you can apply. But you be very careful. They wouldn't be sent to India unless they were thorough Communists. They must be experienced Communists, you see. The government must rely on them for them to be sent out." I said, "All right." So I went.

The eldest one was called Müller. The second one was called Schuster. And the third one was called Schmidt. Müller was 60. Schuster was about 45, and the other one was 36. And the job was to organize the labor for a *Seilbahn*, a *funiculaire*[108] to carry iron ore from the top of a mountain down to the railway, with pylons and all that. They were building them. So I went there. I used to share the house with them. I had a room of my own, and there was a courtyard, and they had their own rooms. And they had their own food. I used to take Indian food from the shop. Cheapest. And I also started feeding the dogs in the place that were thin and very, very badly off. So that went on all right.

The first time I came out with them on Sunday there was Müller and Schmidt. Schmidt did not say a single word, nor did I. Müller spoke. He said, "I was once a disciple of Thälmann the Communist, but since I have seen Communism in the East zone, I'm no longer a Communist. I am a man of Adenauer." I wanted to say, "It's no better," but I didn't say a word. "I think the régime of Adenauer is all right, and see plenty and freedom." Anyhow, I said nothing. He was against

---

[108] Cable car system.

the Führer, very much against him, anti-Nazi.

Then Schuster came and we had coffee together. On the first day, Sunday, I spoke only of India. They asked me questions, good questions. This was the first time they came to India. I gave them my experiences of India. I gave them a few words on Indian tradition. They didn't say anything. The next day, in the morning, Schuster knocked at my door, and he said, "I've spotted you out. You are a National Socialist." I said, "How did you spot that out? I never spoke of National Socialism." He said, "No, you didn't speak of National Socialism, of course. You spoke of India. But nobody except a National Socialist could speak of India as you did." He said, "You know, I'm not against you for that. I was at the Nuremberg rallies. I saw Rudolf Hess two meters away from me, like that. I held the flag in front of him once. I used to go to all the rallies. But of course now I'm a good Communist. Now that I must be a good Communist, I am a good Communist." And he told me about his experiences in the great days. He did this, and he did that, and he did the other thing. "But now I'm a good Communist." He said it so often that I found that it was not true. It sounded false.

And I went up to the works with Schmidt, and we sat near a place they were filling with cement for the pylons. The women used to do that. They had baskets made of iron that were already heavy. I could barely lift one, and when they were full of semi-liquid cement they were even heavier. And they used to go up the hill, slanting like that, 600 women. We watched them work. Schmidt said, "You know I'm from Danzig." I said, "Danzig always was a German town. I learnt Danzig was a German town when I was a kid in school." He said, "Yes, it was 99% German." And he told me in glowing words of the entrance of the German army in Danzig in 1939. He said, "I was there. I cheered them too. And it was wonderful. The Hitler idea was wonderful." I was very reticent because I thought, "Is he provoking me or what? I don't know."

Anyhow, that's all right. Days passed. And one day I thought the three were out, and I went to the courtyard in the morning. It was a Sunday morning, and I bathed in the courtyard instead of bathing in my room. It was so small, my room. It was inconvenient to bathe. I went and bathed under the tap. And just when I was going away, in came Schmidt. I'd just put on my brassiere. I always wear this around my neck.[109] He saw it probably. And I didn't say a word. I went home. In the evening, he knocked on my door. He said, "Mrs. Mukherji, can I just for five minutes have your *Parteiabzeichen* and hold it in my hand? Just for five minutes and give it back to you." I said, "What do you want it for?" He said, "Just to feel the touch of it after all these years." I took it off and gave it to him. He said, "I've known, I've known you for a long time. Don't say a word to Müller. Schuster is reliable, but it's better not to talk too much. You can talk to me if you want to talk."

And of the three, when they left the works after a year, Schmidt was the only one who came to Calcutta and had a cup of coffee with us. And Mr. Mukherji spoke to him and said, "You want the reunification of your country naturally." He said, "Of course I do." "And with what frontiers?" And Schmidt answered, "Those of 1940." Those are the Germans of the East zone.

I came back to Calcutta in '58 when the job was finished. And then I joined the French school[110] in Calcutta and had a job at the French school.

16. BACK TO EUROPE, 1960–71

I left Calcutta in '60. My mother died in '60. She died on the 25th of March '60. I sailed back to Europe in August or September of '60, couldn't tell you exactly, via South India and Ceylon. I took a passage on a Greek ship, third class, and landed in Marseilles.

And then I went to Spain. I was there six weeks, a guest of Otto Skorzeny, and I enjoyed it immensely.[111] I met a very great man in him. He's dead now, may his soul be in peace. He was one of the finest people I have ever met. And I was much honored to have stayed in his house. He invited me after I had sent—which book was it, *Gold in the Furnace*, or no—*The Lightning and the Sun*, I

---

[109] A NSDAP party badge.

[110] The Alliance Française.

[111] SS-*Sturmbannführer* Otto Skorzeny (1908–1975) is celebrated for his daring commando operations during WW II, in particular the raid of 12 September 1943 to liberate Mussolini from the mountaintop hotel in the Gran Sasso where he was held prisoner after being deposed.

think. I sent him one of those books via Hans-Ulrich Rudel.[112] I was in touch with Hans-Ulrich Rudel. I met him in Hanover also. I went to him several times. Very fine man also. Now, of course, I think he's half paralyzed. One leg is cut off, I know that, but on the top of that he had some sort of attack, some stroke since then.

Anyhow, from Spain I came back to France, and I got a job as a stopgap teacher.

And with the money of that job, I started preparing to publish other books. I financed my *Long-Whiskers and the Two-Legged Goddess*.[113] First I worked in Montbrison. That was from January '61 to November '63. In November '63 I was sent to Saint-Étienne. I stayed there till '64. I had trouble, very big trouble, in Saint-Étienne, and nearly lost my job because I had said in class that, "I would rather have died in any German concentration camp, than under the bombardments of the Allies. Rather than at Dresden, for instance, drowned in burning tar in some cellar, the streets having become molten under the heat of the bombardment." I said something like that, and I also put in doubt the things that were told about what the Nazis did. I didn't know that the father of one my pupils was the head of the local section of the L.I.C.A., International League against Anti-Semitism. And I got into trouble. I nearly was kicked out.

But I was not kicked out. I was just sent to another place, to Firminy, and I stayed in Firminy '65, '66, '67, living in Montbrison, of course. I kept my little room in Montbrison because in Montbrison I used to feed a number of cats. I didn't want to abandon the cats until I found someone to feed them in my place. And I stayed in Montbrison till '69 after I no longer had a job in

[112] Colonel Hans-Ulrich Rudel (1916–1982) was the greatest flying ace of WW II, perhaps of all time.

[113] Savitri worked on *Long-Whiskers* from 1957–1961. It was begun in September 1957 in Joda near Barajamda, India and finished on 10 July 1961 in Hanover, Germany. It was published in 1965 in England. From 1961–63, Savitri worked on a German-language book, *Hart wie Kruppstahl* [*Hard as Krupp Steel*]. The title is from Hitler's description in *Mein Kampf* of the ideal German youth. The book was never published, but the manuscript is extant and will be published by the Savitri Devi Archive and Counter-Currents Publishing (*Souvenirs et réflexions*, 12, n1).

Firminy. I used to correct copies for a correspondence course. I used to stay there and continue feeding my cats.

And then I found a job in Ireland, and I was going to sail for Ireland in '69. But at the port, I was told to go back. The Irish authorities thought I was going back to England, and I had been kept out of England on account of my taking part in the Cotswolds camp in '62.[114] Well, I was not allowed into Ireland either. I had to go back.

And I went to Greece. I didn't know where to go. In Greece I had a very small job and a few private lessons. I stayed there a year. And in '70 I came back to France and in October '70, I was the guest of Françoise Dior[115] in Ducey, Normandy, and from there I worked on my French book.[116] I started writing it in '68, '69, '70.

17. LAST YEARS IN INDIA, 1971–78

And then I came to India, landed by plane in Bombay and went from Bombay to Poona on the 23rd of June '71. And from there I continued my manuscript, of course, all the time. And then I went to Delhi. I came to Delhi on the 11th of August '71 and stayed at the Hindu Mahasabha[117] office in one of the guest rooms. I finished my book there. My book was ended in Delhi sometime in August or September, I don't remember exactly, '71.[118]

And then I found a job at the French school in Delhi.[119] I was teaching at the French school in Delhi until August '77. And then they did not give me another job on account of my age only. And now I'm living on private lessons when I get any, and on a tiny little pension that I get, national security for having taught nine

---

[114] On the Cotswolds camp, see the next chapter, §§2–4.

[115] Marie Françoise Suzanne Dior (1932–1993). For more on Françoise Dior, see the next chapter, §§2 and 5.

[116] *Souvenirs et réflexions*.

[117] Hindu Mission.

[118] *Souvenirs et réflexions* was finished in New Delhi on 12 September 1971 (*Souvenirs et réflexions*, 327). It took nearly five years to raise money for the printing. The Preface was written in New Delhi on 28 July 1976.

[119] The Alliance Française.

years, but nine years only, in France.

I've been staying in this flat since '73. Before '73 I was staying in Delhi's South Extension Part 1, and I used to feed a number of cats over there, naturally. And now I go every evening in a scooter to see these cats that are still coming to their feeding place, not knowing that I have shifted to Part 2. And I give them milk and bread and pet food and whatever I have to give them.

And of course, I continue writing. I'm thinking now of writing another book. I don't know if it will be in French or in English. If it's in French it will be called, probably, *Ironies et paradoxes*, about the ironical and paradoxical in certain events of history or in certain lives of people and things like that.[120]

For instance, one paradox is the birth of Goebbels. His father was absolutely against us, a staunch Catholic of Rheydt, Rheinland, and in Goebbels' diaries, you get this phrase, "*Krach mit Vater*"[121] every two lines when he's young. He didn't like him at all. And then Goebbels met Adolf Hitler, and his father liked him even less. Anyhow, his father is one of the greatest benefactors of the Hitler movement without meaning to. And I want to show that so many people do things without meaning to. And sometimes against what they should do.

For instance, Nebuchadnezzar,[122] who stormed Jerusalem in 586 BC and took the Jews all in captivity in Babylon. Of course Cyrus[123] let them go back, those who wanted to go back, in 538 BC. But they didn't all go back. Some stayed in Babylon. Now Nebuchadnezzar, of course, who took them there, thought he was doing a great harm to them. He was destroying the Jewish nation.

In reality, he was doing a great favor to them because they were an agricultural people and a warlike people in those days.

---

[120] According to Savitri's correspondence with O. L. (15 November 1979), the full title of this book was to be *Ironies et paradoxes de l'histoire et de la légende.*

[121] Quarrel with father. Goebbels' father Fritz lived from 1867–1929.

[122] Nebuchadnezzar II (c. 630–562 BC, reigned c. 605–562 BC).

[123] Cyrus the Great (580–529 BC) was the founder of the Persian Empire. After his conquest of the Babylonian Empire in 539 BC, he allowed the Jews exiled in Babylon to return to Jerusalem (2 Chronicles 36:22–23).

They were not great bankers or anything of the kind. The banking of antiquity was in the hands of the Babylonians. We have records of Babylonian banks of 900 years. Babylon was under the Kassite dynasty, an Aryan dynasty, that lasted until 1080 BC. And I must say that the Jews who stayed in Babylon received favor there. They finished by no longer being prisoners. They could go about. They learnt their banking there. That's where they learnt their capacity in banking that they used for centuries later on. Nebuchadnezzar was one of their benefactors. One of the greatest ones.

Another one was Titus.[124] He destroyed Jerusalem completely in the year 70. And Hadrian destroyed what was left of it in 135, after two risings.[125] Well, they had so many risings under the Romans—we normally read of two—but there were a good 150 risings or more. Instead of keeping the Jews in Palestine where they were, these two anti-Jewish Roman emperors made slaves of some of them and sent them all over the Roman Empire, in the slave markets. They took others and dispersed them. They forbade any Jew to remain in Jerusalem. There were a few in Palestine. They persecuted them too. The result was that the Jews were strewn all over the world instead of being in one stronghold in Palestine.

And what would've happened if they had been in Palestine was this: in the 7th century the wave of Islam would have taken them over. There would be no Jews left in the world. They would all be Mohammedans. Except perhaps a few, one little sect, but the wave of Islam was so powerful, it took over the whole of

---

[124] Titus (Titus Flavius Sabinus Vespasianus) lived from 40–81 and was Emperor from 79–81. His father Vespasian (also named Titus Flavius Sabinus Vespasianus) lived from 9–79 and was Emperor from 69–79. Both Vespasian and Titus were occupied with quashing the Jewish rebellion of 67 when Vespasian was declared Emperor by his legions in 69 and departed to claim his throne. In 70, Titus captured Jerusalem and razed the great temple begun in 19/20 BC by Herod the Great (73–4 BC, reigned 37–4 BC), and completed only in 63 AD.

[125] Hadrian (Publius Aelius Hadrianus, 76–138, reigned 117–138) successfully crushed the Bar Kochba revolt of 132–135. Hadrian then leveled what remained of Jerusalem and built a new city, Aelia Capitolina, on the site. He erected a temple to Jupiter on the site of Herod's temple. Jews were forbidden to enter the city.

Christian North Africa. North Africa was Christian. It became Mohammedan overnight, except for the tiny sect of the Copts that are still alive. The Jews would've been the same. There would be no Jewish question at all in the world.

But they were not in Palestine. That's the trouble. Thanks to their enemies, Titus and Hadrian, they were all over the place in Europe. They were in Italy. They were in Germany. They were I don't know where. They had followed the Roman legions, as contractors, of course. They were the best contractors of the Roman legions in Germany and elsewhere. And that is the service these two typically anti-Jewish emperors rendered to them. To those Roman emperors we owe the fact that we have the Jews everywhere.

This is the kind of book I want to write. I think it will be interesting if I manage to write it. It's getting ripe in me, slowly, slowly, slowly. It might take two or three years more.[126] That's all I have to say.[127]

---

[126] According to Savitri's correspondence with O. L., by 15 November 1979, one-and-a-half chapters of *Ironies et paradoxes* had been written, but Savitri's ever-worsening eyesight was interfering with her writing. It is unlikely that the book was ever finished, and the fate of the manuscript is unknown.

[127] Savitri remained in India until 4 October 1981, when she returned to Europe. She died on 22 October 1982 in Sible Hedingham, Essex, England, at Moira Cottage, the home of her old friend Muriel Gantry. She was 77. For an account of her last year and her death, see Goodrick-Clarke, *Hitler's Priestess*, 222–25.

Chapter 2

COMRADES

1. GERMAN COMRADES

I would like to speak of one or two comrades who are alive or dead now. I will not speak of Heinrich Blume, one of the closest collaborators of the Führer, born in 1887, that is to say, two years before him, on the very day Frederick the Great was born, that is to say, the 24th of January. I spoke of him in *Pilgrimage*.[1] He was a wonderful man. He was what you call *Oberregierungs- und Schulrat*[2] under the Third Reich. But I will speak of people whom I met myself in Germany.

One is Gerda Strasdat. I met Gerda Strasdat in the Annastift-Hospital in '56. Frau Marianne Meinecke, a friend of mine, told me about her. Frau Meinecke herself was a wonderful person, a real National Socialist. She must be dead now. She would be I don't know how old. She was much older than I. And she gave me this address. She said, "This girl suffered for us, suffered for the cause." And she did. I met her in her room. She had one arm completely cut off, one leg completely cut off, and half the other leg too. She had, in fact, one arm, the right one, fortunately. And she told me she was reading *Gold in the Furnace*. She knew English. She was 31 at that time, and she looked 21 or 22. She looked much younger than her age. In spite of all that. Pretty face, very nice. And she liked my book. And I said, "Dear me, Gerda. You speak of *Gold in the Furnace*. I only wrote it. It's the title of a book of mine. But you *are* the gold in the furnace."

This is how she happened to get into that state. She was caught by the British, by the British police, after the war. She had been the secretary of a very top National Socialist. And she was asked to tell the names and the hiding places of that man and of several others. She knew where they were. She refused to speak. They

---

[1] Savitri Devi, *Pilgrimage*, 258–70. Savitri met Blume in Hanover on 10 and 11 May 1953.

[2] Senior government official and educational authority.

kicked her and knocked her about. They beat her. They knocked out all her teeth, and they put her in such a state, without her speaking, that even the men who did it could not help admiring her. Then she went to a camp, naturally, a concentration camp of the Allies. It was early '47. After that treatment, her limbs were gangrenous, from the beatings, and they had to cut off one arm and then a leg and then half of the other leg. She was in the state of an unfortunate insect that had been pulled to pieces by naughty children. And still she was smiling.

I admired that woman so much. I saw her later on once at her brother's. She had been discharged from this hospital where she stayed for days and days and months, and she was living with her brother and her sister-in-law. In Seilerstraße, I think, in Hanover. Anyhow, this is one among thousands. There must be thousands like her.

Another one is Olga von Barényi who lived in Bohemia during the war. She's married to a German of what they call Czechoslovakia. It's still Bohemia. She calls herself von Barényi because it's her maiden name. Her father is from Hungary and her mother German, or the reverse, I don't know. She was a writer. She is still a writer. If she is alive. She was very, very ill lately. I don't know. I haven't written to her yet. I'm going to write to her for the Winter Solstice, and I'll have news. She wrote, among others, three very impressive books, *Prager Totentanz, The Death Dance of Prague, Der tote Briefkasten*, and *Das tote Geleise*.[3] They are three books: one about the happenings in Prague, 1945, one about the happenings in Prague later on, and one about happenings in München in our very days. How Communist propaganda goes on in München, and how things happen that people know and why and what. Very interesting books.

The first one, of course, is shocking. It tells you about Czech

---

[3] Olga von Barényi, *Prager Totentanz: Ein Roman aus den Tagen der Prager Revolution 1945* [*Death Dance of Prague: A Novel from the Days of the Prague Revolution of 1945*] (Munich: Schild, 1958); *Der tote Briefkasten: Gegenwartsroman aus der gefährlichen Wirklichkeit der Roten Tschechischen Nachrichtendienste* [*The Dead Mailbox: Contemporary Novel on the Dangerous Truth about the Red Czech News Service*] (Munich: Schild, 1960); *Das tote Geleise* [*The Dead End*] (Munich: Kismet, 1961).

youth, Communist youth, sworn to do as much harm as possible to the Germans after the war, and what they did. Things that Olga saw with her own eyes. Things that she put up with with her own body. She was caught by the Communists and tortured. She showed me her back. Her back is one wound. A red-hot iron was applied to it to make her speak. And she did not speak. And she told me, "It's awful the first two or three minutes. And then, of course, one doesn't get accustomed to a red-hot iron, but one gets a kind of defiant spirit. Some force comes into one," she said, "and one feels, 'I've stood it until now. I'll stand it till the end'" — a sort of a strange force that comes from elsewhere. But she said — and I can understand this very well — "If they had tried this on my dog in front of me instead of trying it on me, I don't know what I would've done." I can understand that.

And she told me that these kinds of things were very ordinary happenings in Prague in those days. She told me about children, German children, 131 of them, taken from a hospital and walled in. They put them in a room, shut the door, walled it up. They died of suffocation, of course. After so many hours, after what torture, nobody knows. Babies and little children, little girls two or three years old, holding their dolls in their arms. She told me — and she put it in her *Prager Totentanz* also — the awful story of people burned alive, hung from the lampposts with a fire under them. A young soldier, an old woman, only because they were Germans. She told me that a young SS man, 17, 18, quite young, was tied to a table in a cinema of Prague with all the people around him, Czechs. And next to him were a pair of scissors and a knife and a container full of vinegar. And every one of the people had to go there, cut a slice off him, and pour vinegar into the wound. Cut it off with a pair of scissors or with a knife and pour vinegar in the wound. Until he died.

Things like that make you ashamed of being White, not Aryan. Czechs may be Aryan. They are Slavs. Whatever they are, they are a White race. We speak of the horrors of the Chinese tortures and things like that. You can imagine that going on in ancient China, at the most in ancient China, not even in today's China. Or in ancient Korea, where it was a feat in the 19th century, a great betterment, that prisoners no longer had their knees crushed to pieces. It was a torture they had before. They suppressed it in the

19th century. It was supposed to be a great betterment. But when you hear this happening in 1945, it makes you ashamed of having two legs and being a human being. That's how it makes me feel. Animals would not do things like that.

Another thing that I also find awful in *Prager Totentanz* is the treatment of the animals because they belonged to Germans. For instance, young boys and girls, Czechs, poking out the eyes of poor German horses because they were *Wehrmacht* horses. One Czech with a kind heart who couldn't bear that on animals tried to stop it. They did it to him. They killed him. And the girl who killed him—it was a girl—she had 180 written in front of her breasts, and she took off the zero and put 181. It meant that she had killed 181 Germans herself. They would take a dog, bring that dog to a heap of corpses. "Now you look for your master." The poor dog would look for his master, whimpering, and he would finish by pulling out the corpse of an SS man killed by the Czechs. "Oh, you are the dog of an SS man! Pour boiling water over him." Things like that. Cut off the paws of poor cats because they belonged to Germans.

I feel so much for this that I feel that Prague should be wiped out. Completely wiped out. By the Russians, by the Chinese, by the Americans, by whoever you like. By extraterrestrials. I don't care by whom. But a place where such things happened—150,000 Germans and so many animals, tortured to death in 1945—this place doesn't deserve to live. And when I heard of the Russians behaving as they did in the '60's, I said, "Well, it doesn't matter." They were their glorious Allies. The Russians had not entered Prague yet. They feasted them when they came. They were their glorious Allies. I couldn't care less if they squashed them under their tanks. What had they done? What had they done?

I tell you, this makes me sometimes sick of being, not a White person, but a human being. Why don't I have four legs and a tail and stripes all over my body and beautiful fur? Why am I not a tigress? Tigresses are much better than that. More beautiful first of all, and then they don't do such things. They are people! People with eyes and noses and mouths, people looking like me and looking like you, that did these things. And I say it's no wonder they did these things, because if they can do what they do to the seals in Canada, to the seals who are nothing to them, who never had an ideology, who cannot have one, who can neither be for nor against any ideology, all the more they can do it to Germans, or to Communists, or to Fascists, or to anything "-ist," anything that has an ideology or that is supposed to have one. I mean to say, the German children had no ideology. Certainly not. But the Czechs would think, "Oh, they are Germans. Their parents had one. They will have one when they grow up. They will be our enemies." It's a different thing. It's a different degree of cowardice to do an awful thing to an animal that cannot be for or against anything and to do it, even to a child, who can be for or against something, against anything, when it grows up. That's a degree of cowardice. They are both awful things. Both cowardly actions.

And I believe that cowardice is the ugliest vice on earth. You cannot be cruel unless you are a coward. Fighting is not bad, fighting honestly. But fighting in a sneaking way, and fighting and doing cruelties, that's cowardice. Cowardice is the worst thing. It's the most despicable vice I can imagine. I'd much rather have some other vices. Laziness. Laziness is not good, but it's better than that. All the other vices are better than that. That's the father of vices. Lying is a mark of cowardice. If you tell lies, it means you don't want to face the consequences of what you have done or what you believe. So you'd rather lie. You are not a liar if you are not a coward. You have to be a coward to have all the vices. You have to be a coward.

I could talk of Frau Meinecke. She died in her bed as far as I know. But she was such a good National Socialist, really. And so kind to all the others. Any National Socialist could go to her house in Hanover and get shelter there, stay there as long as he liked. She would give introductions to him. She would help him to get a job. She would do everything. She had secret meetings in her house, up to 100, 150 people. I went to some in the years '50, '51, '52, up to '60.[4] The last time I saw her was in '71.

Now I'll speak not of great martyrs of National Socialism or

---

[4] Savitri did not enter Germany from her release in Werl in 1949 until her pilgrimage in 1953. She left Germany in May of 1957. She stayed in India until the fall of 1960. The soonest she could have returned to Germany was late in the fall of 1960. The Foreword to *Long-Whiskers* was written in Hanover on 10 July 1961.

great people, but very ordinary people.

There was a girl called Brigitte W— in Germany. She was
about 18 in '71 and she was introduced to me by another very
great National Socialist, Hans E—. Hans E— is a wonderful man.
He introduced me to her. It was a birthday, in fact, for her brother, who was a young boy. He was a young boy then. He must be
a great young man now. We all went to the birthday party. After
the birthday party, Brigitte called me to her room, and in her
room I saw a beautiful portrait of herself. Life size. Head and
breast. I said, "Brigitte, you are as beautiful in your picture as you
are in reality." She was engaged to a young National Socialist of
Flanders. She must be married now and probably a mother. But
she said, "That's not what I wanted to show you." She pulled that
picture out, and behind that picture there was a beautiful picture
of the Führer. I said, "That's wonderful. And you have this in
your room." She said, "Yes. In the daytime I put my picture in
front because the charwoman comes, this one comes, that one
comes, my schoolmates come. (She was going to college.) They
can't see it because it would put my parents into trouble. But otherwise, we all understand each other, and to you I can show it."

The youngest National Socialist I met in Germany in '71 was
five years old, not even quite five. I can see him still. "Heil Hitler,
Tante," putting out his arm. And there are several families in
which this salutation is still pronounced. Not to everybody, of
course. To those in whom they can have confidence. The German
people have learnt as far as I know to be as silent as Japanese, to
hold their tongues. That's the great lesson they learnt from '45, to
hold their tongues.

In '48, I was staying with a family, and I was talking to the father of the family who had three children. Well, one was the child
of his wife, a widow who had lost her husband in Russia. He fell
on the field of honor in Russia. And he married her and gave her
two other children. There were therefore three. The little boy was
about six, and he used to go to school. And I was deploring the
fact that the school was only one hour a day in those days. And
the father told me, "Well, it is one hour a day because they have
dismissed every National Socialist who was a teacher, and they
put teachers in who are not National Socialists, and that means
that one teacher has 4,000, 5,000 pupils, and they can only take

them one hour a day, and that with difficulty."

As he said that, the little boy interrupted and said, "Aber Herr Brücker ist genauso Nazi wie wir." Herr Brücker was his teacher. "Herr Brücker is just as much a National Socialist as we are." And he got such a slap from his stepfather. And I felt sorry for him. I said to his stepfather, "Why do you beat him like that, poor child? He didn't mean anything bad." And the stepfather said, "Yes, but he must learn his lesson. He tells you that Herr Brücker is a National Socialist, which is probably true, and it doesn't matter, if you are one too. But he will tell somebody else tomorrow. He'll tell Tom, Dick, and Harry, and we'll all get into trouble, and Herr Brücker will get into trouble. So he has to keep quiet. He has to learn to keep quiet." And then he turned to the boy. The boy had not cried. He took it without saying a word. A brave little boy, worthy of his father fallen in Russia. And he said, "Well, Gerhard, do you understand this now? Do you understand it? Do you understand that I gave you a slap because you deserved it?" And Gerhard said, "Yes, I do."

That's the spirit. That's the spirit. You have that spirit in Germany. And I can say one thing: I admire Germany in the person of the few National Socialists I met there — and how many is one to meet? — more than I did in 1935. In '35 I heard of all this enthusiasm. I was in India. And I used to say, well, "One day I'd go back to Europe. One day I'll perhaps be able to tell the Führer that I'd be bringing him the alliance of the élite of India." That was all right. There was an atmosphere. But in '48, among the ruins — and I saw something of those ruins. Hamburg was worse ruined than Babylon. I've seen the ruins of Babylon, and I can tell you, they are less ruined than Hamburg was in '48. It was charred walls, nothing but charred walls, and nobody in the streets, black streets. One platform in the station instead of 28. And in '53 there were 28 again, and there was a town. Wonderful people! I was more happy to see the resurrected Hamburg than I was of anything else. I said, "Where did they get that courage? Where did they get that stamina? They are invincible!"

And then not only Hamburg, Nuremberg. Nuremberg has been reconstructed practically as it was. Thanks to boys and girls who, under the bombs, would go to the tops of the buildings and take the measurements in order to reconstruct them after the war.

They did it during the war. And now you get Nuremberg growing out. Well, it doesn't look like the old Nuremberg, of course, because it is not centuries ago since it has been built. But in centuries to come, it will look the same, or more or less. At least they did what they could.

In the Prinzipalmarkt of Münster, in 1536—I'm sorry to say, but this is something that is very disturbing to me—Jan van Leiden, Bernhard Knipperdolling, and Heinz Krechting,[5] the three heads of the *Wiedertäufer*, the Anabaptists, were tortured to death in front of 10,000 people. I detest these foreign creeds that set Germans against Germans and Aryans against Aryans for some quibble, something to do with some ideology that is not even European. I hate that. Anyway, under this Prinzipalmarkt, under the footpath, there are 10,000 people now, descendants of those who watched that, buried under there due to the bombardments. And the Prinzipalmarkt has been reconstructed. The houses with these slanting roofs and gables and all that. It's all there, just as it was. Just as it was. And so many other towns. They have done their best. It's wonderful to see Germany since '48. I couldn't come back until '53. There were only five years between the two, and in five years, I saw such wonders. And the spirit, growing.

2. THE COTSWOLDS CAMP, 1962

Well, I already knew Mr. Colin Jordan and Mr. John Tyndall and the other members of the National Socialist Movement.[6] The NSM existed since 1962. I think it might have existed even before. I was in England in '61 for Easter holidays, and it was not yet the NSM, but some other organization headed by Mr. Andrew Fountaine.[7] And Jordan, I don't know whether he was in it or not. Anyhow, Jordan came to prominence after his great speech in Tra-

---

[5] Jan van Leiden (b. 1509) ruled Münster in 1534–1535. He was a charismatic religious visionary who proclaimed himself king and instituted Old Testament law, including polygamy. After a brief reign of terror, he was deposed and executed, along with his henchmen Bernhard Knipperdolling and Heinz Krechting, on 22 January 1536.

[6] Colin Campbell Jordan (1923–2009). John Tyndall (1934–2005).

[7] In May 1961, Savitri attended a British National Party camp on the estate of its president Andrew Fountaine (1919–1997) in Narford, Norfolk.

falgar Square in July '61. That was followed by the foundation of NSM and the growth of it. And then I met Françoise Dior in '62. Jordan was in correspondence with me, and he gave me her address and asked me to meet her.

And then in '62 I came over to England again, this was in July, as far as I remember. I put up in London at my friend Miss Gantry's, a perfectly apolitical woman, *very* pleasant and *very* understandable. She never spoke a word against us. She's perfectly apolitical. In sympathy, I would say. And I put up [i.e., stayed] with her. And she told me, "Look here, you came to go to the Cotswolds camp. I know you have an international Hitler camp, and you want to go. If I were you, I would not go because look what's in the papers." She showed me a newspaper, and the paper said that any foreigner that goes to this camp will not set foot in England again. She said, "Isn't it a pity? You have so many friends here. You want to see them again. You want to be in touch with them. Look at the risk you are taking." With my natural spirit of defiance, I answered, "It doesn't matter. I'll take the risk. I'm always ready to take the risk—for these kinds of things." And I went.

We had a meeting at the NSM in Holland Park, and we went to the station in separate groups. We were to meet somewhere else. We were to meet at Cheltenham, and from Cheltenham a car was to take us to the camp. All right, we traveled all night and went to Cheltenham. I don't remember if we went at night. We were in Cheltenham part of the day, and that night again we went to a place. I didn't know where we were going. I couldn't have found the camp again. We arrived in the camp. There were tents, and we each occupied a tent, or sometimes two or three in a tent. I was sharing my tent with a Belgian lady whose son was in the movement. Her son was with somebody else. And I remember awakening the next morning. It was Tyndall's voice coming from a tent, and they were speaking to I don't remember who. He said, "What? They are in bed still? Kick them out. Fancy staying in bed all this time until 8:00 like bloody democrats." When I heard that, I thought to myself, "But I'm in bed still. I must get up—quick, quick, quick." So I got up.

And I went to the river. As soon as I possibly could, I went to the river. It was practically deserted—nobody there—and I started bathing in the river. It was freezing cold water. I didn't want to be called a bloody democrat or acting like one. They came and offered me hot water, tepid water. I said, "No, thank you. I'll bathe in cold." So I bathed in the freezing cold water. It was summer of course. I don't know if I would have done it in winter. But in summer it was quite all right. And I came out, and I went up and had breakfast. We had tea. I don't like tea myself, but I took tea all the same. There was nothing else. There was no coffee.

And the camp started. Contact with different people. There were Swedes. There were Germans, of course, a good majority of Germans. There were one or two Italians, one or two Frenchmen, some Belgians, and one or two Americans. One or two Americans, one named Harry May. This Harry May had a swastika brassard on his right arm. He was the only one to wear one. And he showed himself extremely sympathetic and ran up to me and wanted to talk to me. There were others too. He really wanted to talk with me. I thought he was all right. I thought he was. I didn't know.

3. GEORGE LINCOLN ROCKWELL[8]

Anyhow, it went first day, second day, third day, and one day there was a surprise committee for us. They told us there was a surprise. They said, "Be ready. Sit on the benches, and you are going to have a surprise." Of course I was surprised before that to see that Tyndall had vanished. And Jordan, Jordan was not there. So I was wondering why. And they said to us, "They'll come later." Actually on that day—it was the 4th of August or the 3rd, I don't remember; it was very shortly after the beginning of the camp—there was the *Horst-Wessel-Lied* played. There were lights all over the place. It was in a forest. And suddenly, coming up from the river, I saw Rockwell—Tyndall one side of him, Jordan the other side of him. And we all stood up. We stretched out our arms, and the *Horst-Wessel-Lied* was played. And we were so pleased to see Rockwell.

It was written in all the papers, "This man shall not come to England." He was absolutely unwanted by the government, by the system. And the next thing we saw in the papers, "This man is

---

[8] George Lincoln Rockwell (1918–1967).

in England," and he was here. He gave us a speech on that very night. A speech that lasted practically all night. Well, not all night, but with the questions it practically lasted all night. It was the first time I saw Rockwell. I was really thrilled.

He was a great personality, but from what he told us on that very night, I felt, "Poor Rockwell, I wouldn't like to be in his place." Why? Because he became conscious of the value and truth of National Socialism after the war. And after he had fought the war so well on the American side as to get decorations and whatnot. He was a very good soldier. And I wouldn't have liked to be in his place. To have fought National Socialism all these years and then when the war is finished, when the other side has won, to find out that it was the truth. To find out that he had fought against the truth. Really I wouldn't like to be in his place. I'd rather be a little nobody, which I am.

But I liked him for his sincerity and for his courage. It takes courage to say, "I was wrong," especially when one had such a great reputation as he had, decorations and whatnot. He could've kept quiet. He did not keep quiet, because he knew that the truth was the truth, and one has to stick up for it. And he told us all this, his own history. It was after the way he had seen the reaction of the average American to MacArthur and to his policy that he had made an inquiry and found that National Socialism was right. And then he founded and organized this American Nazi Party that is called today the National Socialist White People's Party, NSWPP. It's not the only movement in America. But it is one of the movements, the main movement. There are two or three other little small groups.

At the time, I had been in touch with several of the members of the National Socialist Party of America. Among others, one Dan Burros.[9] I had been in correspondence with him from India. He used to write me enthusiastic letters. And suddenly he stopped. So I asked Rockwell, "What happened to Dan Burros?" And the answer of Rockwell struck me and made me admire Rockwell all the more. He said, "I kicked him out, that one." I said, "Why did you kick him out? What has he done?" "Well, I caught him half strangling a poor dog, and I don't want cowards in the National

[9] Dan Burros (1937–1965).

Socialist movement. To hurt an animal is to be a coward, especially a faithful, trusting dog. So I kicked him out."

That, I thought to myself, is something that the Führer himself could've done. I don't know whether he ever did it, whether he had the opportunity of doing it. But he could've done that. And it was the first time that I ever heard of a political party leader, a man who depends on public opinion to have a following, kick a man out of his party because that man had shown cruelty to an animal. I found that very good. I said, "Bravo, Rockwell, you did the right thing. In fact you did the right thing."

And I was to find out more about the famous Dan Burros a few years later in Montbrison where I was working in France as a stopgap teacher. There was a newspaper on the table one morning. I saw it when I came down to get my morning coffee. And in that paper there were a few lines. A man called Dan Burros had been found dead in New York in his room. He killed himself. And it is presumed that he committed suicide after an article had been printed in the New York papers saying that he, although a member of the National Socialist party, was in reality a Jew. So I was fixed on Dan Burros. That's all.

So now more about Rockwell. I read his book, *This Time the World*, his autobiography.[10] There were passages in it that I liked very much. And there were passages I didn't like so much. The passages I didn't like so much were those about his wives, his children. He could've mentioned the whole lot in a few lines. I didn't see the necessity of talking so long about his private attachment to his first wife and then why he separated from her, and then the second one was a beautiful Icelandic girl, all right. In fact the beautiful Icelandic girl left him when she made him choose between the movement and herself. And he chose the movement. Good for him. But why? Why not stick to him all the same, in spite of all the inconveniences? I find that not very good for a Nordic woman, to leave him for that. She's left him, and the children are with her in Iceland. Anyhow, that's the only thing I would say that was not absolutely well within my expectations of his book. The book is very fine.

---

[10] George Lincoln Rockwell, *This Time the World* (Glendale, California: Parliament House, 1962).

In fact it's quite all right. A very good book.

4. THE END OF THE COTSWOLDS CAMP

I saw the birth of the World Union of National Socialists, WUNS, founded by Rockwell—Rockwell was the first head of it—and by Tyndall and by Jordan and by all these heads of the parties that were there. Of course I joined it. And then I went to London, sent by the others, to pick up some American comrades, an American comrade and his wife. And I found them at the airport, and they went to their hotel, and it was said that we would go next morning to the camp. I knew how to go to the camp by now. But next morning, they showed me the papers: "The camp has been broken up." I said, "Really, the camp's been broken up, so what to do?" He said, "There's no use going. Don't go yourself. You'll only be getting yourself into trouble." I said, "But I left my things there. I left my suitcase and all of my things. I must collect that."

So I went. In spite of all, I went back to the camp. The camp was in a turmoil, but my things were there. I said, "All right, I'm going to collect them." But to my astonishment, the police were there also. And the police took the passports of everyone, and I asked Jordan, "Should I give my passport?" "Well, I can't tell you to not give it, because you have a foreign passport." Of course I had a Greek passport, not an Indian one any longer, because India didn't want to renew it. But I had to have a passport, so I took my old Greek one back again. The police saw it and put some stamp on it that I was not to come back to England again.

And from that day I tried four times to land in England again, and I was repelled every time. I was sent back. I tried by plane. I tried by boat. I tried every way. I was sent back. And it was all the more vexing because I was publishing a book in England at that time, *Long-Whiskers and the Two-Legged Goddess*, a book about cats, but not only about cats. The subtitle of it is, *The True Story of a "Most Objectionable Nazi" . . . and Half-a-Dozen Cats*. It has nine pictures, nine beautiful cat pictures in it. It exists, but of course, I would've liked to have 1,500 copies. I was never given more than 270 copies. I distributed a few. I had approximately 150 in France with my other books. When I left for India in 1971, I had to leave them somewhere. I couldn't take all that by plane. And the friend in whose house I left them died. Her husband died also. And her two daughters just burnt the lot. Not only those books but other books of mine and the last of my doctoral theses. And some books that I valued very much because the people who had given them to me are now dead. One of these books was a present to me by Frau Himmler, Himmler's widow, and other books. They only gave me one or two books, a *Universal History* and *Asiatic Mythology*,[11] one or two books that a friend of mine collected and sent over to me. And he was told, "We burnt the lot. They were either non-interesting or even horrible books." Horrible books?

Now let's talk of something else. Let's talk of Harry May. Harry May disappeared. He disappeared. Nobody knew where he was. He stayed one day or two. And I went and asked Rockwell, "What's happened to this man, Harry May?" "What's his name?" "Harry May." "Oh," he said, "Dear me, Harry May, that Communist." I said, "How did he come here?" I said, "Why did he come here? Why did he wear a swastika on his arm?" He said, "Well, he came to see." And he vanished. I heard of him again. He wrote to me a letter from the USA at my address. I had given him my address in all confidence. I never wrote again, naturally. And I was told that he had been very glad to see me, but that, of course, his ideas were not the same. Well, I could understand that his ideas were different since Rockwell himself told me he was on the other side. And I regretted very much that I gave him *The Lightning and the Sun*. And I saw the copy I had given him. He had underlined so many things. He had taken notes and this and that. So thoroughly, I could hardly understand why, as my book is not so important as to underline all these things. Apparently, he considered it worth underlining. And he sent to me a nasty book of Wilhelm Reich, a dirty Jew who writes about sex. I am not and I never was interested in sex. It's a chapter that has no place in my life at all. Why did you send me that dirty book? I don't know. Of

---

[11] Probably Leopold von Ranke, *Universal History: The Oldest Historical Group of Nations and the Greeks*, ed. by G. W. Prothero (New York: Harper and Brothers, 1885) and Joseph Hackin, et al., *Mythologie asiatique illustrée* (Paris: Librairie de France, 1928). In English: *Asiatic Mythology, a Detailed Description and Explanation of the Mythologies of All the Great Nations of Asia* (New York: Crescent, 1963).

course, I threw away the dirty book. I didn't even take the trouble of wasting my eyesight to read it. And that was that. Why did he send it to me? That made me even more suspicious. Well, there was one good thing in the fact of him sending me that book. It meant that he lacked any knowledge of psychology, because I'm the last person to send such a book to. Therefore he did not have any knowledge of what I am, and that's a good thing. A Communist without any knowledge of psychology is not such a dangerous Communist as one with a knowledge of psychology, naturally.

5. COLIN JORDAN, JOHN TYNDALL, AND FRANÇOISE DIOR

Now let us talk about Jordan and Tyndall. I liked them very much. Both of them. And my great regret is that they are not together still. I liked them very much. And Jordan introduced me to Françoise Dior, former countess of Caumont La Force. Her first husband was a member of one of the oldest French families, noble families, and she had by him a daughter who must be now 20.[12] She was born on the 4th of November, I think 20 years ago [1958].[13] Now Françoise Dior was born in 1932 on the 7th of April. And she grew up under the German occupation. And she had some very nice memories from that. She must've been beautiful as a child. She is a beautiful woman today. But she must've been very beautiful also as a child. And one of her sweetest remembrances she told me was the caress on her blonde hair of an SS man's hand, saying, "What a beautiful little Aryan girl." She was about eight or ten. She remembers that.

Of course, that didn't impress her. That did not impress her. She didn't link this with any ideology at the time. And her great love was French nobility, old France, France before the Revolution of 1789. And I quite understand her, for personally I always was against the French Revolution of 1789. I too was a royalist when I

---

[12] Dior's first husband was Robert-Henri Aynard de Caumont La Force (b. 1925).

[13] Dior's daughter, Christiane Caumont La Force, was born 4 November 1957 and hanged herself on 4 July 1978. Savitri learned of her death only in the latter half of 1979 (Letters to O. L., 16 July 1979 and 19 January 1981).

was eight years old, nine years old. A different kind of royalist, a royalist in favor of the King of Greece. But it was the same thing. I was a royalist to begin with. And so was she. And her dream was to marry into the French nobility because it was nobility. She believed in nobility.

Until she had great disappointments with it. She married a man who was not, well, what we would call a model. His private life was anything but the model of an Aryan, and an Aryan of noble family on top of that. She put up with him for some time, and then she had to divorce.[14] She took the child. She divorced. And slowly it dawned on her that real nobility was not a title. But real nobility was the nobility of blood. If you have the blood and the title, all right. But in that case, your title must give you the feeling that you have to live up to it. You can't have any sort of private life with a title.

But she was already in that milieu, and it was very difficult for her to pull herself out and to live up to the austerity of a real National Socialist. She feels National Socialist, of course. But many times I've told her about the needed austerity of everyday life if one is a National Socialist. She tries to live up to it. At least she tried.

I've not met her for quite a number of years now, more than seven years, and I only know of her evolution through very rare letters. I am at fault. I should have answered her last letter. Owing to many reasons, owing first of all to the fact that writing is difficult for me with my poor eyes, I have not yet replied. I am going to reply for the Winter Solstice.

She's interested in occult things, and she would like to have an occult background, that is to say, a background of experience of — I wouldn't say yoga — but the equivalent of it, to strengthen, not her belief in National Socialism, but her efficiency in supporting it. Of course, if one has developed yogic powers one is stronger, but I don't know exactly what way she's following. She told me she was following a way that was difficult but quick. I don't know enough about it, enough about what she's doing, what she's fol-

---

[14] According to Terry Cooper (personal correspondence, 20 April 2002), the divorce was initiated by Dior's husband because of her infidelities.

lowing, who is the man or the person who is helping her. To give an opinion, I'd have to know all that, and I don't know a word about it.

The only thing I can say is that she did a few rash things in Paris and had herself put in jail. She put up with jail very bravely. She was again in jail in England, accused of having ordered two members of the NSM to set fire to a synagogue, which was not the case. She never gave any such order. And she was asked in her trial, "Why did you give that order?" She said she didn't give it, and she was asked, "Do you approve of setting fire to synagogues?" If she had answered, "I don't approve of it at all," she would've got away with it. She would've perhaps had a month imprisonment. She had in fact something like two years. And she had these two years for the boldness of her answer.[15]

I had given her a piece of information. I had told her that around page 84 of Hans Grimm's book *Warum? Woher? aber Wohin?* it is said that the Führer himself did not approve of the pogrom of the night of the 9th of November 1938. It was organized, or rather supported, by Goebbels on his own account without the knowledge of the Führer at all. It was a movement whose real root was the indignation of the German people because at least two prominent Germans, Gustloff and vom Rath, were killed by two Jews, the last one being the famous Grynszpan.[16]

And it was a reaction to that, just as there was a reaction in 1905 in my own native town of Lyons because the president of the republic, Mr. Carnot, happened to be killed there by an Italian.[17] The Italian quarter was wrecked and ruined. People were even hurt. They tortured Italian pigs, pigs belonging to Italians, that is to say. It was a stupid thing to do and an awful thing to do. They were not the cause of that thing. The same thing, minus torture of

---

[15] Dior was tried at the Old Bailey and in January, 1968 was sentenced to 18 months in Holloway Prison.

[16] Wilhelm Gustloff (1895–1936) was the leader of the Swiss National Socialist Party, who was assassinated by David Frankfurter. Ernst vom Rath (1909–1938) worked at the German Embassy in Paris and was the random victim of Herschel Grynszpan. Both assassins were Jews.

[17] Marie-François-Sadi Carnot (b. 1837), the fourth President of the third French Republic, was assassinated in Lyons on 14 June 1894 by Italian anarchists.

animals, happened in Germany. People were indignant.

But the Führer did not approve of it. He told Goebbels the next day, "You have set my work back for years and perhaps broken it entirely with your stupid nonsense. Stupid nonsense, why? Because this will give a bad name to Germany in foreign lands. And we don't need that bad name now. We need to go forth without any complications. Why do you create trouble?" So, that's what the Führer said. I told Françoise about that. And she remembered it. She remembered the quotation of Hans Grimm, also the page and the book. And she had replied to the judge in front of everybody, "Well, I cannot approve of the burning of synagogues and such kind of things because the Führer did not. And I cannot approve of anything which he did not approve of. And I know he did not approve it because it's written in Hans Grimm's German book, *Warum? Woher? aber Wohin?*, page so-and-so." She got that information from me.

In fact, I myself was asked in Germany in 1955 what I thought about that pogrom. And I told them, "Well, I used to approve of it until last year, 1954." They said, "What, in 1954, you got better knowledge, better sense, and now you understand that it's wrong?" I said, "Not at all. In 1954, the book of Hans Grimm, *Warum? Woher? aber Wohin?*, appeared, and I read it and in that book I saw the Führer did not approve of it. Therefore, I cannot approve of a thing that he disapproves of. That's the only reason why I don't approve of it. Because, in the time, in 1938, I was in North Bengal preaching for the Hindu Mission. And when I heard of the pogrom, well, I said, 'All right, good for them. Some damage to some Jewish shops, and what of that? Doesn't make any difference.' But now I know the Führer was against it, I am naturally against it." My answer angered the people I was talking to in Germany, people who were not National Socialists, more than if I had said I approve of it, even more.

So I can understand the reaction of the judge in Françoise Dior's case. He gave her two years, and she put up with it, and she scrubbed the floor in the prison. She was made to do the most heavy work, and she did it joyfully.[18] People insulted her.[19] Peo-

---

[18] According to Terry Cooper (personal correspondence, 20 April 2002), Dior did cleaning work only once in prison, then complained to

ple caused her to have a very bad time, and she said, "I don't mind at all. I'm doing this for my Führer." And I liked that. I told Françoise, "I'm proud of you," when she told me that she was in prison.

Now, I cannot say more about her because I have not been in touch with her for many years. But she was sincere. She is sincere, I think. And even if she does not always understand all the implications of National Socialism, well, who does? It's no business of mine. My business is to try to be a good National Socialist myself and not to criticize anybody.

About the dealings between Françoise Dior, Jordan, and Tyndall, it's better to ask Tyndall himself, or Colin Jordan.[20] It's no business of mine at all. And I really regret that whatever happened might've contributed to the breaking up of the NSM, and I deplore that very, very, very much. But I think that if the people in the NSM had been a little more attached to the ideology, whatever may happen in the private sector could not influence their attitudes, and they could've stayed together all the same. There was no reason for the falling apart between Jordan and Tyndall, and they have stayed apart.

Tyndall is now heading the National Front in Britain. I'm very glad of that. I'm very glad the National Front is against entry of more and more and more complete non-Aryans or mongrels. Colin Jordan wrote to me lately telling me that Tyndall accepts the membership of Jews in the National Front — if they are English

---

the prison doctor about her health. Her doctor in Paris sent a letter certifying that her health was delicate. From then on, she worked in the prison jam factory, which she enjoyed so much that jam-making remained a hobby once she was released from prison, sometimes to the distress of her close friends.

[19] While in prison, Dior's fellow prisoners nicknamed her "Nazi Nell." Prison nicknames, however, are not uncommon and not necessarily mean-spirited.

[20] In 1963, Dior was briefly engaged to Tyndall. She then broke her engagement and took up with Colin Jordan. They were married in a Nazi ceremony in London on 6 October 1963. In August 1964, Tyndall split off from Jordan and the National Socialist Movement, launching the Greater Britain Movement. Tyndall maintains that the split was purely political and denies that it was motivated by the loss of Dior to Jordan.

Jews, of course. I did not answer his letter. I don't know whether that's true or not, and therefore I'm not repeating it. I'm just saying that Jordan wrote to me to tell me that. I did not reply to him. I don't know what to say. I'm not on the spot, and I don't wish to judge. I hope it's not true. I hope it's a mistake. I hope it's misinformation and not any gesture of Jordan's purposely directed against Tyndall. I hope that the difference, the falling apart, is a thing of the past completely now.

6. IMMIGRATION AND MISCEGENATION

Whatever it is, anything that can contribute to the stopping of the inrush of non-Aryans into England and their settling there and their marrying there and their mixing with English people, anything like that is very good. But they should've thought of it long before. This invasion of England by non-Aryans and this awful damage to the Aryan race in England is in reality, in my eyes, a sort of divine punishment for England raising her hand against Adolf Hitler. That's what a country gets when it turns against Adolf Hitler and against his people.

Unfortunately, his own people are having the same trouble with the *Gastarbeiter*.[21] I wouldn't mind so much if the *Gastarbeiter* in Germany were only North Italians, say. Lombards are Aryans. Or if they were really good Greeks. Not all Greeks are really good. Some Greeks are mixed, like some Italians are mixed. In most countries of southern Europe, you get people who are not perfectly worthy of marrying northern Europeans, Aryans. But you have a number of Turks among the *Gastarbeiter*. And that's the trouble. Turks and whatnot, anything you can imagine, anything you can imagine.

I wouldn't be astonished if you have North Africans. There are so many in France. I don't know if they are invading Germany also, but France has about two or three million North Africans, Berbers and Arabs. Well, of course, these people have been breeding very heavily since the occupation of their country by the French. In 1830, they were not so numerous, and they never needed to go outside the frontiers of North Africa, of Algiers. Now I think they are 10 times more numerous or 15 times more

---

[21] Guest workers.

numerous than they were in 1830. And they need space. Well, instead of invading their neighbors, they invade the former protecting countries. And they marry French girls. Well, it's the fault of the French girls. It's not the fault of the Arabs. Because the French girls are not so natural, if they haven't got the sense of a tigress, who will not mate with another species unless she is forced to. Or the lion.

They tried an experiment in the zoo in Vienna. Before the war, the zookeepers were party members. Everybody who had a government job in Austria or the greater Reich was generally a member of the party. After the war it seems they dismissed all the zookeepers who had been Nazis. Now fancy that. As though they were going to make Nazi propaganda among their animals. The animals don't need it. Animals are naturally Nazis. At least the higher animals, the big cats, the felines. They took it into their heads to do an experiment, and they put an unfortunate lioness with a tiger. Well, the poor tiger didn't want the lioness, and the lioness didn't want the tiger, but what could they do? They are animals. Men can't keep control of their instincts. I mean to say, many men cannot. But I speak of big felines. And they mated, and the product was a feline, and they called that a "tigro."

Well, if I say a human being hasn't the sense that a tigress has, that is to say, willfully goes with a person of another race, it's not the fault of the person of the other race, it's the fault of the woman. I disapprove strongly of these French women who go around with the North Africans or anything else, any other non-Aryan, and of the English women in Cheltenham. That's a small place in the West of England where I went before going to the Cotswolds camp. I met two perambulators with half-Negro babies in them. In a small town like that. How do those things happen? How do these women come to do these things? That is what puzzles me. And if they do, well, they are not worthy to belong to the Aryan race. They should be dismissed.

If I were the dictator of England I would send them to work in some place where they have need of workers. Instead of sending a foreign worker, I would send them. After sterilizing them, because it's no good mating them with an Aryan afterwards. I suppose you know that the people who breed dogs, say Alsatians or something like that, do. If an Alsatian bitch has been with a mongrel dog, they do not mate her with an Alsatian again. If she's impregnated once it's sufficient. She's no longer useful for breeding purposes. They might keep her if they like her. I don't see why they shouldn't keep her, poor dog. Why kill her? No, certainly not. I'm not for killing her. But they don't mate her again. They don't have her mated again.

7. MATT KOEHL[22]

I like Matt Koehl. I admire him. He's a very worthy successor of Rockwell, and he has an advantage over Rockwell. He's a German. It's not Rockwell's fault, of course, but in my eyes, that's an advantage. I wish I could become a German one day myself if there was such a thing as reincarnation. I don't know whether I'd like to be a German or not. But at first glance, I'd like to be. On the other side, I don't know if I would like to be a German if I had to put up with the discipline in the German family. Suppose my father was an anti-Nazi. It can happen in Germany, you know. Suppose my father was an anti-Nazi and gave me slaps and kicked me about because of my ideas. That could happen. I wouldn't like it to happen. I'd rather be something else, but a Nordic race of course.

To speak of Matt Koehl: I like his articles. I read his articles in *White Power*. I like *White Power* immensely. I think it's one of the best papers that comes out in the USA. And I find that whatever he says is perfectly logical. Another thing: he never speaks of himself. He speaks of the ideology. And his book is very good. Very, very good really.[23] I have nothing to say except one thing: I'd like to meet him. I've never met him. I'd like to meet him very much. I think he's most efficient.

There's one thing I don't like in the movements of America. There are too many. I don't like this idea of small National Socialist groups that exist only because somebody wants to be at the head of them. I'd like them to all meditate on the example of Streicher, Julius Streicher, the one of the Nuremberg martyrs who said "Heil Hitler!" in front of the gallows. They were his last

---

[22] Matthias Koehl was born in 1935.

[23] Savitri is likely referring to Koehl's pamphlet *The Future Calls* (Arlington, Virginia: National Socialist White People's Party, 1976).

words, his words before that being, "One day the Bolsheviks will treat you as you are treating us." Now, "Heil Hitler!" and he went up, and they hanged him. Well, this man Streicher had a party of his own. He was the head of, well, I would say, a national socialist party, a party with the same ideas, when Adolf Hitler was rising. But he felt that Adolf Hitler was the man, that he was worth more than Streicher was. Streicher was sincere and *disinterested*, and this disinterested attitude is *the* attitude for a National Socialist. What did Streicher do? He went to his followers and told them, "The party is dissolved. I am dissolving it. There's no more party at all. You go join the NSDAP. I'm joining the NSDAP myself. Hitler is our Führer, Führer of all the Germans." And he dismissed his own people and told them to join our party, the growing party, the party of the future. Well, why don't these small leaders, those who are conscious at least of the efficiency of Matt Koehl, tell their followers to join the NSWPP?

There's another thing I feel rather shaky about, and I felt that already under Rockwell. It's the insistence, in some of the literature supposed to be National Socialist from the USA, on the ideas of "Christian" and "White." Even the title of Matt Koehl's organization, National Socialist *White* People's Party. Well, if I were a Jewess, I would join it. I would infiltrate. I would try to destroy it from inside, if I were a Jewess. And I would get in because I'm White. Isn't that so? It's a funny thing to see that more Jews have not thought of it. Well, good for us if they're not so clever as they were once. If they're going down, good for us.

But White is not necessarily Aryan. The Arabs are White. Real Arabs, not mixed with Negroes. But too many Arabs are mixed with Negroes because they have harems, and they like a variety of females. Unfortunately, a variety of females makes a variety of offspring. But those who are pure Arab are White. Berbers are White. Berbers are Mediterranean people. They were in North Africa before the Arabs came. Jews are White. Jews are Semites. They are the first cousins of the Arabs. They might be enemies, but they are the first cousins of one another, or should be. The Assyrians, the Akkadians, all these people of Mesopotamia and of North Mesopotamia, of the upper Euphrates, in antiquity, they were White. Hittites were White. I don't know how far the Hittites were Aryans, or have Aryan mixture. I don't know. Their language may be Aryan, but that doesn't mean to say that they were. Many people speak an Aryan language. Negroes speak English today. Who doesn't? That doesn't mean they are Englishmen. Anyhow, White does not mean Aryan.

The trouble is that in the USA today, the situation is such that the people's consciousness, simple people's consciousness, is White and Black. If you say "White," they understand. They wouldn't understand the word Aryan, half of them. But it's dangerous, because Jews are White. And they are much more dangerous than Negroes. A clever Jew is much more dangerous than a Negro. Negroes are like children. Leave the Negroes to themselves, absolutely to themselves, without any foreign influence, and they are not dangerous at all, except that they breed fast. Well, put them in another surrounding. Put them in another place, and don't give them any development aid. That's one thing I would say: this aid to the undeveloped should be stopped completely. Completely.

And even more I would say, I'm not for all this aid even to the developed. When I was in France as a stopgap teacher we had propaganda: such-and-such a society for *retardates*, backward children, sick people, etc., etc., supporting, giving money for them to be pushed along, to be not so undeveloped. Even Whites, even Aryans who are not really up to the mark, deficient, shouldn't be encouraged, and encouraged to breed at that. I'm all for the steps that Adolf Hitler took, or wanted to take. He didn't take them, in fact. He couldn't take them, really, because the church was against him. Especially the Archbishop of Münster, von Galen.[24] Von Galen used to preach against the measures he wanted to take from his pulpit. These people should not be encouraged to live, because you cannot get a real strong Aryan society if you have these people in it, and if they breed. If they don't breed, all right. If you have a weak person that doesn't breed, it doesn't make any difference, but don't allow them to breed. Anyhow, that's one thing, White instead of Aryan.

Another thing is that mixture of Aryan and Christian. I have had very good propaganda sent to me from an organization called Sword of Christ in America asking for the liberation of Ru-

---

[24] Clemens August Count von Galen (1878–1946).

dolf Hess. Nothing better. But telling us that it's from the so-called Christian point of view. I wrote to them. I told them what I thought of it, and they replied telling me that the Jews, the Israelites of antiquity, were originally Aryans. But how can they believe that? I know that's a theory. It doesn't come from them. It comes from a man called Saint-Yves d'Alveydre, a Frenchman who wrote a book a hundred years ago with a queer theory like that.[25] He also mixes up Hebrew words and Sanskrit words. "They look like each other, therefore they come from Sanskrit." They don't come from Sanskrit at all. It's just like so much stuff you read from old missionaries in India, telling you Hinduism comes from Judaism. Why? Why is it? One of the gods of India is Brahma. "Brahma is Abraham." His wife is Sarasvati. "Sarasvati is Sarah." All right! They put two words together, and it's finished. There's no good etymological connection between Brahma and Abraham. Absolutely none. But still they put one where there is none. And Saint-Yves d'Alveydre did exactly the same to support this theory that the ancient Israelites were Aryans. They were not Aryans at all. They were Semites, and they always were Semites.

They may be mixed with Aryans now. That's a different thing. And that is one of the reasons for their efficiency. When they mixed with Aryans. Especially when an Aryan marries a Jewess, the child is a Jew. The child is a Jew from his mother, not from his father. If an Aryan marries a Jewess, the child is a Jew according to Jewish law. And he gets some of the characteristics, some of the virtues from the Aryan race, along with some of the characteristics of the Jewish. He might get efficiency in trade from his mother and some sort of idealism, disinterested idealism, from his father. And then he's doubly dangerous.

That's what I have to say on Matt Koehl.

---

[25] Joseph-Alexandre Saint-Yves d'Alveydre (1842–1909) was an influential 19th-century French esotericist. His teachings on Agartha, the mysterious Himalayan headquarters of occult masters, and his concept of "root races" influenced, among others, Helena Petrovna Blavatsky (1831–1891), the founder of the Theosophical Society. The book Savitri mentions is *La Mission des Juifs*, 2 vols. (1884) (Paris: Éditions traditionnelles, 1990).

Chapter 3

RELIGION

On Christianity

1. GREEK ORTHODOX CHRISTIANITY

I'll be very frank about Christianity. I used to go to church. I'm christened in the Greek Orthodox Church. And I used to go to church until I was about 23, until I became conscious of being a National Socialist. The church was not really a church in those days. It was just a room in my native town. Now the Greeks of Lyons have a real church and a beautiful one. I go sometimes. I still go when I'm there. I used to go, but not because I loved the values of Christianity. I never could accept the values of Christianity. But, I liked the church. I liked the church because it was national, supposed to be national at least. I had been told that forever: "The national church of Greece is the Orthodox Church. Modern Greece is the daughter of Byzantium. It's the continuity of what was Byzantium once, what the Turks have destroyed. The Greek nationality would not be alive if it hadn't been for the church and for the monasteries under Turkish dominion for 400 years." And this, and also the beauty of Byzantine music and of Byzantine singing. I used to go to church, and I liked it. And I like it still. But as far as the values of Christianity, that's a quite different thing.

By the way, I really believe that a very great number of modern Greeks don't believe in the values of Christianity at all. Many of them might not even believe in the facts that they are celebrating, for instance, Easter, the resurrection, and things like that. If you really ask them, if they are sincere, they will tell you, "The church tells us so, but it seems rather queer to believe, rather difficult to believe." It doesn't matter. They are attached to the church just because it is the national church.

My second doctoral thesis was on a Greek philosopher, Theophilos Kaïris, born in 1784, died in prison in 1853. He was put into prison by the Greek government for openly not believing in the Orthodox Church, the national church. The real theme of my thesis was not so much the person Kaïris, but the Greek mentality regarding religion. The modern Greek mentality is exactly the same as that of Ancient Greece. Socrates was condemned because he did not believe in those gods in which the city believed. Had he not been an Athenian, nobody would have cared in Athens. Had he been an Egyptian, a Persian, an Assyrian, nobody would have cared whether he believed in the gods of Greece at all. It was natural that he should believe in his own gods. Each country had its own. And there was harmony between them all. They used to borrow each other's gods now and then, when they really wanted the services of a god, against illness or something like that. That is antiquity. That is modern Greece.

No modern Greek would find it necessary to convert a Turk to Christianity. He's a Turk, well, all right. It's natural for a Turk to be Mohammedan. He's a man from Western Europe, and it's natural for a Western European to be a Protestant or a Catholic. He's a foreigner. A Catholic, even a Greek Catholic, is a foreigner. You can hear a Greek tell you, "Well, we have three foreigners in our building. There is a Catholic on the first floor. There's a Jew on the third floor. And there's an American on the ground floor." An American, a Jew, a Catholic: they're all foreigners.

Well, I had this spirit myself, as an adolescent. Although it was not my father's spirit. My father was not a believer at all. He was christened, but he didn't believe it. He was what you call a freethinker. My mother was a follower of the Church of England as an Englishwoman, but she was more and more and more going towards skepticism, agnosticism, as she grew older. In the end she used to say, "Well, I don't know whether the soul exists or not, whether we have a soul or not. That is a metaphysical problem that's beyond my comprehension."

2. CHRISTIANITY AND NATIONALISM

And what I had against Christianity from the very start was, first, that it was not national. It was not national. We had something before it in Greece. Why didn't we stick to that? We had something as beautiful, and more beautiful, than it. We had the worship of the sun. We had the worship of gods that represented natural forces. We had the worship of the forces of the universe.

We were in harmony with the universe and not with man. It was not man-centered. Our religions were not man-centered. No religions of antiquity were man-centered. Except one. Judaism was not only man-centered, it was Jew-centered.

The other religions were, of course, national. But at the same time they were cosmic. Anything that has to do with sun worship or moon worship or worship of forces of nature is naturally cosmic. And the man of antiquity never thought anything of worshiping somebody else's gods. The Pharaoh Amenhotep III, when he was sick, couldn't find any solace by the means of the god of medicine, the god of healing, of Egypt, Khons the son of Amon and Mut. No. But he heard that Ishtar of Nineveh was good for healing. She had healing powers. He brought the statue of Ishtar of Nineveh from 2,000 kilometers away. He brought it to Egypt. And it seemed that she cured him. She stayed two years in Egypt, and then she was sent back with her priests to Nineveh.

That was the spirit of antiquity. Freedom, no intolerance at all. No lack of toleration. None of that, "If you don't belong to us, you're damned. If you don't have our religion, our belief, you're damned." None of that in antiquity. None of that before Christianity.

The Jews are quite a different thing. The Jewish religion is quite a different thing. The Jewish religion is national, tribal. Yahweh, Jehovah is the God of the Jews. The Jews will not say, "If you don't belong to Jehovah you are damned. Oh, no. Oh, no. You are a Moabite, it's quite natural you worship Chemosh. You are an Ammonite, you worship Milcom, quite natural. You're a Philistine, you worship Dagon, you worship somebody else, Philistine gods. But if you are in our *Bezirk*, in our region, you must be destroyed. This place is only for us."

That's the Old Testament. I don't want to expatiate on that. I only ask those who don't believe me to open the Bible and read Deuteronomy chapter seven, the first verses of chapter seven. That's all in it.

Now I didn't like that very much. It has one advantage only, that is to say, it is forbidden for a Jew to marry a non-Jew. Not that the non-Jew is bad. Sometimes he does marry non-Jews. For instance, Mahlon, son of Naomi, married Ruth, who was a Moabitess.[1] And that very same Moabitess married Boaz,[2] the son of Rahab of Jericho[3] who herself was celebrated for taking in the Jewish spies of Joshua.[4] Anyhow, they were taken in sometimes. "Your God is my God, and your people will be my people," said Ruth to her mother-in-law Naomi when, after the death of her husband, she followed Naomi to Judea. But it was an exception. Generally it was forbidden for the Jews to take women in Canaan. Although racially they were same. There was no difference between the Jew and the Canaanite, racially. But they were worshippers of different gods. And it was feared that they would entice their husbands to worship their gods. That was the great idea. In that way, of course it kept the Jews among themselves. It was a good thing, from a racialist point of view.

3. INTERNATIONAL RELIGIONS AND RACE-MIXING

What I have against international religions — be it Christianity, be it Islam, the two religions that sprang from Judaism, be it even Buddhism that sprang from an Aryan creed — is that they are international and that they have no objection to interracial marriages. In Buddhism it's not generally done. You don't see an Indian Buddhist marry a Japanese Buddhist. A Japanese Buddhist wouldn't like it anyhow. Japanese people are really racialists. But you could see Arabs with harems of women of all nationalities. The Arabs of Spain, the founders of the Caliphate of Cordova, were no Arabs at all after the third generation. The very son of Musa ibn Nusair, the conqueror of Spain in the early 8th century, was called Abdul Aziz. He married a Visigoth woman, Egilona, the widow of the last king of the Visigoths.[5] And his son married another Aryan, or part-Aryan, and his son the same thing. After three generations or four there was virtually no Arab blood at all in the rulers of Cordova. And you get the same thing in other countries. You get intermarriages of Arabs and Negroes. Abyssin-

---

[1] Ruth 1:4; 4:10.

[2] Ruth 4:13.

[3] Matthew 1:2.

[4] Joshua 2:1-7.

[5] Roderick (c. 670-c. 711) was from 710-711 the last king of the Visigoths. Musa ibn Nusair lived c. 640-c. 715, his son Abdul Aziz c. 670-717. Egilona's dates are unknown.

ians are a mixture of the two. You get a mixture of Arabs and anything that's Mohammedan. If you are a Mohammedan you can marry any Mohammedan. And if you are a Christian, there's no reason why you shouldn't marry any Christian. According to the church it's not forbidden. It's not forbidden at all. And I don't like that.

I was always shocked by the National Socialist propaganda, very opportunist propaganda, saying that, "We have nothing against Christianity. We are very good Christians." That always shocked me. The one thing that I underlined when I read the 25 points for the first time—the 25 points was at the basis of National Socialism, for the public at least—is point 24, "We stand for a positive type of Christianity." What does the Führer mean by positive Christianity? Probably: aid one another. All the institutions like NSV,[6] the Winter Aid, Aid to Mother and Child, all these things represent what the public can consider as positive Christianity: love your neighbor. All right.

And then comes the end of point 24: "The party is neutral in matters of religion. We admit any kind of religion, provided it does not shock the moral feelings of the German race and does not go against the state." Well, I thought of this, and I said to myself, "Any religion that allows marriage with view to reproduction between an Aryan and a non-Aryan, provided they are both christened in the same church, is naturally against the moral feelings of the Germanic people and against the interests of the state, and Christianity is one of these religions. A Catholic Negro can marry a Catholic of any country including a Catholic German. Why not? They are both Catholics."

I knew a couple, a mixed couple like that. The woman, a beautiful, young, blue-eyed blonde Aryan, the daughter of a German soldier of the First World War and of an Alsatian woman. Unmarried. Doesn't make any difference. An Aryan. She met in some bar-room in Lyons, my native town, a perfectly brown, dark brown Dravidian of South India, considered by other Indians of upper castes as an untouchable. And he was a Catholic, and she was a Catholic, and the two married. And they had four children,

---

[6] NSV stands for *Nationalsozialistische Volkswohlfahrt*, National Socialist People's Welfare.

three sons and a daughter. Fortunately the children are not married. I hope they never marry. They were very happy together it seems. The man was not bad. I have nothing against him. But I would've liked him to marry a Dravidian untouchable, a Dravidian *harijan*, they call it, like himself. And she should've married a Frenchman, an Alsatian, or a German. She was a German herself. But because they were Catholics they got married. If they had not been Christians at all, if he had been worshipper of Mariama— Mariama is a mother goddess of South India, one of the numerous mother goddesses of South India—and she a worshipper of Wotan, like in antiquity, they never would have come together. There you are. That is the advantage of these national creeds. They keep each one in his place.

And when they don't, well, it's an exception. Or else the two people are very near each other. You had, for instance, probably intermarriages between people who worshipped Thor in antiquity and Slavs. How did the Poles come about? Poles are Slavs with a mixture of German. They are not pure Slavs, and so many Russians are not pure Slav either. The Russians, the ancestors of the Russians, before Christianity worshipped another god with a hammer also, with four heads, Perun. Perun and Thor got along very well together. They were neighbors. They symbolized the same thing. Well, why not? They were brothers. They were very near in all this.

And of course you had the Gauls marrying Germans in the Merovingian days. Before the Gauls became Christians, they had their own gods. They had some international gods, cosmic gods, the sun and the moon, naturally. The sun and the moon. There's a lovely little dialogue in a French tale, a short story of Anatole France, of a Gaul who followed Caesar to England. And they are both coming back, and the Gaul saw with his own eyes the shattering to pieces of the Roman fleet on the coast of England due to the tide. And he knows the moon governs the tide. And he tells Caesar on his way back, "You see, the moon is a very powerful goddess, and she loves the Gauls. She's on the Gauls' side." And Caesar laughs and says, "Well, everybody considers the moon as a goddess. We do. The Greeks do. Everybody does. Even the Carthaginians did. And that moon, you say, belongs to the Gauls, but she's now shining over Rome." And the Gaul looks at him and says, "Shining over Rome, the moon? It must be a different moon." That's national spirit. I would say that. Real tribal spirit. It might look rather naïve to a person who lives in the 20th century. But it has its advantages. It has its advantages.

The Gauls very quickly married Romans, and led to Gallo-Romans. But some of them also married Germanic people. All the North of France is Germanic. And I'd like to point out that not only the North of France but all of the aristocracy of Europe, all the kings and queens of Europe from the early days on, are Germanic. Even the Russians. Who was Rurik?[7] Rurik was a German, or a Swede. It's the same thing. Who were the rulers of Italy? Well, the German emperors, of course. Who were the rulers of France? The Merovingians, the Carolingians, and the other ones. They were all descended from Germans, from Franks who conquered France. France was called France because of the Franks, and Franks are Germans.

They were Christians. That was their downfall. That is to say, they did not stay purely Germanic because they were Christians. They shouldn't have married people from the South of Europe. They should have married from the North of Europe. And you have some of the greatest emperors of Germany who married foreigners. For instance, Otto II. Otto II married Theophano, the daughter of Romanos II of Byzantium, the sister of Basilius, the exterminator of the Bulgarians, as we call him, Basilius II.[8] She was his sister. His other sister, Anna, married the recently Christianized Russian Vladimir, and Russia became Christian, officially at least, from that day.[9] The sign of Christianity is, in the begin-

---

[7] Rurik (c. 830–c. 879) was a Viking warrior who founded the first Russian state of Novgorod in 762. His descendants ruled Russia until 1917.

[8] Otto II, King of the Germans and Emperor of Rome (955–983), reigned from 961–983. Theophano (c. 959–991) married Otto II in 972 and bore the title of Empress of Rome until her death in 991. Her father (or on some accounts, godfather) Romanos II, Emperor of Byzantium (940–963), reigned from 959–963. His son, Basil II, Emperor of Byzantium (958–1025), reigned from 976–1025.

[9] Anna, Princess of Byzantium (963–1011), married Vladimir, Grand Duke of Kiev (c. 956–1015), in 988 or 989 to seal a military and dynastic alliance. One of the conditions of the marriage was Vladi-

ning, intermarriage. And I don't like that.

Of course, I know there are some National Socialist groups in the USA like this Sword of Christ group in Arkansas that tell you the Bible doesn't encourage interbreeding. The Bible doesn't encourage it, perhaps. It doesn't encourage interbreeding of Jews with non-Jews, with non-Jews *religiously*. But it doesn't mind a Jew marrying a Semite who's converted herself or himself to Judaism. And you get converts to Judaism in the days of Christ and afterwards. Who was Timothy? Half Greek, half Jew. And there were many of these God-fearing people. They called them in the Bible, the New Testament, God-fearing. They were half Jew, half Greek, or proselytes, people who were living near the synagogue who were not circumcised but still worshiped Yahweh. And this, all this prepared Christianity.

That's what I have to say about Christianity. I'm not against it. I don't want to say that I would like to bring people away from it. If they have nothing else, let them have it. But I think on principle it's incompatible, not with National Socialism only, but with any attitude centered on race, centered on nation and race. In order to be a nationalist and a Christian, you have to distort Christianity. You have to consider it as a national religion, like the Irish do. The Polish do, in spite of Communism. Like the Spanish do. In that way they are all right. Nothing will happen to them. But it is due to a misunderstanding of the spirit of Christianity, of the spirit of Christianity as it has come to us through the legend of Christ, perhaps not through the historical Christ, if it is true—I don't say it is, but some people think it is—that the historical Christ was really a Jewish nationalist fighting the Romans.

4. ROBERT AMBELAIN ON CHRISTIANITY

[I wish to recommend three books by Robert Ambelain.[10]] They were lent to me by this French lady. They are extraordinary,

---

mir's baptism. Vladimir was the great-grandson of Rurik.

[10] Robert Ambelain, *Jésus, ou le mortel secret des Templiers* [*Jesus, or The Fatal Secret of the Templars*] (Paris: R. Laffont, 1970), *La vie secrete de Saint Paul* [*The Secret Life of Saint Paul*] (Paris: R. Laffont, 1971), and *Les lourds secrets du Golgotha* [*The Heavy Secrets of Golgotha*] (Paris: R. Laffont, 1974).

and they are all the more convincing in that the man is not a Jew. He's an Aryan, but he's pro-Jew. He's a very good Hebrew scholar. He knows Hebrew as I know French or English or Greek. And he is an historian. And a high graded Freemason, on top of that. What really gets up his nose is the antagonism between Christianity, especially Medieval Christianity, and the Jews. He says that, "May his blood fall on us and on our children,"[11] was an interpolation. "The Jews never said that. Why were they persecuted for saying that when they never said it?" Personally, I don't care if they said it or not. To me, it is quite immaterial.

To him, the person of Jesus is the son of a Jewish anti-Roman agitator, and he was himself an anti-Roman agitator and nothing else. No teacher of any sort of religion. Just an anti-Roman who was condemned to death by the Romans on the cross. Well, it's perfectly true that if he were really condemned by the Jews, according to Jewish law, on the charge of blasphemy for calling himself God, he would not have been crucified. He would've been stoned. The Jewish custom was stoning, *lapidation*, and not crucifixion. Of course he never called himself God. He always said, "the Father and I," "There are things I do not know but the Father knows."[12]

But even if he had called himself God and he were condemned by the Jews for blasphemy, he was crucified by the Romans. He was condemned by the Romans, not for calling himself God but for saying that he was "King of the Jews" and for resistance activities. He was a Jewish *maquisard*.[13] According to Ambelain, his father also and his grandfather also. His grandfather Ezekias was supposed to have been crucified under Herod.

Now according to Ambelain, Paul was no insignificant little Jew. He was one-fourth Jewish and three-fourths Idumean, that is to say, Arab, of the dynasty of the Herods. He was the grandson of Herod the Great by his mother Cypros. And he was neither in the Arab gang nor in the Jewish. He was circumcised. He had himself circumcised when he was aged. That is to say, he was not circumcised as a baby. He had no place among the Jews, and Jews

---

[11] Matthew 27:25.
[12] Mark 13:32.
[13] Guerrilla fighter.

didn't like him. They did not like neophytes who come when they are older and for perhaps non-religious reasons. So he tried to found a sect of his own. According to Ambelain, he took the person of that Jewish agitator and made him into a mystic figure, added to him all the characteristics of the age-old vegetation gods, Mithra, Osiris, Adonis, and others. The disciples of Jesus already had spread the rumor that he was resurrected, so half the job was done. He only had to say, "Yes, he was resurrected, and he rose up from the dead for the salvation of the world." He made him into a world figure, when in reality he wasn't even a Jewish figure. And by his doing that, he spread an influence of Jewry on the whole world. You have a perfect Aryan girl, a German named Ruth or named Sarah, or you have an Englishman named David. You have an Englishman, Isaac Newton, called Isaac. What is all that? What is that stuff? You have a man called Johannes. Johannes is Jokannan in the Hebrew. Jokannan is John. The whole thing has changed.

After the spreading of Christianity, after the acceptance of Christianity as a state religion by the Roman emperors after Constantine,[14] it seems that *then* the gospels as we know them today were written. They hadn't got the same ones. There is no manuscript of any gospel except one or two, what they call the Apocrypha. And even then, there's no manuscript contemporary of Christ in the world. The first ones are of the 4th century AD. Those we have, Matthew, Mark, Luke, and John (well, in reality, there were other names), date from the 4th century AD. The gospels that the Christians used to use before that date, they were taken back to Constantinople by order of Constantine. In packets of 50. And packets of 50 of the new ones were given to them, the new ones we have today.

And there are queer things in them. For instance, in the gospel according to Matthew, Christ was born under Herod.[15] Herod died in the year 4 BC. Therefore, he was born before 4 BC. Maybe 5 or 6 or 7 BC. According to Luke, he was born under the magis-

---

[14] Flavius Valerius Constantinus (c. 271–337) reigned from 306–337. Constantine's conversion followed the Battle of the Milvian Bridge in 312.

[15] Matthew 2:1.

trateship of the Roman Quirinius.[16] Quirinius ruled Palestine before Pilate, that is to say, in about 6 AD.[17] That is to say, if Jesus
were born in 4 BC he would be at least ten years old. Which is the
right date of birth? Why does one say this and one say that? Anyhow, this Ambelain has picked the gospels right through, the canonical ones and the apocryphal ones that have survived in Cop-
tic translation, in Slavonic translation, Ethiopian translation, in all
sorts of translations. He has gone through them all. And it has
given a figure of Jesus that is not at all the classical one.

The Jews are the ones behind the institution of Christianity.[18]
I'm quite sure of that. It was a means to emasculate the race.
There is a contradiction between the principles of Christianity and
warrior behavior. They can't go together. If you have to love your
enemy like yourself, you can't fight. And the first Christians did
not fight for the Romans. But there was a compromise. When
Constantine wanted Christianity to be the state religion, he said,
"Call the bishops." The bishops said, "All right, we accept it, but
we have to accept to fight for you. It will no longer be an offense
to fight for the Roman Empire." That was a compromise, an unhealthy compromise. All compromises are unhealthy. You can't
have them, can't have them.

The gentle Jesus of the Christians, the classic gentle Jesus never
existed. I believe in Ambelain's theory. The real Jesus was a Jew
fighting for his own race, a very respectable man. I have nothing
against him. I much prefer him to the classical image of Jesus, in
fact. He didn't want the salvation of the whole world. He wanted
his country to be out of the Roman Empire. I understand that. I
quite understand his struggle. But that struggle doesn't interest
mankind. It interests the Jews. And the Jews found out, of course,
that the best way to put him onto mankind was to give him sort
of a mystical personality, a personality of peace and what mankind wanted, and to assimilate his qualities with the qualities of

---

[16] Luke 2:2.

[17] Publius Sulpicius Quirinius (d. 21 or 22) ruled Palestine from 6–
11.

[18] This is the argument of Savitri's *Paul de Tarse*. Savitri's suspi-
cions were shared by the American classicist and White Nationalist
writer Revilo P. Oliver. See Revilo P. Oliver, *Reflections on the Christ
Myth* (Uckfield, Sussex: Historical Review Press, 1994).

the already existing gods.

Now 1400 years BC, there was a religion, existing still in Christ's days, the religion of Mithra, the Iranian god. In fact, in the very words that are attributed to Christ at the moment of the consecration of the bread and wine, "He who does not eat my flesh and drink my blood has no eternal life," we have the exact replica in the cult of Mithra 1400 years before: "He who does not eat my flesh and drink my blood has no eternal life." And this was discovered by Tertullian, the Christian father of the Latin church in the 2nd century.[19] And Tertullian, of course, found an explanation. He had to find an explanation. How is it that Christ and Mithra speak the same language? He said, "Oh, no, that's not the fact. Christ is right, but the devil put these words into the cult of Mithra 1400 years before out of mockery of what was going to be one day Christianity."[20] The devil did it. That's an explanation. It's no explanation in my eyes, anyhow. In reality, it's the Christians who took these words and applied them to their own master. Without that, their own master wouldn't be a god. He would just be a human being. And the crucifixion would have a quite different meaning. Crucifixion: he was condemned for rebellion against the Romans, that's all. The Christians made him into a sacrificial scapegoat. He was taking on the sins of the world.

5. CHRISTIANITY AS MAN-CENTERED

The message attributed to Christ is kindness to all men. But only to men.[21] Animals are never mentioned in the gospels. Whether the person at the center of the gospel is the historic Christ or another person, invented by further commentators, especially Paul, it is a fact that no miracle is reported in favor of a creature that is not human. On the contrary, you get a fig tree that refuses to give Christ some figs out of season. It's mentioned in Mark.[22] The fig tree did not give figs. It was out of season. And

---

[19] Quintus Septimus Florens Tertullianus (c. 155–c. 225).

[20] See Tertullian, *De praescriptione haereticorum* [*On the Prescription of Heretics*], ch. 40.

[21] For more on Christian anthropocentrism, see *Impeachment of Man*, ch. 1, "Man-Centered Creeds," and *Souvenirs et réflexions*, ch. 3, "Anthropocentrisme et intolérance."

[22] Mark 11:13–14; cf. Matthew 21:19.

Christ curses the poor fig tree, and the next day it's gone completely withered. For not giving its figs out of season. What did he expect it to do? Did he expect the fig tree to give him figs out of season? And if he was so powerful why didn't he just give the fig tree the power to give figs out of season? That's something that used to shock me. That fig tree withered, cursed by the founder of Christianity, because it wouldn't give figs out of season, against the laws of nature.

And the poor Gadarene swine.[23] Here is a pack of people possessed by devils. The devils won't get out of them. They tell Christ, "We will only get out if you allow us to go into the swine." There was a herd of swine. Well, first of all, what business did a man have keeping a herd of swine in Judah? What was he bringing up these swine for? What was he herding them for? To sell them to the Romans, I suppose. For people who used to eat pork. The Jews never eat pork. Anyhow, Christ allows these devils to enter these poor swine that have done no harm to anybody. And they go mad, and they throw themselves into the Sea of Galilee, from the cliff. I didn't like that. Whether it's true or not, I don't know. But I didn't like that. So many things I never liked in Christianity.

6. CHRISTIANITY AND INTOLERANCE

Another thing that I have against Christianity is that it was not taken freely by Europe. It was imposed on us. It was the fault of our princes, for different reasons that have nothing to do with religion. Constantine became a Christian in 313. Before him, ten years before, Tiridates III, King of Armenia, became a Christian also.[24] And aren't the Armenians proud of that! "We are the first Christian nation," so they say. That is to say, Tiridates III was the first Christian king. I don't know whether the Armenians fol-

---

[23] Mark 5:1–14.

[24] Savitri says Tigran II, although it was King Tiridates III (238–314) who introduced Christianity to Armenia after his conversion in 301. The year 303 is also given as the date of Armenia's conversion, perhaps because it was the year of the consecration of the cathedral of Echmiadzin, the holiest site of the Armenian Church. Tigran II (the Great) was born in 140 BC and ruled from 95 BC to his death in 55 BC.

lowed him or not at once. Certainly the Greeks did not follow
Constantine at once.

There were Christian communities already all over the Roman
Empire. There were other communities too: Mithraic communities. Cybele, the mother goddess of Asia Minor, had many followers too. And these other religions were called religions of salvation. They had the idea of a god put to death and resurrected,
risen from the dead, for the salvation of mankind. The idea that
you have in Adonis, Osiris, and Tammuz, in those cults of Syria,
of Egypt, and of Babylonia.

The fact is that Europe did not become Christian at once. First
of all, why did Constantine become a Christian? His life was not a
Christian life, absolutely not. He had his wife killed, on simple
suspicion of adultery, not proof.[25] He had his own son killed.[26] He
had so many people killed. Not Christian. But he was a Roman
Emperor, and he wanted the unity of the Roman Empire. Unity of
blood, there was none. Unity of language, there was none. And
there could be none. There could've been unity in the worship of
the Emperor, but the worship of the Emperor only interested the
Romans. It didn't interest the Syrians a bit. It didn't interest even
the Greeks. I wonder if the Greeks did not even resent a temple to
the goddess Rome on the Acropolis. There is a temple of the goddess of Rome on the Acropolis of Athens. A round temple. The
ruins are there still. I don't know how the Athenians liked it.
Anyhow, there was no unity. The only unity that could be was
a unity of faith.

Now there were several faiths of salvation. Why didn't Constantine pick Mithraism? Mithraism was already very, very widespread among the Roman soldiers. Even some emperors later on
were going to be worshipers of Mithra, the Aryan god, Sol Invic-
tus, the invincible sun represented by a man with a Phrygian cap
and a bull sacrifice. Well, the religion of Mithra would have taken

---

[25] Flavia Maxima Fausta (c. 293–326) was the daughter of the emperor Marcus Aurelius Valerius Maximianus (c. 249–310, reigned
286–305). She married Constantine in 307 and bore him three sons
and two daughters.
[26] Flavius Julius Crispus (c. 305–326) was the son of Constantine's
mistress Minervina. He was likely killed for adultery with his step-
mother Fausta.

centuries to spread because the priests of Mithra were no fanatics. They didn't say, "Outside the cult of Mithra you are all damned." They never said that. It would have taken centuries. The cult of Cybele also. Any cult except Christianity would have taken centuries to forge the cultural and religious unity of the empire. And even Christianity took centuries, but at least under Constantine there was a hope that within a few decades officially the Mediterranean would be Christian. And that was a fact. It was imposed.

There is no manuscript of any of the canonical gospels, Mark, Matthew, Luke, and John, older than the 4th or 5th century. What was there before? Other gospels, Apocrypha, of which there are pieces to be found now and then, and some of them quite different from the canonical gospels. What happened to the originals? They were collected from all the churches under Constantine, under the supervision of Eusebius of Caesarea, the great court historiographer and Bishop.[27] And they were collected by batches of 50, and new batches of 50 of the gospels we know today were sent out to the churches. There were very many alterations in them for the Roman Empire to have *one* faith.

And then of course the crosses of Christ were found by Helena, Constantine's mother.[28] She dug somewhere in Jerusalem. Now Jerusalem was completely destroyed by Titus in the year 70. So much so that there was no trace, according to Flavius Josephus, of its streets.[29] One didn't know what was where before. It was completely flat. It was reconstructed afterwards. So in the 4th century, the emperor's mother, Helena, who was a Christian, digs somewhere in Jerusalem and found three crosses, wooden crosses, intact. How did they stay intact? Although the land is dry. I admit the land is dry. But 300 years, more than 300 years after the crucifixion, three crosses absolutely intact? That's funny. They put a dead man on each one, and when they put him on the cross that was Christ's cross, the dead man became alive again.[30] So they

---

[27] Eusebius of Caesarea (c. 264–c. 340).

[28] Flavia Julia Helena, later Saint Helena (c. 250–c. 330).

[29] Flavius Josephus (c. 37–c. 100), *Wars of the Jews*, 7.1.1.

[30] Saint Helena toured Palestine circa 326–328. There is no mention, however, of the discovery of the cross either during her lifetime or that of her son Constantine. By the middle of the 4th century, however, a number of stories of her discovery of the cross were in

say. That's how they found the real cross. And when you go to Jerusalem as a pilgrim, you can buy a piece of the real cross. There are so many pieces of the real cross to be sold that if they were all genuine, the cross would have been kilometers long and kilometers wide. Anyhow, that was Christianity for the Mediterranean people.

"No jobs of high significance unless you are a Christian" — Constantine. And then came Theodosias, long after Constantine.[31] You have in between the attempt of Emperor Julian to give another chance to paganism, to the Greek or Latin paganism.[32] Unfortunately that failed. That failed in the year 363. Julian only ruled from 360 to 363. He was probably murdered on the battlefield, because he received a spear from behind. And they said it was a barbarian captive that did that. Since when were barbarian captives taken into cavalry charges and given spears in their hands? It's a story. He was murdered, probably by some Christian. Anyhow, after him Christianity was again the religion of the Empire. Then comes the Emperor Theodosias who died in 395. He shut the temples. He forbade as much as he could forbid. He forbade the Oracle of Delphi. Already in Julian's day, Delphi was an abandoned place. Now, in the 6th century, under Justinian, the last philosophical schools were forbidden, the Greek philosophical schools.[33] You were not to teach anything but Christianity. Antiquity was forbidden.

Naturally it continued on the sly. They say there was still worship of the gods in Greece in the 14th and 15th centuries. In those days Prussia, land of Frederick the Great, land of Bismarck, was still pagan. Prussians were Christianized in the 14th and 15th centuries, and so were the Lithuanians. They were pagans. Scandinavia was Christianized in the 11th century under Olaf II of Norway and Erik of Sweden.[34] They were Christianized by fire

---

circulation.

[31] Flavius Theodosius (c. 346–395) reigned from 379–395.

[32] Flavius Claudius Julianus, 331–363.

[33] Flavius Petrus Sabbatius Justinianus (c. 483–565) reigned from 527–565. Justinian prohibited the teaching of pagan philosophy in 529.

[34] Olaf II of Norway, later Saint Olaf (995–1030), King of Norway from 1015–1028, converted to Christianity in 1010. Erik ruled Sweden

and sword, just as Germany was under Charlemagne.[35]

Charlemagne fought the Saxons for 30 years to make them Christians by force. Widukind defended Germany and defended the old faith.[36] He was vanquished. Well, the Franks were better organized. They had better weapons. They were efficient as warriors, and they were perhaps more united. They had the schooling of the Byzantines. They were very much in touch with the Byzantines. In fact, they speak of a prospective marriage between Charlemagne and the Empress Irene of Constantinople, of the Eastern Roman Empire.[37] It didn't come through anyhow. But the Germans were Christianized by fire and sword.

In 782, 4,500 German chiefs were put to death, beheaded one after the other after a solemn mass and a lot of pomp on the banks of the Aller in Verden in North Germany because they didn't want to take the new faith. They refused it. They were all beheaded. The river Aller must have been red with blood. That was 782.

In 772, ten years before, the old high place of the sun for all North Europe, not for Germany alone, the Externsteine, was stormed by Charlemagne, and the sun room destroyed. The roof was blown off. He had no dynamite of course, but he put ice in a kind of little channel. He dug a channel all around and he put water there. It was in the middle of December. The water became ice. Ice is bigger. It takes more volume than water. The roof was shot off. You can see the ruins of it now.[38]

---

from 966–995. He returned to paganism at the end of his life. The process of Christianization was taken up again by his son Olof, who reigned from 995–1022.

[35] Charlemagne (c. 742–814) was King of the Franks from 768 on and Roman Emperor in the West from 800 on.

[36] Widukind (d. 807) was a Westphalian nobleman and leader of the Saxon resistance against Charlemagne until he accepted baptism in 785.

[37] Irene of Athens (c. 752–803) ruled the Byzantine Empire from 797–802 after blinding then murdering her son, the emperor Constantine VI (770–797). She was deposed and exiled in 802. Since it was not legal for a woman to rule the Roman Empire, Pope Leo III crowned Charlemagne Roman Emperor in the West in 800, marking the final severance of the Eastern and Western Roman Empires.

[38] Savitri recounts her visit to the Externsteine in *Pilgrimage*, ch. 9, "The Rocks of the Sun."

And in 785 you have the famous Capitulary of Paderborn, the rules and regulations that Charlemagne imposed on Germany, or on the part of Germany he had conquered. He didn't conquer eastern Germany, of course: "Whoever runs away to the woods in order not to be christened is to die, penalty of death. Whoever burns the dead instead of burying them according to Christianity's new rules: the death penalty. Whoever reads the runic scriptures is to be killed. Whoever listens to runic teachings is to be killed." There's a list like that of I don't know how many things you mustn't do. "Whoever refuses to do this or to do that, whoever doesn't have his children christened: penalty of death."

That's how Germany was Christianized. That's how Scandinavia was Christianized. That's how, in fact, all the countries of the North of Europe were Christianized. Christianity was not liked by the Nordic race. The Nordic race didn't like it. There were certainly things in the Bible that shocked them. Even if nothing else, the story of Lot and his daughters.[39] That was shocking enough. And then the polygamy of the old Semites. The Nordic race is by tradition monogamous. They probably didn't like that. There were so many things. And of course stories like how Jael killed her enemy during his sleep. That was so anti-Aryan, so shocking. How could they accept that?

The result was that the Catholic Church very wisely forbade the faithful reading the Bible. It was not allowed to read the Bible in the Middle Ages. Of course it was not allowed. I can understand the Catholic Church. And what I can't understand was when the Bible was allowed to be read, after Luther, after the Reformation, how did people remain Christian? It's the Bible that put me against the Jews. It's not anything else. It's not *Mein Kampf*. I didn't own *Mein Kampf* in those days. When I was a child I was made to read the Old Testament and the New Testament by my pious aunt. There were so many things that shocked me.

And that's what I have to say. Christianity was not taken by Europe spontaneously, at least not by the Nordic race. And even the Mediterranean people had their own beliefs. They had their own superstitions. They carried those superstitions into Christianity. There's nothing more superstitious than a southern European

---

[39] Genesis 19:30–38.

even today, among the masses. The Marian cult, the cult of the Virgin Mary, is nothing but the cult of the Great Mother of antiquity, transposed. They stuck to it. They gave it another name, that's all. They made Christianity according to themselves.

But what is awful is that it is a religion that inherited, from its Jewish origin, intolerance. A typical Jewish product. Although the Jews never did these things, because their policy was not conversion or death, but death in any case if you are not a Jew and if you stand in the way of the expansion of Jewry, like the Canaanites. In Europe there was not that. You could save your life by becoming a Christian. If you don't want to become one, or if you work against it, in the Middle Ages, it's the stake. You're burnt at the stake. So many people were. It was not done in the Greek Church. I must say, to be just, in the Orthodox Church you have no burnings. You get it in the Catholic Church. You get it in the Protestant Church. They're no better. One is as good as the other. Some burnt Catholics, others burnt Protestants, or heretics, or whatever you like. You have the awful story of the Cathars from the South of France, early 13th century.

I much prefer our old, old European religions. European or non-European, anyhow, all religions of antiquity, of that free antiquity of which Adolf Hitler speaks on page 507 of *Mein Kampf*, the German edition of 1935, in which he says, "The Ancient World, which was much freer than it is today, became unfree with the entrance of Christianity."[40] He's perfectly right. You don't get persecution of religions for the religion's sake in antiquity. You get persecutions for political reasons. That's quite different. Socrates was killed because he was an Athenian who did not believe in the gods of Athens.

On Hinduism

7. HINDUISM AND NATIONAL SOCIALISM

I embraced Hinduism because it was the only religion in the world that is compatible with National Socialism. And the dream of my life is to integrate Hitlerism into the old Aryan tradition, to show that it is really a resurgence of the original Tradition. It's not

---

[40] See ch. 1, §12, n. 84 above.

Indian, not European, but Indo-European. It comes from back to those days when the Aryans were one people near the North Pole. The Hyperborean Tradition.[41]

Well, I'm not a full Hindu. I'm a National Socialist. To me it's quite sufficient. I'm a European heathen. I'm one of those who would've fought Christianity in the 4th and 5th centuries. The great man I admired in my youth was Alexander the Great, my first love. My second love is Emperor Julian. Adolf Hitler is the third one. I put him above the others, but chronologically he's the third. The first book I wrote in English in India is called *A Warning to the Hindus*.[42] It was written in '37. It was translated into six Indian languages. It's not dedicated to an Indian. It's dedicated to Divine Julian, Emperor of the Greeks and Romans, 360–363, the one who wanted to bring back the old Greek and Roman religion after Christianity had been ruling for — well, I don't know — say 50 years. The Christian religion was instituted as the religion of the Roman Empire in 313. It was too late in 360. It was too late.

Now I must tell you something that I recently read this morning. I have a French friend.[43] Well, she could be my daughter or, according to Indian standards, even my granddaughter. She's much younger than I, 38. And she's now in the South at her guru. She has a guru. Or rather the disciple of a dead guru. Her guru is dead. And she was visiting the ashram of the famous Ramana Maharshi.[44] Ramana Maharshi is really *the* greatest, or perhaps one of the greatest, one of the first or second of the two or three greatest sages of modern India. An extraordinary man. He did not teach. He taught only through his radiations. He was perfectly silent. He was vowed to perfect silence. That's a very queer thing to say, but he did teach like that. I know people who saw him and who said, "If silence

---

[41] Savitri accepted the theories of Bal Gangadhar Tilak, *The Arctic Home in the Vedas* (Poona: Kesari, 1903).

[42] Savitri Devi, *A Warning to the Hindus* (Calcutta: Hindu Mission, 1939).

[43] Miriam Hirn.

[44] Ramana Maharshi (1879–1950). His ashram is located in Tiruvannamali in Tamil Nadu, South India. For a vivid description of Ramana Maharshi as well as photographs, see Paul Brunton, *A Search in Secret India* (New York: E. P. Dutton, 1935), esp. 138–142 and 280.

can have meaning, that man shows it."

Anyhow, he used to speak sometimes, of course. He was not silent completely. This woman asked his *shishya*, his disciple, "What did Ramana Maharshi say about Adolf Hitler? Did he ever mention him?" And the disciple answered, "Yes, he considered him as a *jnani*."[45] A *jnani* is something extremely high. A *jnani* and a *rishi* are the same thing, or practically the same thing. They're Sanskrit words. *Jnani* has the same root as *gnos*, the Christian sect, the Gnostics, the people of knowledge. A *jnani* means a man who has complete knowledge, who knows everything, infused knowledge, intuitive knowledge, if you like. He is divine through his intuition. Like God, he knows everything through intuition. Well, I was extremely pleased to hear that said by a very great *rishi*, a very great Indian man, a sage, about our Führer.

It's not what you have in Europe. Here in India, nobody says anything against him, except people who are brainwashed by European ladies. Apart from that, the masses of India don't care. It's something foreign. They have their own little, small, petty lives to think of, the poverty and the struggle from day to day. Some of the intellectual Indians like him very much. My landlord likes him very much. My landlord's son likes him very much. Or else they have an idea like this. Satyananda Swami was the founder and head of the Hindu Mission, for which I worked for years, fighting Communism, fighting any religion of equality and especially Christian missionaries, in the name of Hindu tradition. Satyananda Swami used to say, "Adolf Hitler is the reincarnation of the god Vishnu." Vishnu is the aspect of the Hindu trinity who goes to keep things from rushing to destruction. To keep them back, to go against time. Time is destruction. You have to destroy in order to create again, but there are forces that try to postpone destruction. And he said Hitler was the reincarnation of that force. And he was. He was. But it's a nice thing to hear, a very refreshing thing to hear from a Hindu sage.

I told him, "I came here because I'm really a pagan, a worshipper of the sun, and I believe in the pagan reaction of Emperor

---

[45] For more on the Ramana Maharshi's opinion of Hitler, see Savitri Devi, "Hitlerism and the Hindu World," *The National Socialist*, no. 2 (Fall 1980): 18–20, 18.

Julian. And I came to India to get, if possible, a sort of tropical equivalent of what we had in Europe before Christianity. And I am not a disciple of any Indian, I'm a disciple of Adolf Hitler." He said, "Good, good. Adolf Hitler, he's as much a Hindu as any of our Hindus. He's an incarnation of the god Vishnu." There you are. It was extremely surprising and refreshing to hear that in 1936. And he said it during the war too. In Kubila he gave a speech in '42. He openly said, "What we need here in India, as everywhere in the world, is National Socialism." He openly said so. And I said to him, "Satyananda Swami, you'll get into trouble with the British police." He said, "I couldn't care less if I did. I told them the truth."

In fact, Hinduism is for the Aryans of India a means to be able to rule. According to tradition, the Aryans should rule here. They don't, because tradition has been abandoned for years and years and years. India is going away from tradition, like the whole world. We are in the Dark Age, and India is going to the dogs, and the whole world is going to the dogs. Except a minority who are fighting against time, against the current of time. And I hope that we'll win. We will have to win. We can't help winning. But I don't know whether we'll win just now and if the avenger Kalki, as the Hindus call him, is going to come very soon or whether he's going to come in centuries. Because centuries are also very soon in the infinity of time. A century is nothing. And ten centuries are nothing. In fact I feel that myself. When I feel the struggle of Christianity to master Europe 1,500 years ago, I resent it as though it were now. I feel the struggle of Widukind as though it were now.

In Europe I feel at home with National Socialists, but with non-National Socialist Europeans, and especially with the people who are against it, I feel much worse than I do with indifferent people here. Here at least if they are not for it, they are not against it either. They don't care. They let you alone. They don't run after you because you are a Nazi, you know. That's your right. And in the war time, those who were for Hitler, they would take his picture and put it among the gods. Every Hindu house has a little shrine for the gods, with pictures of the gods. And they put his picture there with them. And those who were for Stalin, Indian Communists, would do the same with Stalin. Nobody did this with

Churchill, funny enough. It was Stalin or Hitler.

Here we can believe in whatever we like. There's no common belief among Hindus. One Hindu doesn't believe in any god at all. He's a perfect atheist, materialist if you like. Another Hindu believes in one god. Another believes in 33 million gods. Another one believes in a couple, god and *shakti*, god and consort. In fact, every god in Hinduism has a consort, meaning the two aspects of energy, the positive and negative, like electricity, negative and positive. That's what it means in fact. It comes down to science.

There's a book recently published, and I want to read it. The Greek Ambassador here told me he would lend it to me. It's his, but he has lent it to somebody else. It is called *The Tao of Physics*.[46] I'd love to read that. In fact, the idea of the expanding and contracting universe that the modern physicists believe in: that you get in Hinduism; that you get in Hinduism. Not after each *manvantara*, each succession of four ages, but after several successions of four ages, that is, the time comes when the universe expands, expands, expands and grows very, very wide, and the time comes again when it absolutely comes to nothing. It's very heavy. The whole universe is extremely heavy, and it has hardly any volume and begins again. That's creation and destruction. That's the explanation of creation and destruction by the old Hindu sages.

8. REINCARNATION

Now reincarnation is one of the only two beliefs that unite all Hindus of any caste, from the Brahmin to the untouchable, that is to say, the *harijans*.[47] They call them *harijans*, that is to say, "people of God." But every creature is a person of God. It doesn't mean anything. They're outcasts, the lowest outcasts, generally the aborigines. What is a *harijan*? He's either an aborigine, or else he's a man of any caste who has done something awful or whose ancestors have done something awful, and was outcasted. And when you were outcasted in India, your descendants are outcasted also, for all times to come. From the topmost Brahmin to the lowest *harijan*, everybody believes in reincarnation.

---

[46] Fritjof Capra, *The Tao of Physics: An Exploration of the Parallels Between Modern Physics and Eastern Mysticism* (New York: Dell, 1975).

[47] The other common belief is, presumably, the caste system itself.

That is to say, there is in every living creature, not in every man—reincarnation is for animals and plants also, not only for people—there is in every living creature a visible body and more than one subtle body, and these subtle bodies separate from the rest of the physical body at the time of death. And they constitute what they call the ego. That ego, if it is not already merged into the universal ego—that is to say, if a man is not what the Hindus say "liberated"—that ego takes a new birth, in some other body, animal or human or plant. Plants live. Even minerals have some kind of life. There is nothing in the world that's not absolutely soaking in some kind of life, some kind of vibration. So the belief is not that when you are good you are reborn in a higher social status. That's nonsense. You will not be born rich if you are poor. If you wish to be rich, if you are good, you don't become rich in the next life, not necessarily. It might be the contrary, that the rich man is reborn as a beggar. He is reborn in that state which will be the best for his spiritual evolution. If it is better for his spiritual evolution for him to be born in a very low social status, he will. And the low social status does not mean in India a low race. There are Aryans and there are non-Aryans. There are Brahmin beggars. And there are untouchables who are millionaires. It has nothing to do with money. And that's one of the things I like the best of it. An Aryan, or supposed Aryan, say, a Brahmin, if he is a beggar and he goes to marriage ceremony, they put him inside at the best place, the most honorable place, with the other Brahmins. If a multi-millionaire untouchable goes to a marriage ceremony, he'll be put outside with his fellow untouchables. He will not be given a better place because he has money. Money or learning. Even learning. Brajendra Nath Seal[48] was a scientist, a very great scientist. He was a Seal. That's a very low caste in Bengal. Seals are a very low caste. He was never given greater status.

Learning can be acquired. Money can be acquired. Only blood cannot be acquired for the Hindu religion. And that's what I like in the Hindu religion. It's the only real, living religion compatible with National Socialism. It gives priority to what cannot be ac-

---

[48] Sir Brajendra Nath Seal (1864–1938) was a renowned Bengali philosopher associated with the Brahmo Samaj movement. His work focused on comparative religion and philosophy of science.

quired with any means. You are born with a race. You can't change your race whatever you do. You get reborn if you are not perfect. That is to say, if you have not gone through all the experiences resulting from the algebraic sum of your good and bad deeds.

Good and bad mean nothing. Good is what is according to the nature of your soul. And bad is what goes against nature. That's all. In Hinduism, you do not have to kill your instincts. Not at all. In fact, if you go to a yogi and ask him to be your master, he asks you some questions. Among the questions there is this, "How strong are your instincts?" If you tell him, "I have no instincts, very little." He says, "That's no good for you." The stronger the instincts you have, the better, because the stronger means the more and greater energy you have. You have to take that energy upwards. You have to transform it. Well, it's the theory of Nietzsche. It's exactly the idea of Nietzsche. The superman does not have to kill his passions. He has to canalize them for a higher purpose. Dominate them. Not let them dominate him but dominate them. That's a Hindu idea too.

Now you get reborn. Unless you are finished with the processes completely, you will get reborn. Some people are not reborn, but they wish to be reborn for the good of creatures. Again, not of man, but of all creatures. And they are reborn where they want to be. They choose their race. They choose their family in which they are getting reborn. They choose their own life beforehand. And they get reborn. These are what the Buddhists call the *Bodhisattvas* and the others who are not reborn at all, they are called *Arhats* in the Buddhist terminology.

Now, generally when you are reborn higher, you are reborn not higher in a social status, but higher in race. It will take centuries and millennia for a man of a lower race to become an Aryan. Generally an Aryan is reborn as an Aryan. Unless he has done awful things, then he might be reborn very low. I suppose the men who tortured Streicher, for instance, would be reborn as Negroes. It wouldn't astonish me at all. They would deserve it. Certainly they do. Especially if they were Aryans. If they were Jews, not so much. If they were Jews they would be more excusable. If they were Aryans, less excusable.

I'm not a strong believer in anything that I cannot either see or prove with my own strength. I just take reincarnation as an hypothesis, a theory, if you like. But I do think that of the many, many theories that have been put forward to explain the unexplainable, reincarnation is the most plausible. It is at least the one that can be the best exploited for National Socialism. I told you of Khudiram, didn't I?[49] Telling me that he was a Shudra, and even if he was still a Shudra under the New Order it wouldn't matter to him because he was born in the Shudra family because of his past sins in past lives. And he said, "Well, whatever I am in the New Order, I believe in the New Order because it's true."

True or not, I don't know.[50] But I know that if we had this kind of belief in Europe, and if a European of more or less pure Aryan descent could think, "If I'm good in this life, and if I stay good in future lives for another 500 years, I might become a German. What a lovely thing to be. Or I might become, say, a Swede." I wouldn't say a Swede like certain Swedes are today, because not all of them are perfectly Aryan in behavior. Some of them take drugs and do I don't know what. "But an ideal Swede, an ideal Nordic European, I'll become that one day. Before I get liberated completely." It would be a very good sort of propaganda. It's better propaganda than what we get in Christianity. Heaven and hell. And of course hell, if you don't believe in the church.

9. YOGA

Hinduism holds that there is no watertight separation between man, animal, plant, or whatever it is.[51] There is one universe and one life permeating everything. And the individual has one thing in common with the universe and that is what they call the *atman*, not the soul, not the ego. The ego is the totality of his subtle body. The *atman* is something different. It is that which in him is of the same nature as the soul of the universe. There's a spark of divinity in every living creature, not only in every man. We can act as though that spark of divinity were nonexistent. Or he should, if he wants to develop more spiritually, strive to become more and

---

[49] For more on Khudiram, see "Hitlerism and the Hindu World," 18–20 and *Defiance*, 202–3, 337.

[50] The truth of reincarnation, not of the New Order.

[51] See *Impeachment of Man*, ch. 2, "Pessimistic Pantheism."

more conscious of it. And yoga is just nothing else but the science of making a person conscious of that.

There are different kinds of yoga. There's Hatha yoga. Hatha yoga is what you do on your body. You act on your body. There is Karma yoga. Karma yoga is one of the teachings of the Bhagavad-Gita. Not only of the Gita. You get it in National Socialism. I'll tell you what Karma yoga is. Karma yoga is: Act with your body for the interest of the universe, according to the scheme of the universe, the divine scheme, and without any passion, without any personal attachment or disgust or enthusiasm or anything. Just do it because it's duty. Act in the name of duty alone. That's Karma yoga.[52]

Well, I was thrilled when I read a few of the writings, letters to Princess von Isenberg, of Otto Ohlendorf, a few letters he wrote before his death. He had that spirit. And he was the head of the *Einsatzgruppe D* of the four famous *Einsatzgruppen*, acting in Russia and acting in Poland especially. They were all SS men, naturally. And they show from the rules and regulations which Otto Ohlendorf told the judges when he was judged by the Americans how near they were to Hinduism. Without knowing it or knowing it, I don't know. Probably the chiefs knew it.

The *Einsatzgruppen* had very dirty work to do: mass executions of anybody who was opposing the German army, even children. Of course if the child is six, and can shoot, and shoots, well, we can't let him live. You have that experience with the Americans in the Vietnam War. I was told by an eyewitness that the Americans went to someplace in North Vietnam. They came in tanks, four or five tanks, perhaps more. They left their tanks and distributed candies to the kiddies. The kiddies took the candies, ate them, and then, perhaps eating them still, went under the tanks. They were young Communists with ideals, brave children. I admire them. Brave children, six, seven, eight years old. They put what they had in their hands under the tanks, and the tanks blew up and the children under them. They gave their lives for their cause. Well, if you catch a child like that, are you to keep it or are you to kill it? It's a powerful enemy, a convinced enemy. What are you to do?

---

[52] For more on Karma yoga, see *Defiance*, ch. 12, "The Way of Absolute Detachment."

The *Einsatzgruppen* had to do that, against partisans in Russia, partisans in Poland, partisans who were harassing the German army from right, left, behind, and front. What could they do?

And Otto Ohlendorf said, "If any of us showed the slightest pleasure or the slightest disgust in what we did, we were degraded and sent home." That is the spirit of the Bhagavad-Gita. That's what you call Karma yoga. All these SS men, whether knowing it or not, they were Karma yogis. They were getting salvation. They were mastering themselves, mastering their feelings, putting themselves in the proof, in the *épreuve* we call it in alchemy, for purification by their action.

And then you have Bhakti yoga. Bhakti yoga is the yoga of devotion. You feel devoted to something. And in devotion you raise yourself higher.[53]

Well, I tried Hatha yoga years and years ago, '36, '37 with a South Indian Brahmin who happened to be at that time the curator of the Museum of Lahore. Lahore was in India, of course.[54] And I was teaching in Jallundhar not far away from Lahore. He taught me breathing exercises and the beginning of Hatha yoga. Now, I progressed very quickly, and I reached a stage at which I felt that my body didn't exist. I had no body. I was just a column of vibrating energy, up and down, according to respiration. And I felt I could pass through walls. No material obstacle was a real obstacle to me. And that's it. But, after my exercises, I had pains behind my eyes, as though somebody was pulling my eyes from inside. And I told that to this guru of mine. He said, "If you feel that, stop. Hatha yoga is not for you. You need very strong nerves for that. Your nerves apparently are not strong enough. You get this eye trouble.[55] Take another form of yoga." I said, "What form

---

[53] In addition to Hatha, Karma, and Bhakti yoga, there are three other generally recognized forms of yoga: Jnana yoga (the path of wisdom associated with the Upanishads), Mantra yoga (which exploits the consciousness altering power of sound), and Raja yoga (the royal path, the system of Classical Yoga set down by Patanjali in the *Yoga-Sutra*).

[54] After the partition of India and Pakistan, Lahore was in Pakistan.

[55] Savitri suffered from eye problems throughout her old age. She had glaucoma and cataracts, and by the time of her death she was

of yoga?" He said, "Don't you love anything?" I said, "Yes, I do. I have a cause." "Then work for your cause, work for whatever you love. But work in detachment. Try not to feel upset if you are unsuccessful. Try not to feel pride if you are successful. If people blame you or insult you, be indifferent. If they praise you, don't feel pleased. Feel indifferent. Feel, 'All right, they praised me.' Don't feel exalted if people are praising you. Every praise is really not right. I mean to say, it's not to the mark, because you are not perfect. You are not liberated. You have a body still."[56]

To have a body, to be born, according to a Hindu, is bad. It's a sign of sin. If you never sinned you wouldn't be born. You sinned in your previous lives, therefore you are born. Even if you are born a Brahmin. If you are born Brahmin, you have all these weaknesses of a body. You eat and you sleep. You do all that the body has to do. Therefore, it's not a good thing.[57] Once I gave Mr. Mukherji a dhoti, the equivalent of a sari for a Bengali male. I never saw Mr. Mukherji wear a pair of trousers, dressed in the European style. He always wore a Bengali dhoti. I gave him a dhoti for his birthday. He refused it. He said, "Give me that at the time of the festival of the goddess Durga." "All right." "But my

---

nearly blind from the degeneration of her optic nerves.

[56] From the context, one might infer that here Savitri is talking about Bhakti yoga, but she is describing Karma yoga. Savitri did, of course, engage in Bhakti yoga as well. Bhakti yoga centers on the cult of the incarnations of Vishnu, and Savitri regarded Adolf Hitler as the ninth avatar of Vishnu. Her devotion to Hitler was, therefore, a form of Bhakti yoga. Her book *Pilgrimage* is the best record of her Bhakti practices. Before her return to India in 1971, Savitri tried unsuccessfully to raise funds from her comrades in Europe to create a temple to Hitler in New Delhi. Thus the title of Nicholas Goodrick-Clarke's biography of Savitri, *Hitler's Priestess*, is quite well chosen.

[57] It should be noted that Savitri shared Nietzsche's rejection of this life-denying and pessimistic aspect of Hinduism and Buddhism. See Savitri Devi, *Impeachment of Man,* ch. 3, "Pessimistic Pantheism," on Hinduism; ch. 4, "Joyous Wisdom," offers a world- and life-affirming alternative. Savitri deals mainly with Akhnaton's philosophy, but the chapter's title (borrowed from Nietzsche's book *Die fröhliche Wissenschaft,* sometimes translated *The Gay Science*) and her use of the phrase "faithful to this earth" (a Nietzschean *Leitmotiv*) make clear her inspiration. See also *Defiance,* 232 and 353.

birthday, I don't celebrate." "But why? You came into this world." "I want to get away from it. I want to go back to the subtle, utmost part of myself. The divine spark should merge into the ocean of divinity, that is to say, the soul of the universe. I don't want to be an individual any longer. Individuality is a prison. Therefore, I act" — he acted all right — "I act. But I try to act with detachment." And that is the detachment.

I didn't do Hatha yoga any longer. I was told not to do it. I was told that Karma yoga was my line. I had to do what I could for what I love, and do it with detachment. That is to say, I should not have felt upset in 1945. I did, of course. But I shouldn't have been. I should have felt it was necessary. It had to happen. I should have felt different. I couldn't feel that. I was not advanced enough to feel that. Very few people were.

Human and Animal Sacrifice

10. HUMAN SACRIFICE

I used to cry and keep silence on the 12th of October because that was the day Columbus landed in America. And I was against it. I didn't want Americans to be spoilt. I knew they had beautiful monuments. They had human sacrifices, of course. I couldn't care less. It was among themselves. And the victims used to like it. The victims found it an honor. It was an honor to have your chest cut open and your heart pulled out and offered to the gods. All right, if you like it. If you consider it an honor, carry on. I don't care. I never would have stopped that, if I had been the Spaniards.

If the Spaniards had been National Socialists, it would have been different. Supposing Europe had kept its old national religions and never became a Christian Europe, and of course, the Spanish or some Europeans would've gone to America and conquered America. All right. They would've taken a lot of the gold. They would have exploited the people, quite right. They are the strongest. The strongest exploit the weakest. But they would've left the gods and the monuments as they were. And that's all I liked. I would've liked to be able to see Tenochtitlán, that is to say, Mexico City, as it was in 1519 when the Spanish landed there. It must've been beautiful, these pyramids, with the temple on the top, and these stairs — down, down, down, down.

Of course, when the victim was killed and they sent his body downstairs, people used to cut it up and eat it. Well, I couldn't care less. That's not worse than eating a piece of beef for me. Not worse. If you offer me one or the other to eat, I'd say, "Neither, please. Neither." And after all, if you have to eat some flesh, I'd rather eat the flesh of an enemy than of a creature that never did a thing against me, that doesn't hate what I love and doesn't love what I hate. Say a lamb. What is more beautiful than a little lamb? The Aztecs used to eat their sacrificial victims. Well, they didn't used to eat them completely. They used to take a little bit off, just as what they call in Hindi a *prasad*, a part of the offering, and the offering was a warrior. It was always a warrior, a warrior whom they had defeated. Now the warriors liked it.

I don't know if you know the story of Tlahuicol. Tlahuicol was a Tlaxcalic warrior of the 15th century. Not under Montezuma II who had to deal with the Spaniards, but under his grandfather, Montezuma I. That is to say, between 1440 and 1469. He died in 1469.[58] He was a great warrior, this Tlaxcalic warrior. Tlaxcala and Tenochtitlán, two cities in Mexico, were always at war. Tlaxcala was defeated. The warriors were taken, and they were to be sacrificed, not in the ordinary war god festival, but in the fire festival. That was much worse. In the fire festival, the victim was made to fight alone with a wooden sword against five Aztec warriors with stone swords. They didn't know metal. Metal was not known. They couldn't make steel. They had iron but they didn't know it. They knew gold and silver and stones. They were living in the Stone Age, if you like. But they had beautiful works of art. They used to have clothes made of feathers and whatnot. They had an art. You only have to see Aztec art. So he was there, and generally the warrior was defeated, naturally: five with stone swords against one with a wooden sword. But this one was not defeated. Once defeated, he was supposed to be thrown into a fire and half burnt, pulled out with some hooks or tongs or something, and then his breast opened and his heart pulled out and offered to the fire god. That was the procedure.

Now, Tlahuicol knew it very well. To the amazement of eve-

---

[58] Montezuma I, 1398–1469; Montezuma II, c. 1480–1520, reigned 1502–1520.

rybody, including Montezuma I, he defeated with his wooden sword the five Aztecs with their stone swords, one after the other. Montezuma I said, "Stop! This man is more than a man." Nobody had ever done such a performance. "Now, Tlahuicol, I don't want you to be sacrificed. You are too precious. Take command of my own army, and you won't be sacrificed." And Tlahuicol answered, "What? To march against Tlaxcala tomorrow? My own city? Never. Let the feast continue. Let the ceremony continue."

Well, I find that so wonderful, so beautiful. And he was a non-Aryan, mind you. He was a non-Aryan. He was a Red Indian. I found him worthy of having his story told — to another Aryan, an English friend I had then — on the top of the Externsteine. She came to Germany, and we went to the Externsteine together, and I told her.[59] We were talking of Mexican things. I said, "Wait till we come to the top of the Externsteine, and there in the Sun Room, I will tell you the story of a sun worshipping warrior, Tlahuicol of Tlaxcala. He deserves it. Aryan or non-Aryan, he deserves it." Well, I used to be feeling that way.

And when I think of the inquisition in America, so many people burned alive and the horrors, the same horrors as in Europe, in the name of the ghastly Catholic Church, I felt disgusted. I felt, "Better these sacrifices in which the victim himself thought it was an honor at least." He had nothing against it.

Like the *suttees* in India, the widows who were burnt alive, of their own free will, according to religion. I don't say a pressure was not put on some of them, but as a principle, as a law, they were only victims voluntarily. I wouldn't have stopped that if I were the British. There are so many other things to stop, not that. Stop that last. It was the first thing they stopped. There was one in my husband's family, one *suttee*. Only a few years ago, perhaps 20, 30 years ago.[60]

Well, when Mr. Mukherji died, I cut off my hair, clipped it off.

---

[59] The friend was Veronica Vassar (d. 1972), to whom Savitri dedicated her *Akhnaton: A Play*. The event took place on 7 July 1954 (*Pilgrimage*, 316, n).

[60] This would have been a very unusual occurrence, as *Suttee* was rare to begin with and generally practiced only by Kshatriyas. Indeed, it is prohibited to Brahmins by the Padma Purana.

That's why it's not so long now. It was a year and a half ago, a little more than a year and a half ago.[61] It grows slowly at my age. So I haven't got enough hair now long enough to make a mop. I'm letting it grow. When he died I cut it off, very short. And I went to the ceremony. He was burning. He was on a funeral pyre. Like the old Vikings were, like we were all in Europe in the old days before Christianity. And I stood by the pyre. And I said to myself, "What if I had to sit in the middle of it like the old *suttees*?" It takes courage. It takes a tremendous courage to sit in the fire.

Unless you have the capacity by yoga to take your etherical body and put it away. And I think some people have that capacity, because when the Buddhist monks were burning themselves alive in Vietnam, I remember the death of Thich Quang Duc on the 12th of June 1963.[62] It is another thing I saw on the television, somebody else's television. You could've seen the serene expression of that monk. He lighted the fire himself, with a lighter. He poured himself and the wood with kerosene and lighted the fire. And he stood in the flames. You could see him on the television. He had the serene indifferent expression of myself when I was supervising a class. The boys were doing their own tasks. I was looking on so that nobody copied somebody else. That kind of expression. And then he got blacker and blacker and blacker, carbonized, and dropped. Without a scream, without a struggle.

And I think he had the capacity of taking away what they call the etherical body among Theosophists.[63] It is the body that feels,

[61] A. K. Mukherji died on 21 March 1977 in New Delhi.

[62] Thich Quang Duc immolated himself in Saigon on 11 June 1963. Savitri probably saw Malcolm Brown's series of photographs on television. These photographs were seen around the world and won The World Press Photo of the Year 1963 award. Savitri may be giving the date she saw the photographs on television. Generally, her recollection of dates is remarkable.

[63] Savitri's connection to the Theosophical Society is worthy of investigation. Two of her books, *A Son of God* and *Akhnaton: A Play*, were published by the Theosophical Society. In *Pilgrimage*, Savitri makes it clear that she was quite familiar with the activities of the Theosophical Society in India and in Iceland, even as she denounces "Theosophy, Anthroposophy, the Rosicrucian Order, Freemasonry"

because our physical body doesn't feel. It's the etherical one that does, the first subtle body, the grossest among the seven subtle bodies. If he had not that capacity, he couldn't have done that. Put your finger in the fire and see what you feel like. Let alone your whole body. I imagine the burnings of the Middle Ages were horrid. They must have been screaming. They were tied, of course.

11. THE IMMOLATION OF CATS

But what I find even worse than that in the Middle Ages, at least in France and Germany and Belgium and so many other places, was the burning of live cats.[64] You see, whatever was revered, whatever was good, in pre-Christian Europe was considered bad in the Middle Ages after Christianity ruled. And cats were among the things. The number 13. The number 13 was good in Germanic tradition. Then it was a bad number. Cats were well-kept and loved in pre-Christian Europe. In Christian Europe they became the embodiment of the devil, especially black ones, because when you caress a black cat in a storm, it gives out sparks. So that was very bad. That was devilish. And they burnt cages full of cats on the Saint John's festival, that is to say, the Summer Solstice. They were thinking they were feasting Saint John. It must've been horrid. Poor cats in the cage and then the cage burning. The bars would get red hot. The poor cats were inside. Or else they had a pole, and the cats would run up the pole and fall down and back into the fire. It was entertainment for people.

In France it was done, and in France there is a place called Saint Chamond, 20 kilometers from my native town. The inhabitants of Saint Chamond are not called Saint Chamondais. They have a name that is nothing to do with Saint Chamond. They are called *chasse-minets*, meaning to say the pursuers of pussies. *Minet* is a pussy. Those who pursue, run after pussies. Up till 1875, they had a custom that apart from Saint John's day they tied

---

(*Pilgrimage*, 265–66). It is also noteworthy that the second and all subsequent editions of *A Son of God* were published by the Rosicrucian Order as *Son of the Sun*.

[64] For more examples of this disgusting practice, see Robert Darnton, *The Great Cat Massacre and Other Episodes in French Cultural History* (New York: Basic Books, 1984), ch. 2, esp. 83–85, 89–96.

a poor cat by its tail above the fire. And the string burnt, naturally. The string was the first thing to go. It was the lightest thing. The poor cat would fall into the flames and then run away. And they would run after the burning cat, through the streets, *chasse-minets*.[65]

I heard of all that when I was a child. It put me absolutely against mankind. And when I started hearing of some movement in Germany, the National Socialist movement, "It's inhuman!" "Inhuman?" I said, "Goodness me. I'm going to go into it. If it's inhuman, I like it." "It's inhuman." "Well, well, very good. I wouldn't have touched it if it were human. It's inhuman? All right."

The Jews

12. THE JEWS AS INSTRUMENTS OF THE DARK AGE

The Jew, originally, was not different from other Semitic people. He was just as good as they are. I have absolutely nothing against him. I mean to say, the real Jew in antiquity. He believed in a God of his own. And he didn't think twice of praying or sacrificing to the gods of other people. You get that in the Bible. Again and again and again in the Bible you have examples of Jewish kings—they are called bad in the Bible, of course, all bad— sacrificing to gods of Syria, to Astarte or to different Baalims. "Baal" means "god" in Syrian religions. And the average Jew had no scruples about that. Only Moses and the prophets are the ones who made the Jews what they are. Really, what distinguishes the Jews from other people of antiquity is the intolerance that was given to them through the Mosaic law and through that command of Deuteronomy: "People you come in touch with and people that your God will give into your hands, don't spare them, don't make friends with them, destroy them. Destroy whatever opposes you."[66] That is the new thing. And most of the Jews didn't stick to it. So many times you get in the Bible: "They are a

---

[65] According to Darnton, the residents of Saint Chamond were also called "Courimauds," from *cour à miaud*, chasers of cats (*The Great Cat Massacre*, 83).

[66] Deuteronomy 7:1–3.

hard-necked people." "They will whore after other deities." And
they did whore after other deities. Take the story of the King Ma-
nasseh.⁶⁷ He erected altars to all the stars in heaven and bowed
down to them. He worshipped the stars. Everybody did the same
in those days. And you get worse than that, especially in the 6th,
7th, and 8th centuries BC. Excavations have turned up heaps of
children's ashes in Palestine. It was the custom among the Semitic
people to sacrifice their firstborn by fire. An awful thing. I don't
condone it. I wouldn't do the same. But the Carthaginians, the
Tyrians, the Sidonians, all these people did it. The Jews are one of
them.⁶⁸ They did the same. And God, of course, was angry. Jehovah was angry. These were not the orders of Jehovah. They had to
be different from the other people. They hadn't ought to do what
the others did. But you get heaps of these places. And there's one
awful place south of Jerusalem called *ge Hinnom*.⁶⁹ It's the original
word for *Gehenna*, hell. Hell because I suppose if you were passing by when they were sacrificing you must've heard the screaming and smelt the burning. It must've been awful, really.

But the Jew has become what he is now through Moses and
through the prophets. Through the prophets, in order to make
them a different people. And the prophets were extremely re-
sentful of any other people who opposed the Jews. You only have
to read in the Bible the prophet Nahum. Nahum, when he hears
of the fall of Nineveh in August 612 BC, is rolling with pleasure.
"Woe to the bloody city," he says. "She's punished now, she's
fallen."⁷⁰ He probably didn't hear it at once. There was no radio in
those days. But perhaps three months later, after the fall, he heard
that Nabopolassar of Babylon and his son, young Nebuchadnez-

---

⁶⁷ 2 Kings 21:1–5.
⁶⁸ For instance, Kings Ahaz (2 Kings 16:3) and Manasseh (2 Kings
21:6) burned their sons as offerings.
⁶⁹ *Ge Hinnom* means the Valley of Hinnom or of the son of
Hinnom, who was a person of ancient Israel. It was also called *To-
phet*, the place of bones. See Jeremiah 7:31 and 2 Chronicles 28:3. Josi-
ah converted the shrine into a garbage dump (2 Kings 23:10). It was
also where the corpses of executed criminals were discarded, which
gives a very this-worldly aspect to the threat of *Gehenna*. See Isaiah
66:24, Matthew 23:15, Mark 9:43, and Luke 12:15.
⁷⁰ Nahum 3:1.

zar who was then 17, had stormed Nineveh and set it on fire.[71] He
was pleased.

I have nothing against the Jew as long as he stays in his place.
That is to say, as long as he is a Jewish nationalist. A Jewish nationalist, proud of his race. All right, I'm proud of mine. The Negro should be proud of his too. Every creature should be proud of
what he is. But what I resent in them, and what is a sign of the
Dark Ages, is that they are used for the purpose of this Dark Age
of deracializing everybody. What I resent in the Jew is not that
he's proud of being a Jew. All right. I can have a cup of tea with
him, and he'll talk of his pride. I don't mind that. But I resent it
when he starts telling me that I must consider race as nothing. I
must be an internationalist and an interracialist, while he is not.

What I resent is this. On the 15th of September, 1935, the Nuremberg laws were promulgated in Nuremberg, interdicting any
Aryan from marrying a non-Aryan and especially a Jew. The
Jews are allowed in Germany as guests only. They are not allowed to raise the Reich's flag, the flag of Germany. But if they
wanted to raise their own flag, the flag of Israel — Israel did not
exist yet, but it existed among themselves — they had a flag of
their own. The Jew in Germany can raise his own flag. And if the
neighbors object, they will have to deal with the German police.
The German police will protect the Jew against public opinion. He
can raise his own flag, but not the German. He's not a German.
When people all over the world heard that — I was in Calcutta at
the time — they raised hell. "Oh, awful racialism! Look at the tyrant Hitler, persecuting the Jews." He wasn't persecuting them at
all. He was giving them what should be given to them, and that's
all. They are foreigners in Germany. They have the right to be
proud of their foreign origin, and they are not right to call themselves Germans. They are not Germans. That's all right. That was
1935.

Twenty years later in Israel, a law comes out: interdiction for a
Jew to marry a non-Jew. Nobody raised hell then. It was perfect.
Nobody said a word. Why didn't they make the same kind of

---

[71] Nabopolassar became King of Chaldea in 630 BC. He freed
Babylon from Assyrian rule and was the founder of the Neo-
Babylonian Empire. He reigned from 626–605 BC.

fuss about that as they did with the Third Reich? Why? One law is as good as the other. I approve of both. They approve of none. If they approve of none, and if they raise a fuss for the first, they should raise a fuss for the second. And that is the success of the Jew: "I am a racialist, but you mustn't be." That's the sign of the Dark Age. He's an instrument. An Orthodox Jew who keeps to himself, all right. I like that one. But I resent the other one that keeps to himself, or lets his family keep to themselves, and goes out of his way to propagandize the Aryan and any race that is not his and tell them, "Your race is rubbish. You mustn't believe in it. Believe in mankind, mankind, mankind. All men are equal. All men are loveable. You can marry anybody."

13. ALEXANDRIAN JUDAISM

The rise of Jewry as the great powerful political factor and cultural factor and, unfortunately, religious factor in the world doesn't date from Christianity. It dates from the 4th century BC, from Alexandria. And the proof of it is that you have Jews of the 3rd century BC with Greek names like Aristobulus. It is a Greek name, but he is a Jew, who dared to write in those days, long before Christianity, that all the marvels, all the good things of Greek philosophy really come from Judaism. They come from Moses. Pythagoras, Plato, all these great thinkers of Greece, they were influenced by the Jewish scriptures. So Aristobulus says. Of course, it's not true.[72] And after that you get Pseudo-Aristeas.[73]

---

[72] Aristobulus probably lived in the second half of the 2nd century BC. He is the earliest Jewish thinker to show interest in Greek philosophy. His commentary on the Pentateuch, which is known only through quotations by Clement, Anatolius, and Eusebius, offers an allegorical interpretation of scripture and claims that Homer, Hesiod, the Orphic writings, Pythagoras, Plato, and Aristotle borrowed their ideas from the Old Testament by reading an alleged (and wholly fictional) Greek translation that predated by centuries the first Greek translation, the Septuagint, which was undertaken in Alexandria in the 3rd century BC at the behest of the Macedonian pharaoh Ptolemy II Philadelphus, who reigned from 282–246 BC. See *Fragments from Hellenistic Jewish Authors, Volume 3: Aristobulus*, ed. Carl R. Holladay (Atlanta: Scholars Press, 1995).

[73] Pseudo-Aristeas is the author of the fraudulent *Letter of Aristeas*,

You get so many writers.

And you get Philo the Jew,[74] who is one of the first ones to speak of the *logos*, the word, the incarnate word that is going to become the second person of the *Sainte*[75] Trinity in Christianity. He's preparing the way for Christianity without knowing it. And who goes to Rome with a Jewish delegation when he's not far from 100, under Caligula?[76] And what did they go to Rome for? To ask the Roman Emperor to dismiss Flaccus, Roman governor of Egypt.[77] Why? Because Flaccus says that the Jews are no citizens of Egypt. They are something different. Flaccus said, in other words, what our Führer said also. The Führer said the Jews are no Germans, point four of the 25 points. Flaccus said the same. He said, "The Jews are a people apart. They have nothing to do with average Egyptians. I'm the governor of Egypt. I'm not the governor of the Jews. They must be considered as foreigners. They must be treated as guests, as foreigners." And for that Flaccus was dismissed by Caligula.[78]

---

which seeks to establish the veracity of the Alexandrian Greek translation of the Old Testament, the Septuagint. Indeed, he seeks to establish that the translation was more authoritative than the Hebrew original! The author is thought to be an Alexandrian Jew of the 2nd century BC who poses as a Greek of the 3rd century BC, when the Septuagint was created. See *Aristeas to Philocrates (Letter of Aristeas)*, ed. Moses Hadas (New York: Harper & Brothers, 1951).

[74] Philo Judaeus, a.k.a. Philo of Alexandria, c. 30 BC to c. 50 AD.

[75] Holy.

[76] Gaius Caesar Augustus Germanicus, nicknamed Caligula ("Little Boot"), 12–41 AD, reigned from 37–41.

[77] Aulus Avilius Flaccus was the Roman governor of Egypt between 32 and 38.

[78] Savitri is conflating two separate incidents. Flaccus was dismissed in October of 38, then tried, exiled, and eventually killed by Caligula because of anti-Jewish riots that broke out in Alexandria in August and September of that year. One of Flaccus's innovations in maintaining order was to confine the Jews to one quarter in Alexandria, thus creating the first Jewish ghetto. It should be noted that Caligula had no love of Jews, and in fact enraged the Jews by ordering a statue of himself set up in the Temple in Jerusalem. It is likely that Flaccus was removed for simple incompetence in maintaining order, not for his actions against the Jews *per se*. The Jewish side of the story

The same attitude in those days as now. They don't want to be called foreigners, but among themselves they are foreigners. And it is quite sufficient for an English Jew or an American Jew — or a Jew from England, a Jew from America — to sit in a seat on one of the El Al planes, he's automatically an Israeli citizen. He lands, no trouble. No trouble at all. But when he's in France, he says, "I'm French." When he's in Canada he says, "I'm a Canadian." When he's in the USA he says, "I'm an American." But he gives one-tenth of his income to Israel. He's logical. He does what he can to get on, to get on in the interests of his race. We should imitate them in that way. We should be as logical and as efficient in the defense and in the support of our Aryan race as they are of theirs. Then there would be no Jewish question, no question.

---

is told in Philo's *Against Flaccus*. History does not record Flaccus' side. Philo's visit to Rome took place in AD 39 and dealt not with Flaccus, who had already been deposed, but with the practice of setting up statues of the emperor in synagogues. See Philo's *Embassy to Gaius*. Both texts can be found in *The Works of Philo*, trans. C. D. Yonge (Peabody, Mass.: Hendrickson Publishers, 1993).

Chapter 4

LIFE IN THE KALI YUGA

1. THE NATURE OF HISTORY

I have never shared the opinion that history is a linear unfurling with continuous progress. I don't believe in progress at all. I never did. In 1925, at the university, we had that subject in one of the four exams that go to make a university final exam. In those days it was four. And for the third one, the subject they gave us was the idea of progress, and what I wrote then, I could sign today after all these years. That is to say, after 53 years I could sign the same writing. I said in that writing, "I don't believe in progress, except in technical fields." Yes, we have electricity. In Babylon they didn't have it. They used to light themselves with something else, probably with naphtha, petrol. They had ample supplies of petroleum in antiquity also in Mesopotamia, or else with something else, I don't know what, but anyhow they had no electricity. They had no electric fans. They had no hot and cold water. But excavations have proved that in Crete, 3500 BC, they had sewers and hot and cold water in their houses.[1] There were wonderful arrangements for water in Crete. So anyhow, in the technical domain, I admit there is a certain progress, with ups and downs.

But in all other domains, I don't believe in progress at all. I believe in regression. According to the not only Hindu, but ancient, theory of the cycles, I believe that history goes in cycles. And it's always the same thing. It begins again and again and again and again. It starts with a perfect age in which there's no need for violence because everything is all right. The visible world is a reflection of the invisible, which is perfect, or of that which is perfect in the invisible. They call that in Sanskrit the Age of Truth, the Satya Yuga.

---

[1] The date is 1500 BC, i.e., 3500 years from the present day. This is a slip that Savitri makes four times.

And the second Yuga is less good than the first, lasts less long. The first Yuga is very, very long: tens of thousands of years. The second one is long, but not quite so long. And there you already have the germs of decay in it. The germs of decay are in anything material, anything visible. Even when you come to the subtle material world—invisible, but material still—there you already have decay. You have no decay in the One, the universal substance behind everything. That does not decay. It is something eternal. But all the rest—wherever you go outside of the One—you have the germs of decay. In this second Yuga, called the Treta Yuga in Sanskrit, you get certainly something very good. Compared to us it would be wonderful, but compared to the Satya Yuga, that's already a step lower.

And then you get to the Dvapara Yuga. The third one is already full of violence. You get wars and violence and all sorts of treachery. You get some characteristics that you have now, but to a lesser degree, and you have some races already existing. I think the Aryan used to exist already in the Dvapara Yuga. It is the youngest race of all. But still I suppose it existed then. Much better than now.

Now since some few thousand years BC—some say 3000, some 4000 BC, that is to say, the date of the entrance of the first Aryans into India—you get the Kali Yuga, the Dark Age.[2] And we are nearing the end of the Dark Age. I don't know when the end will be. Maybe in a few centuries. But we are nearer the end than we are to the beginning. That's all I can say. And the Dark Age is what you see around you. Technical progress, maybe. But in all other domains, perfect decay.

Decay in intuition, for instance. People can learn a lot by reasoning, and that is such today. They have been doing so for centuries. But before that, intuition was much more developed, and they could learn things directly. You didn't need so much reasoning and so much research. You didn't need any research at

---

[2] Again, Savitri dates an event that probably took place 3000 or 4000 years from the present as 3000 or 4000 BC. Although Savitri may be following Tilak's dating of the Aryan invasion to between 3000–5000 BC (*The Arctic Home in the Vedas*, ch. 13).

all—any scientific research, for instance. There were even some instances in the old Hindu epics, according to which they could fly. They had some appliances. I wouldn't call them aeroplanes. But something. They called it *havavahana*. A *vahana* is an appliance to go. A car is a *vahana*. Anything that goes. In the buses in Delhi or Calcutta, you have the Indian government's kind of *vahana*. A thing to go. *Hava* is air. Instruments to go in the air. You have a reference to those in the *Ramayana*.

The *Ramayana* is long before the Kali Yuga. I don't know how many thousands of years. It corresponds to some historical fact. At least it might be over 4000 BC, a little over 4000 BC, when the Aryans came, because Rama is an Aryan.[3] He's an Aryan king who conquered the South and conquered Ceylon. Ceylon was the stronghold of Dravidian power, the Dravidians being technically far in advance of the Aryans of those days. But they hadn't got the Aryan virtues. And Rama is said to have conquered Ceylon with the help of flocks of monkeys. The king of monkeys made an alliance with him. Who were the monkeys? Probably the aborigines of India. The aborigines, very primitive people, made an alliance with the Aryan king against the Dravidian stronghold. It's quite possible that it corresponds to such a fact as that in history.

Anyhow, we know a lot more about it. But we know that there were achievements, even in the technical field, far older than what we can imagine, and realized through more intuition than research. Nowadays intuition is getting slower and slower, and less and less. Some people have it, of course. But the people who have a lot of intuition are fewer and fewer. And fewer and fewer people are conscious of the One, the substance beyond all existing things, visible and invisible, what the Hindus called *brahman*. *Brahman* and *atman*. *Atman* and *brahman* are the same thing. *Atman* is the soul, if you like, the soul of the universe. Not a person, anything but a person, anything but a personal god. That consciousness is given to a few people, even in our Yuga.

---

[3] The Aryan invasion was closer to 2000 BC, i.e., 4000 years before the present, and probably took place after 1500 BC. (But see n2 above on Tilak's dating.)

In fact, I have a friend who is now in the South, in an ashram.[4] An ashram is a gathering of people who are interested in religious subjects. And the head of that ashram was conscious of that.[5] In fact, our French friend is getting conscious of it herself. Through some exercises, breathing exercises from yoga, you can get conscious of it. But not everybody can. Only a few can, even with exercises. And very few can without exercises. Well, in the Satya Yuga, in the early ages, this consciousness, this supernatural consciousness, was a common thing. Well, not supernatural. It's natural. But consciousness of what is above the visible world and even above the invisible, above the subtle world: the One. People were more conscious of it than they are now. I don't know whether they lived in caves or not. It didn't matter if they did. You can live in a cave and be much more advanced spiritually than people who live in palaces.

The proof of this is that the ancient Germans were very highly civilized people, far in advance, I think, from that point of view, to the Mediterranean so-called more civilized ones. And the ancient Germans didn't live in caves. They lived in forests, in houses made of wood, without a single nail. They didn't have any nails. I've seen some of those reconstructed German settlements not far from Bielefeld in the woods. They are wonderful. I wish every German could see them. And how they are arranged. The family has a house of its own. And there is a house for the gathering of the community, the village community. There is a house for the head of the village. It's wonderful. But they hadn't any electricity, of course. They used to light themselves with I don't know what. But they used to light themselves. They had lights. They had water. They used to bathe. They were very advanced people in every domain. Technical things are not to be the criteria of real civilization. Real civilization is something much, much more advanced than that.

So, we are in the Dark Age. Technical civilization is advancing, and real civilization is going backwards. Real civilization had one characteristic all over the world: no race-mixing.

---

[4] Miriam Hirn.
[5] Ramana Maharshi.

You wouldn't have gotten an ancient German marrying an Etruscan or even a Greek, unless it were a Greek of the same race as himself. Because the real ancient Greeks, the invaders of Greece in the 13th century BC, came from the North of Europe, and they were Nordics. There was no harm in marrying Nordics. But the Greeks who were there before, the Cretan civilization, were Mediterranean people who were very beautiful indeed, but they were not Nordics. They were something different. As for the Etruscans, they were no Aryans at all. Which doesn't mean that they were not capable, that they were not a fine race.

You can be a fine person without being an Aryan. And you can be a wretched person while being an Aryan. There are some exceptions, of course. What I think of when I speak of racial superiority, it's a statistical affair. Statistically, you get, say, 80 or 90% Aryans that you can recommend, and you might get 5% Africans. But you'll get some. You get some in all races. You get perhaps 20% of other races. You might get 50% of the Semites or of the Mongoloids. I don't know about Semites. There are some fine ones. Take the history of Arabia, the history of Islam, and you get fine characters.

Even in the history of the Jews you get fine characters, now and then. The famous Bruriah,[6] for instance—the Jewess who lived in the early centuries AD. AD or BC, I don't remember—anyhow, she was a fine woman. There are some. Well, in our day the Führer himself said that the best Jew he ever knew was Otto Weininger,[7] who discovered all the nasty things that his own race had done, wrote them down in a history, and committed suicide. He didn't want to be a Jew. Committed suicide. Then you have Martin Buber, who was mentioned in connection with the trial by the Soviets of the so-called war criminals of the

---

[6] Bruriah lived in the 2nd century AD. She was the daughter of Rabbi Hananiah Ben Teradion and the wife of Rabbi Meir, also known as Rabbi Meir Baal HaNes. She is one of several women mentioned in the Talmud as a sage.

[7] Hitler did not know Otto Weininger (1880–1903) personally, but admired his book *Geschlecht und Charakter* [*Sex and Character*] (Vienna: Braumüller, 1903).

SS.[8] He was friendly with SS men, although he was a Jew. He didn't have any intermarriage. He didn't marry his children to any of them. Nor did they theirs to any relatives of his. But on the intellectual plane, they were getting on very well together. He did no harm to anybody. He did no conspiracy. He did not try to destroy the Aryan race. Well, let him live in that case.

We are only against people who are harmful. And we don't hate them. There's no need of hating them. We don't hate bugs. We fight them. We don't hate lice. We fight them. They're harmful. They bite us if we don't kill them. And they infect us with disease. Mosquitoes: the same thing. You don't want swarms and swarms of mosquitoes. You have to do something to make them go away, at least to get rid of them. It's the same thing with races that do harm to ours. We defend ourselves, and that's all.

But in this Yuga, this Dark Age nearing its end, you get more and more power in the hands of those people. That's natural. And there will be a racial struggle somewhere. I can see it coming. I can see it coming in the USA. I wouldn't be at all astonished if one day, not tomorrow, perhaps not in 50 years, but perhaps later on, the USA had a National Socialist government, made of Americans, after a terrific fight with the other races. By Americans, I understand Nordic Europeans who have immigrated amongst Americans. I wouldn't be at all astonished. It could happen anywhere else.

Of course, I think America will precede Europe in that way, not for any other reason but because in America the pressure of the dark races is much more powerful. I've never been to America, but I can imagine you meet Negroes everywhere. Well, you do in Paris, but you don't so much in the French countryside. Although I know a village in France called Chambly, 600 inhabitants, 600. Of those 600, two girls have married Negroes. Two

---

[8] Martin Buber (1878–1965) lived and worked in Frankfurt am Main and published five books during the Third Reich. He moved to Palestine in 1938. He agreed with the National Socialists that Germans and Jews were distinct national communities. Savitri's source is André Brissaud, *Hitler et l'Ordre Noir: Histoire secrète du national socialiste* [*Hitler and the Black Order: Secret History of National Socialism*] (Paris: Librairie Académique Perrin, 1969), 285. (See *Souvenirs et réflexions*, 291.)

girls, two. Two out of 600. It's enormous, if you think of it. And there are more than two in the place where I used to teach, in Montbrison, with 10,000 inhabitants.

It's the fault of the Catholic Church, or of the Christian churches in general. The Negro is a Christian. Why not marry him? That's what happened. It happened to one girl in Montbrison. And I told her mother, "She's expecting a child from a Negro, all right, have her abort it and be finished. And may she never touch any man again. I would not advise an Aryan man to marry her after that. And just stay like that." And the mother said, "Yes, but abortion is a crime, you see." I don't believe it's a crime in that case. It's the best thing to do. No, she wouldn't on Christian grounds, and on Christian grounds with a man who was a Hottentot, if you please. The Hottentot being a Christian they married, and now they have five children. There you are, five French children. They are called French. They're born in France. They're called French. They marry French girls. Look at the danger of it. That is the thing that the Aryan race should react against, and I think it will react against sooner or later.

And if a new Yuga is to begin, if there is to be a world catastrophe, after which a new Yuga is to begin — a new succession of four Yugas, what they call in Sanskrit, *manvantara* — the first one will be perfect. Therefore the first one cannot have any struggle. It can only begin in an Aryan victory. But when, I don't know. And through what ordeals, I don't know either. There will be a terrific ordeal. The Hindus believe in the coming of the same one who always comes. It's the god himself. It's some inspiration from the force that they call Vishnu. They say Vishnu is a member of the Hindu trinity. There's Brahma, Vishnu, and Shiva. Vishnu is nothing else but the force of the universe that keeps things together, that is against change. And change is a form of creation. There must be another force, an antagonistic force, that's Shiva, who goes for change. Change in order for new creation, the new appearance of form. They are connected. The two are connected. You can't have one without the other. And Brahma is of course the unthinkable, the unthinkable soul of the universe, the One out of whom everything comes, the creator, if you like.[9] We'll call him creator. It's not really creation *ex nihilo*.[10] It's something that corresponds to a sort of emanation. In one of the Upanishads, the Chandogya Upanishad, the One says, "*Bahu syam prajayeyti*" — "Let us become multiple. Let us become many."[11] And it is he himself who makes himself many, who takes on forms, invisible forms, and a visible one after that.

We have been in the Kali Yuga since about 3500 BC.[12] It started then. It will last another perhaps two centuries. After the third or fourth World War — I don't know — when the Dark Age will end, there will be a new world, few people. There will be Aryans and non-Aryans, all right. But the proportion between Aryans and non-Aryans will be better in favor of the Aryans. Because a great number of people will be dead. A great number Mongoloids will be dead. The best will survive. The Kali Yuga will last. We mustn't expect the end tomorrow morning. We can expect for tomorrow morning only topical, that is to say, partial resurgences. Like in Germany. Germany was a partial resurgence, just for 12 years. It didn't last. It couldn't last in this era. This is a time when nothing good lasts. According to the laws of evolution, of manifestation, things don't last, because the quality of the people is bad, and you cannot make a good omelet with bad eggs. Even the best cook cannot do it. The eggs are stinking. Now in this period, you have 50 stinking eggs and one good egg, all over the world, if you take the world population.

2. THE SIGNIFICANCE OF ADOLF HITLER

Hitler was a throwback, something that belonged to none of the ages. But his movement is typical of this Dark Age. If he had come in the Satya Yuga, in the Golden Age, in the past long ago, he would have been at home. They were all like him in those days. Everybody lived according to the laws of nature. He went against time. He went against the current of time, and he was

---

[9] Savitri is identifying Brahma, the creator, with *brahman*, being or the substratum of the universe, which Savitri also calls the One.

[10] Out of nothing.

[11] Chandogya Upanishad, 6, 2, 3.

[12] Savitri probably means 1500 BC.

one of the latest ones. There's one that the Hindus are expecting, but not only the Hindus. The Christians say Christ will come again. Somebody will come. The Parsis say Saoshyant will come. Muslims say the Mahdi will come. The Buddhists say Maitreya will come. They're all expecting somebody. If Adolf Hitler had been that somebody, he would've won the war. Even if he had the whole world against him, he would've won. But he didn't win. The only reason why he didn't win was that he wasn't that somebody. He was the forerunner of the one to come.

He said it himself. He said it himself. He knew it. He knew what he was saying. He said it in 1928 in a conversation with Hans Grimm. He said, "I know that somebody must come forth and meet our situation. I have sought him. I have found him nowhere; and therefore I have taken upon myself to do the preparatory work, *only the most urgent preparatory work*. For that much I know: I am not he. And I know also what is lacking in me."[13] And he knew he was going to fall. Kubizek tells that in his book, *Adolf Hitler, mein Jugendfreund*.[14] When he was 16 he went with Kubizek to the theater and saw *Rienzi*, the opera.[15] It was 1:00 in the morning. He came out of the theater, and instead of going home, he said to Kubizek, *"Gehen wir zum Freinberg."*[16] The Freinberg was the mountain near Linz where they used to

---

[13] Hans Grimm, *Warum? Woher? aber Wohin?* (Lippoldsberg: Klosterhaus Verlag, 1954), 14. On the tape, Savitri quotes only a fragment, in German. I have substituted her English rendition of the whole passage from *The Lightning and the Sun*, 430. She renders it in French on page 201 of *Souveniers et Réflexions*.

[14] August Kubizek, *Adolf Hitler, mein Jugendfreund* (Vienna: Stocker, 1953); in English: *The Young Hitler I Knew*, trans. E. V. Anderson (New York: Tower, 1954), 96–98.

[15] *Rienzi* is Richard Wagner's third opera. It is based on the life of Cola di Rienzi (c. 1313–1354), who became the popular dictator of Rome and would-be restorer of the Roman Empire. He was overthrown by a conspiracy of the aristocracy and the papacy, restored to power, then overthrown and killed in a popular uprising supposedly provoked by his own excesses. Wagner's opera portrays him as a popular leader undone by the Pope and the aristocracy.

[16] Let us go to the Freinberg.

go spend their Sunday afternoons. At 1:00 in the morning! Through the fog. But Kubizek followed. They both went there, through the fog. Time came when they were on the summit of the Freinberg. The fog was below. You could see nothing but fog and stars. And then Kubizek says in his book, "Then he caught hold of my hand and spoke to me with words that cannot be retold, so great they are, and he unfurled in front of me, his own future and the future of our German people." He was 16. He knew he was going to fall. He said, "Like Rienzi, I'll go up." Rienzi was a Roman of the 14th century. "I will be carried up by popular love, and I'll fall." He knew it. He couldn't do otherwise. He had to fight all the same, because a fighter is a fighter. Of course, he couldn't say that to the public. He had to do his job. And his job was this: Go against the current of time. Show that the Germans could go against the current of time. They are the ones. They are the best Aryans in Europe.

Not because they are the purest. Swedes — well, up to now — are equally pure. Now they are taking in all sorts of non-Aryans. There is a hateful Catholic organization here: Mother Teresa, supposed to be a lover of children. They gather all the children they can, and if you want to adopt an Indian child you can. They adopted 300 in Sweden last year. Only last year. Little girls and boys of low castes generally, as dark as possible. They adopted them. First of all, they are uprooted from their surroundings. They will never hear a word of Bengali or of Hindi again in their lives. They'll be Swedes. But they are non-Aryans. The masses of India are non-Aryans, and they'll probably marry Swedish girls and boys. You get the end of Sweden. These beautiful Europeans. And that's encouraged. That's encouraged by the Indian government. This government is nothing but under the *impôts*, under the orders, of the international Jew. There's strong Freemasonry here.

3. KNOWING THE FUTURE

My idea of the future is this: If one lives in the eternal present, one *knows* the future. One doesn't see it as we see it through reasoning, but one just is *conscious* of it. You have examples in history of this. One is the Grand Master of the Templar Knights and some of his followers.[17] They were burnt alive, some say on the 11th, some say on the 18th of March, 1314. It is said that the Grand Master in the flames spoke and said, "I call you to God's tribunal, both of you, the Pope, Clement V, within a month, and the King, Philip the Fair, within this year." And it was true. They both died. The Pope died on the 9th of April and the King died on the 29th of November of the same year.[18] How did that man know it? It was perfectly true. How did he know it?

Long before him, how did Confucius know about modern China? They say Confucius was asked by his disciples, "How long will your doctrine rule China?" And he said, "Twenty-five centuries exactly." After 25 centuries exactly Mao Tse-Tung came. With Mao Tse-Tung, the rule of Confucianism, the rule of the spirit of Confucius, was put to an end. The Chinese does not any longer live for his ancestors and in respect to his father and mother. He lives for the thoughts of Mao and the application of the thoughts of Mao. So he was right. How was he right? How did he know it? Why didn't he make a mistake of at least two or three centuries? He didn't. If he was on the margin, it was a margin of 50 years.

This is knowing the future. Unfortunately I have not that capacity. I don't live in the eternal present. To live in the eternal present, you have to be much higher than I am. Probably the Führer lived in the eternal present, because according to Kubizek he knew when he was 16 he would rise and fall like Rienzi.

But very few people do live in that way. For those who don't, well, the future is a matter of reasoning, of conjecture. Suppose this and suppose that. From the data of the present and from the data of the past, you do some comparisons and you try to deduce the future. But this is nonsense. Nobody can deduce the future from the present and the past. At least the far future. Per-

---

[17] Jacques de Molay (1244–1314) served as the last Grand Master of the Knights Templar from 1293–1314.

[18] Philip IV (The Fair) (1268–1314) reigned from 1284–1314 and died on 29 November 1314. Pope Clement V (Bertrand de Goth, archbishop of Bordeaux, b. 1264) was Pope from 1305–1314 and died on 20 April 1314.

haps the near future. And in small things of everyday. Supposing it is known that in the locality there is a shop that shuts on Monday. Well, I'm perfectly sure, practically sure, that if I go on Thursday, I'll find it open. That's very easy. That's the future, the very near future and a very paltry kind of matter. But to tell you whether there's going to be a war before the end of this century or not, nobody knows. Because any event in the future depends on many factors, and the most obvious factors are not always the most important. Not always the most important.

There was a very great speech or sermon of the Bishop of Meaux, Bossuet.[19] He was known as one of those who spoke the most beautiful French. He is given to the children of the college, college boys and girls, to read for his French. And he used to give sermons on the deaths of great people. There is one famous sermon of his on the death of Henrietta Anne of England, who had married the brother of the King of France, Louis XIV.[20] And she lived in Cromwell's day. And there's a passage of that sermon about Cromwell and about the trouble he had. He died of a stone, not in the bladder, but in the tube that goes down from the bladder to the lower parts of the body. In French it's called *urètre*.[21] Well, Bossuet says this stone, a tiny little stone, if it had been anywhere else in Cromwell's body, wouldn't have made any difference. But it happened to be just in that tube. And he died.

Now of course the death of Cromwell was something important in English history, and it was not foretellable. You couldn't see it 20 years before. Who knows what will happen to this person or that person? From a tiny little cause like this, a physiological cause. And that goes for the future. If Roosevelt

---

[19] Jacques Bénigne Bossuet (1627–1704).

[20] Bossuet's 1670 *Oraison funèbre de Henriette d'Angleterre*, on Henrietta Anne of England (1644–1670), wife of Philippe of France, Duke of Orléans (1640–1701), is not to be confused with his 1669 oration on the death of her mother Henrietta Maria of France (1609–1669), the wife of King Charles I of England (1600–1649, reigned 1625–1649), also mother of Kings Charles II (1630–1685, reigned 1660–1685) and James II (1633–1688, reigned 1685–1688) of England (*Oraisons funèbres* [Paris: 1689]).

[21] Urethra.

had died 20 years earlier, world history would've been different. He could've died. Nobody knows. Life and death are in the hands of forces that we don't know anything about. World history would've been different.

They say political assassination is generally useless when one wants to suppress a movement. The movement is represented by a man. One kills that man. Some other man appears. It depends. Political assassination is generally useless because it comes too late. It always comes too late. The knowledge that this man is dangerous is the cause of his assassination. If somebody, knowing the future, had known that when the man was a baby and killed the baby, history would've been different. Suppose somebody had killed Stalin when he was six. History would've been different. Or anybody, any great man. You know the great man too late, and you get rid of him too late. You need to have insight. To have insight, you have to live in the eternal present, and that's not the affair of most people. But if you lived in the eternal present and could know that this man's going to be dangerous for this purpose, and you want that purpose—you want that thing, you love the ideology or whatever you like, that state of things—and you want to get the man out, get him out as a child before he knows himself what he's going to do.

That's what I have to say of the future. So I cannot say anything about the future. I just don't know it. I'm not living in the eternal present. All I know is this: do, every one of us, what we can now. The future is made of many factors. One of the factors is now. And whatever one does, counts. Whatever one says, counts. Whatever one thinks, counts perhaps even more.

I actually believe that thought is a force.[22] Thought is something that comes from our nerves. It's a sort of radiating force. It's waves, if you like. There are waves of thought. We emit waves. These waves have an effect. A very small effect, of course, smaller or bigger depending on the person. But it has an effect. I would say why don't you try to do one thing: Get together every day, or every two days, or every week, or twice a week at the same place and especially at the same time. Time is

---

[22] Cf. *Pilgrimage*, 92–93.

very important. And intensely think. Don't do anything else. Intensely think about what you would like to happen. You have to think all the same. All the people united in one place have to think the same thing. Intensely think what you want the future to be. Intensely think of, say, something simple. How to change the status of the USA or of Canada or of North America. How to do it. Think that. Think, "Superior forces of the universe, help us to do this or that, to reveal the responsible people for the mess in which the Aryan race is now in, and how to get out." I think that is useful.

I really think that the only thing we can do is to wait. Make ourselves strong, and create among ourselves a superior layer of people able to command, able to take the lead of the race one day in each country. People who are nearer in their daily lives to the ideals of the Führer than any others.

4. THE EXAMPLE OF THE FÜHRER

Study the life of the Führer. Study his ideals. There are certain things he never did. I really think he was quite right. For instance, the Führer was a vegetarian, a perfect vegetarian. He didn't smoke, and he didn't take any alcohol. How many of us do the same, what percent, how many? He didn't ask anybody to do it. He says in the *Tischgespräche*, "If I had made these items a condition of belonging to the NSDAP, I would've had nobody. Therefore, I could not make them a condition."[23] But he felt that they were things important in life. Of course, if you drink no alcohol your blood is pure, more pure, and you are stronger than if you do. It's artificial. It's a kind of drug. Of drugs, of course, he had no knowledge. No knowledge.

He gave up smoking when he was a boy. He said, "Isn't it a shame to spend money on cigarettes when I'm so much in need of butter?" He threw his last pack of cigarettes into the Danube in Vienna and bought butter instead of cigarettes. I think that

---

[23] *Hitler's Table Talk, 1941–1944: His Private Conversations*, ed. Hugh Trevor-Roper, trans. Norman Cameron and R. H. Stevens (New York, NY: Enigma Books, 2000). I cannot locate Savitri's quote in this edition.

was quite right. Of course, some people can buy both, but it is not good for the lungs. And the fact that people smoke necessitates and causes experiments to be done on poor dogs to see how long it will take for the poor dog to get cancer of the lungs by smoking. They put a kind of thing on his nose. He doesn't ask for it. He doesn't want to smoke. And they pour smoke into him. All these awful things are done because people smoke, and the doctors want to know about it. They should do experiments on themselves, or on smokers. Not on dogs. I'm absolutely against that.

The Führer forbade all these experiments. If you have to do them, do them on enemies. I would say better than that, do them on "lovers of science." People who are in love with science, let them suffer for what they love. I would be glad to suffer, if at the cost of me being vivisected there would be, for instance, the reunification of Germany. I'd accept at once. I wouldn't accept for anything else, mind you, unless it could be for the suppression of vivisection for all times to come and everywhere in the world. Then I would accept.

Another thing: the Führer used to consider that there was what he called "the sacred flame of life." You get that in Kubizek's book, *Adolf Hitler, mein Jugendfreund*. How, during his youth, during his preparation for life, in that den that was Vienna in those days, with all its temptations, he never fell for any temptation of a woman. He was strong. He wanted to keep his force for something better. Afterwards, when he was settled in life, whether he knew that kind of experience or not, I don't know, and I think nobody can know. Nobody can tell. Nobody was there. But if he had it, it's all right. All right. It was his own business. But he did not waste his energy, as so many people nowadays do, when he was young, when he could use it for something else. I don't think he could've done what he did if he had wasted his time. It's a waste of time and energy in anything one does without a real purpose.

Apart from that, he did not drink, although he was a man of a cold country. He never drank. He was not a tyrant. He was not a fanatic. He allowed people who did drink to come into his party, Robert Ley, among others. He didn't tell Robert Ley not to drink.

But of course, I think he would've appreciated him more if he had also been a teetotaler. He took coffee. I don't know if he took tea. I know he took coffee, the Führer. But coffee now and then. He didn't make a habit of it. He didn't intoxicate himself with any kind of thing. He kept his body as fit as possible.

People nowadays tell me that in the USA there are children of 12 who are already addicted to drugs. Why do they do it? I was offered morphine when I was 17 in Greece by a Greek woman. I said, "No, I'll never take a drug in all my life." As far as alcohol, well, I took Samos wine and Malaga wine once or twice in my whole life. And once it played me a bad trick. It was a birthday party in Athens, and I brought a bottle of Samos wine. I like Samos wine. I like these old wines, cooked wines. I don't like ordinary wine or champagne. Cooked wines I really like. I brought it to this young man, the son of one of my friends. And it was a party. There were Germans. There were English people. There were Greeks. And she said, "You brought the wine. You'll have a little, just a little, a bottom of a glass, with us." I said, "Don't ask me to take any wine. I don't put up with it. I get nervous, and I get—I don't know what to say. I get excited. So don't ask me." "Oh, just a little bit. Just a little bit. Just a centimeter." "All right." I took a centimeter. And I drank it with delight. Although it burns. I'm not used to it, so it burns my stomach. But it was nice. Samos wine is very nice. And then, after this party, we were all asked to sing a song. And some Germans said to me, "Well, you know German, you must know German songs, sing a German song." Well, I said, "All right." And I sang,

> Wir sind die Sturmkolonnen.
> Wir gehen drauf und dran.
> Wir sind die ersten Reihen
> Der deutschen Revolution.
> Sprung auf die Barrikaden.
> Der Tod besiegt uns nur.
> Wir sind die Sturmkolonnen
> Der Hitlerdiktatur!

> [We are the storm columns.

We are the go-getters.
We are the first ranks
Of the German revolution.
Jump on the barricades.
Only death defeats us.
We are the storm columns
Of the Hitler dictatorship!][24]

I left out the greater part of the song. That is the beginning
and the end. I sang that. Some people were delighted, but some
were not. It would have been better if I had not drunk any wine
at all. That's what happens to me when I drink even a little wine,
and I can't control my speech. *In vino veritas*.[25] And that's not the
point. I don't mind if a good person drinks a little bit of *Schnapps*
for Christmas or something like that, on a great occasion.
Christmas meaning the Winter Solstice, of course. It does no
harm. But drinking every day and drinking too much. I know
that in cold countries people drink a lot. You can put up with it
in cold countries. You can't in hot countries. You can't in hot
countries at all. You get ruined. But it's not so bad as drugs.

I think the Führer's life was abridged at the end by the stuff
Theodor Morell gave him.[26] He had confidence in Theodor Morell, as his doctor. I'll tell you the source from where I got it. I
remember comrade F—,[27] SS-*Sturmbannführer* who was impris-
oned in Landsberg. I met him in Uelzen in 1953 when he was
just liberated from prison. And he showed me a letter, a letter
from Karl Brandt, to him—Karl Brandt was also a doctor, an SS
doctor[28]—telling him, "Please can you do anything for him? Can

---

[24] The title of the song is "Wir sind die Sturmkolonnen."

[25] In wine, truth.

[26] Dr. Theodor Gilbert Morell (1886–1948) was Hitler's personal
physician from 1937–1945. Hitler's life was, of course, "abridged at
the end" by suicide, but Savitri's point was that Hitler's health was
harmed by Morell's treatments. See David Irving, *The Secret Diaries of
Hitler's Doctor* (New York: Macmillan, 1983).

[27] The name is unintelligible.

[28] Dr. Karl Brandt (1903–1947) was Hitler's escort doctor from
1934–1944, and from 1942–1945 was General Commissioner for Public

you help me in this way? I'm sure that Theodor Morell is just poisoning the Führer with all his medicines. Tell the Führer not to take that stuff, if you possibly can." So be very aware. Of course he had confidence in this Morell. Unfortunately, they say he abridged his life. That's possible. I don't know. I can only speak of the letter I saw in F—'s hand, a letter addressed to him by Karl Brandt who was also a very high-ranked SS man and a doctor.

Another thing is the vegetarian question. I think it's better if you follow the example of the Führer in that way. Now you tell me that in cold countries it's difficult. It's difficult for some people. Myself, I never took meat. I didn't like it. I didn't like the idea of it. I didn't like the sight of the quarters of animals hanging in front of the shop. It used to disgust me. But I took fish when I was young. I took fish, not every day, once in a while. Once in a while, on festivals. Or when I went to see people who had fish. I didn't refuse. I had fish. And it was a struggle, an interior struggle on my part, to give up fish. Even now, sometimes, when I take some fish for my cats — take a box of sardines for my cats, for instance — I'm tempted to take the oil for myself. I love the oil, fish oil. They used to give me cod liver oil when I was a child. Some children don't like it. I used to relish it. I don't know why, but I used to relish it. They gave me a spoon, and I said, "Give me another spoon of it." I liked it. Well, no accounting for taste, of course. The Führer gives us that example, neither meat nor fish. All right. If we can do it, I think it's very good. It's good for the health, and it's good to feel that one is doing as the Führer did. I believe it.

And I believe it is also a good thing to feel that we are not contributing to the industry of the slaughterhouse. I've never been to Chicago, but I've read descriptions of the stock herds of Chicago with all the animals in a row and killed *en serie*, one by one.[29] They are killed by Negroes. But whoever kills them, they

---

Health and Sanitation. He was executed for his role in Hitler's euthanasia program.

[29] In *Pilgrimage*, Savitri mentions reading about the stock herds of Chicago in Georges Duhamel, *Scènes de la vie future* (Paris: Mercure de

have a struggle of death, on a string, one after another. It's horrible to think of. And these flows of blood. It's disgusting. It disgusts me from an aesthetic point of view. Now there's another point of view. In Europe, they are not Negroes who kill them. They are people of our own race. And to think that by eating meat, we are forcing some people of our own blood to do that disgusting work, killing creatures eight hours a day, and then going home. And to think that these people have wives and children at home. I wouldn't like to be the wife of a slaughterer, but there are some women who are. And they're our people. They're our sisters, our sisters in blood. Could we not do something to suppress that obligation of some of our brothers and sisters in blood to do that dirty work? If we could do it, I think it would be a good thing.

Anyhow, the great idea behind that is the example of the Führer. I believe in him, and I believe that everything he did is something to look at. There's something contained in it for our own discipline and betterment.

5. BABY SEALS

One thing also, there are certain things going on, especially in Canada. I cannot end this speech without saying that. It's something that hurts me so much and still makes me shudder every time I think of it. We should follow the spirit of the Führer in every way. And one thing that would've made the Führer indignant, if he had known it, is that massacre, that mass massacre of seals on the coast of Canada. I've not seen it. I've seen pictures of it. And it's more than enough for me. Poor baby seals, so beautiful, such trusting creatures that you can tame them if you like. Just killed. And how killed? A knock on the head, and their skin pulled off while they're alive, practically alive. Their skins stolen from them. To steal their skins, mass massacres of these beautiful creatures. Trusting creatures that do no harm to anybody.

And one has the cheek of criticizing us for treating our ene-

France, 1930); in English: *America the Menace: Scenes from the Life of the Future* (New York: Houghton Mifflin, 1931) (*Pilgrimage*, 85, n).

mies badly. And sometimes without us doing it. Take the Malmédy case. These SS men who were so tortured in prison that
van Roden, an American of Dutch origin, had to come to Germany to investigate the case.[30] Some of them were not even in
Malmédy, and some of them there had no part in the shooting of
some American prisoners. They had nothing to do with it. And
still, just because they were SS men of that same division or
what, they were tortured in a most awful manner. They had to
be condemned. Well, criticizing people for torturing, for using
their enemies badly, and allowing in one's own country what
goes on with the seals: that should be something to stop.

There were ten million seals. Now there are 800,000. Whatever is going to happen to the rest? I can see them. I can see them,
see them skinned. I can see their corpses skinned, lying on the
snow in pools of blood. Take away that sight. That's an awful
thing. And what's even more awful than that, is to think that
some Aryan men do it for two-and-a-half dollars each. How can
they do it? They are disgracing their race. Every Aryan who
does something horrid disgraces his race. Disgraces his children
first.

In old China, a man who did something wonderful was re-
warded. He was made noble. His sons were not noble. His fathers were. His fathers were responsible for his birth. They were
made noble. He was perhaps a peasant. He did something extremely good. And the Emperor gave him nobility. It went
backwards. There were very many good things in old China.

There was another thing I can tell you of in five minutes, just
in parentheses. You have a doctor when you are sick. You go to
the doctor when you are sick, and you pay him for what he says.
In old China you didn't do that. Every family had a family doctor. And they used to pay him a small sum as long as they were
well. He didn't do anything. He just received the money from so
many families, as long as these families, these family members,
were all well. Once somebody fell sick, then they called the doc-

---

[30] Judge Edward L. Van Roden reported some of his findings in
his article, "American Atrocities in Germany," *The Progressive*, February 1949, pp. 21ff.

tor. The doctor's pay was stopped. They did not pay him any more until the person got well. If he took a long time to cure the person, he had no pay. If he wanted his pay, he had to cure the person quickly. I find that much more reasonable than what we have now. He had an interest in curing the person quickly. Now a doctor has an interest in making the person stay sick as long as possible to receive some pay. Isn't it so?

There was some wisdom in antiquity in all countries. And of course, among our own people—nobody has to learn from me these things—you all know of the wise women of the ancient Germans. There were wise women, in ancient Germany, four or five or six centuries, up to 30,000 BC, prehistoric Germany, prehistoric Europe, North of Europe. And they were very celebrated in the art of healing, as well as in the counsel they could give, in the advice they could give for governing. So, that much for history.

6. Sex, Marriage, and Family Life

There's this widespread propaganda, in order to destroy our race—it's willfully done—propaganda of the excellence, of the indispensable character of sex. Even to children. Telling people that if you don't have that, well, what are you missing? And that is disastrous. That is disastrous, because it's one of the signs of the Dark Age. As said by the Hindu scriptures, if the marriage bond is no longer duty, but pleasure only and money, it's the beginning of the end. It's the Dark Age. And that's what they preach. They preach, "Enjoy yourself. You ought to have a good time. You're on earth to have a good time."

No, we are not on earth to have a good time. We are only individuals. We are on earth to serve that which is eternal in us, and the only eternal thing in anybody is the race. You are immortal if you have children. And children of your own kind. You are immortal if you have works. I don't say works that are known. In the old cathedrals of Europe, if you look at the sculptures, you have some little details that are perfect, as sculptures. The workman who sculpted those, sculpted that wonderfully 800 years ago, in the 12th century, that man is immortal. You don't know his name, but he's immortal all the same. His work lasted. And the work doesn't last as long as the race. The race will outlive the work. Work is something that depends on climate. In a damp country, a sculpture will not last as long as in a dry one. But race, if it's kept pure, will last.

And that is the reason, of course, for the bondage of marriage, and it's not to be made a plaything. It's not to be made a pastime. It's a sacred thing for a purpose, in the spirit of the Führer. He said he was all for early marriage and for many children of good Aryan blood. He told the people that were not of perfect Aryan blood or who were deficient in a bodily way, "You can't have children. You are not to have any. You can adopt an Aryan child."

I like the propaganda of the NSWPP: "Adoption not abortion." When they go picket in front of the abortion clinics and tell the people, "Don't do any abortions of Aryan children. We are not so numerous, proportionately to the others. The Negroes multiply ten times as quick as we do." In England also, and that's a danger. That in itself is a danger. Don't abort Aryan children. Let the mothers have them. The mother doesn't want the child, all right. Find a couple without any children who is willing to take it. Or even a couple with children willing to bring it up as a brother or sister of their own children. Why not? Why not?

If I had money—I never had a fixed job, you see—if I had had a fixed job with a fixed income, I would've liked to adopt an Aryan child myself and bring it up in my own spirit. I would've inquired into the family. Failing that, when Mr. Mukherji had a job and when I thought it was stable—it wasn't of course, but I thought it was in those days—I told him, "We are outside the pale of breeding and all that. We are faithful to the caste system, both of us. All right, we don't want any intimacy and any children. But I wouldn't mind adopting a little boy or a little girl of your caste, an orphan of good Brahminic stock." He didn't want that. He didn't want to take the responsibility, probably feeling that his financial situation was not stable. In fact, after the war, he had no job at all. He had some kind of earnings during the war. But after the war, he no longer had any earnings at all. And he was right. He lived his last years on his astrology. And an astrologer in India doesn't earn so much as that. There are so many astrologers here.

But I'm all for this propaganda: no abortion, adoption instead of abortion, quite good. And encourage people to have children, not one or two, but more if they can afford to bring them up decently. And what does it mean to bring them up decently? Bringing them up decently means: cleanly-lodged, I don't say lodged in luxury; well-fed, as they need to be fed for their health; and given a good, sound education, a general education and an ideological education. And that's all. It doesn't mean to have a TV. You can live without a TV. You can live without a radio.

There's our *Kamerad* in France, Marc Augier de Saint Loup, author of several books, and author of a trilogy on the fight for our ideology in Russia: *Les Volontaires, histoire de la LVF*, the *Legion Volontaire Français*; *Les Hérétiques, histoire de la SS Charlemagne*; and a third book called *Les Nostalgiques, The Nostalgic People*, very good books.[31] He has no radio in his house, and no TV. He doesn't want the appliances, just as I don't want them myself. I never had a radio. I listened to the radio during the war at my landlord's place. I only listened to one thing: the Führer's speeches. I never listened to anything else. And Mr. Mukherji used to come to listen with me, although his German was anything but good. But he wanted to hear his voice. That's all. But you can live without that.

Instead of spending so much on these kind of things, which after all are just propaganda, and the enemy's propaganda, why not spend that on an extra child? Have an extra child. It's very good. Have, I would say even, a pet. It's good for children to be brought up with a young animal. It teaches them to love creatures, to love nature. If you have a garden, plant something beautiful in your garden. It's a good thing to put children in

---

[31] Marc Augier (1908–1990) was the author, under the pen-name Saint Loup, of the trilogy *Les Volontaires, histoire de la L.V.F.* [*The Volunteers: History of the French Volunteer Legion*] (Paris: Presses de la cité, 1963); *Les Hérétiques, histoire de la SS Charlemagne* [*The Heretics: History of the SS Charlemange*] (Paris: Presses de la cité, 1964); and *Les Nostalgiques, aventures de survivants* [*The Nostalgics: Adventures of the Survivors*] (Paris: Presses de la cité, 1967), as well as many other books.

touch with nature, to keep them in touch with nature. Teaches them to love nature, and love of nature is one of the things that Adolf Hitler had. Germany still, in spite of all the devastations of after the war, has one-third of its surface covered with forest. It's one of the very few countries in Europe that has that. Sweden of course. Sweden has a small population. But more simple living, not so much artifice, not so much uselessness in life, and more concentration on health, beauty, ideology, truth. Health, beauty, truth.

Well, that's what I believe for the future. And the only thing we can do now, I think, is to prepare ourselves by sticking to ourselves. That is to say, either not breeding at all or breeding people of our own race. Not breeding at all, if we have any defect. I consider a defect some mixed ancestry, or else some weakness. Personally I opted for this solution for myself. My mother is one of the daughters, one of the 14 children, of a couple of first cousins. It's allowed according to the English church. They were Church of England, both of them, English people of old descent. My grandfather descended from a Viking of Jutland, who came to England in the 10th century. He was not a Christian, but then they became Christians, of course. They intermarried with the British people. They became Christians, those Vikings. When they became Christians, it was not forbidden to marry between first cousins. Well, it was not forbidden at least after the Reform of Henry VIII, when it became the Church of England. And my grandfather Nash and my grandmother Nash were son and daughter of two sisters. One of the sisters married a Nash, and the other sister married a Morgan. And they were the father and mother of my grandfather and grandmother. Well, the 14 children all died as babies, except three. And of the three, one died at 15 of tuberculosis of the lungs and tuberculosis of the bones. She had tuberculosis of her bones all her life, poor thing. Never married. The other aunt never married either, but she was strong. Always suffering from stomach pain, though. My mother is the only one who married, and she only had me. Well, I thought that with this heredity, it's not necessary for me to continue the line. So I didn't do anything to continue it. That's all.

7. Detachment

Another thing is detachment. It is what I like immensely in the idea of the SS and especially in the idea of the élite of the SS, the *Einsatzgruppen* in charge of all the dirty work in defense of National Socialism, in Poland and Russia especially. We heard of it during the trial of Otto Ohlendorf. And I have the honor of knowing the family of Otto Ohlendorf. I was the guest of his widow several times, and I met his children when they were quite young.

Otto Ohlendorf was the head of *Einsatzgruppe D*. Of course he was condemned to death and hanged by the Americans with the other six of Landsberg in the night between the 7th and the 8th of June 1951, in spite of people asking to be hanged in his place or in the place of the others. Among those people was myself. I wrote to McCloy, the High Commissioner of America, in that connection.[32] But there were better people than I. There was a Catholic priest who had been interned for anti-Nazi activities during the war in a concentration camp. He offered his life for them, on other grounds, of course, on grounds of Christian love. Whatever it is, they rejected his demand, and they rejected the demand of several other people in Germany, and they rejected mine. As a sign of stupidity, McCloy sent me a book about the career of the seven, and with a small letter, written by his secretary, of course. He wouldn't take the trouble of writing to me. "If you knew the career of this man, you wouldn't try to offer your life in the place of theirs, or even in the place of one of them." I'd gladly be hanged in the place of one of them, any of them. And I found that so stupid. Ridiculous, laughingly ridiculous. I am a person who tells the people outright, "I am a National Socialist, and in the place of these seven people I would've done what they did, and perhaps worse. You don't want to do anything unreasonable. You don't want to do anything that would worsen your position in Germany. You have now the cold war with the Bolsheviks. You want to strengthen Germany against the Bolsheviks, your former Allies, your gallant Allies of before '45. You'll get the curses of all Germany for killing these seven peo-

---

[32] John McCloy was US High Commissioner in occupied Germany.

ple. If you kill one insignificant National Socialist from the other end of the world, who is not even a German, nobody would care. You will have Germany's approbation because you saved the seven, and that would be all right." They didn't even listen to that argument, which was a very reasonable argument. They didn't listen to me.

Otto Ohlendorf said in his trial—to come back to him—"If any of us showed pleasure in what he was doing or disgust, pleasure or disgust, he was degraded and sent home. We should act only on the ground of duty. We had to act with indifference, because we had an order, and *Befehl ist Befehl,* an order is an order. It's our duty to obey the order. We obey, finished. We don't think about it any longer. It's finished, we do it, and we go do what we have to do later on."

That is the spirit of the oldest philosophical poem written in Sanskrit by Aryans for Aryans. It's the Bhagavad-Gita. The Bhagavad-Gita says, "You are a fighter by nature. You belong to a fighter's race." The lord Krishna, the god, tells that to the hero Arjuna. He has taken the shape, the form, of Arjuna's charioteer to accompany him to the war. And Arjuna is reluctant to fight, because he is fighting his own kinsmen. Krishna tells him, "Take victory and defeat as equal. Take pleasure and pain as equal. Take success and failure as equal. Be indifferent, but throw yourself into the battle with courage in spite of that." This is said in chant number two. In chant number four it is said that whoever acts—any kind of action, be it the most violent action—but not for himself, not for his personal interests, not for the interest of his family because it is his, not for the interest of his country because it is his, not for the interests of mankind because he's a man, but purely in the interest of all living things in the universe, in the interest of the universe, and also, dispassionately, without any feelings or enthusiasm or passion, hatred, love, just because he feels it is his duty, his higher duty. He feels that it is not the duty of every man, because in Hinduism, all men have not the same duty. Duty is a matter of who he is and how he is to act. The duty of the priest is not the duty of the king's minister. The duty of the warrior is not the same as the duty of a mother. Each one has his own duty, *svadharma.* Well, whoever acts in the name of his *svadharma*, his own duty, without passion, and in the interests of the whole universe, whatever he does, he does not sin. That action will not fall into his karma. That is to say, that action will not be a determinant factor in his next birth or his rebirth or his lack of rebirth. It will exist as though it didn't exist. He can do whatever he's told, or whatever is considered as his duty. That I find wonderful.

And that is the spirit of National Socialism. Otherwise, Otto Ohlendorf wouldn't have said in his trial to the face of the Americans, "We acted like that." He didn't tell them, "We acted in the spirit of the Bhagavad-Gita." They wouldn't have understood, first of all. Half of them don't know what the Bhagavad-Gita is. But he said the same, and I had the honor, at his house, to read a few letters of his written a few days and a few hours before his death, his correspondence with the Princess von Isenberg, Eleni von Isenberg. And I must tell you one thing, those letters are absolutely detached. He knows he's going to be hanged in a few days or in a few hours. He doesn't care. He couldn't care less. He has done what he could according to his conscience. He has done his duty. Fate is fate. That spirit, that spirit is our spirit. That spirit is our spirit. And I've seen it also in other National Socialists. Great ones have all the same spirit. It was cultivated especially in the SS, which was the élite of National Socialism, but it must be cultivated at every level if possible, to the extent it is possible. I really like these people.

8. ARYAN SOLIDARITY

I wouldn't criticize the Führer, but I criticize the people who tried to keep down Russia. They should've been allies of the Aryan Russians—Slavs, the real Slavs—not despise them. Slavs may be inferior to Germans, all right, but they are not non-Aryans. The real Slavs. And the real Slavs got on very well with the Germans in antiquity. Thor with his hammer got on very well with Perun, the four-headed Perun with his hammer, who was the god of the Poles and the god of the Russians, the Slavic equivalent of Thor. It's only when they became Christians of different churches that they started quarreling. They used to get on very well, the Germanic people and the Slavic people. Well, they should've tried today.

[I am told that there's a pan-Aryan movement in Russia.] It would be very good. It would be very good if they could take over Russia. There's a former SS French correspondent of mine who wrote to me not long ago saying the Russians should've packed off Marx and kept Stalin. Instead of that, they put Stalin into the dustbin and kept Marx. It was a mistake. Quite true. Quite true. Stalin at least was Russian, but his wife was Jewish and his brothers in law, the Kaganovich brothers, were Jews. His daughter was half Jewess.[33] The Russians are conquered. Communism is Jewish.

[Some people say the Russians freed themselves of the Jewish yoke.] I don't believe that. As long as you have Jews at the top. At the top you have Jews there. Of course the Russians are anti-Jewish by nature. When Mr. Mukherji was in Russia, he had a friend called Ligachov. Ligachov was expelled from the Communist party for three years for calling a man who stepped on his toes in the tram a "dirty Jew." He said, "You dirty Jew." That was reported. He was expelled for three years from the Communist party. He was a Russian, not a Jew.

There are many things that we could take from the Jews. I very often said if we had some of the virtues that the Jews have, there wouldn't have been a Jewish question. And one of them is this: solidarity. If a Jew goes bankrupt, other Jews will bring him out, three times. He can be three times bankrupt. He will survive with the money of the other Jews. In my native town, there was a Greek who tried business and failed, the son of friends of mine. His father and mother gave him some money. He wanted to go into the cloth business. Well, the cloth market in Lyons, as well as everywhere else, is a monopoly of the Jews practically. This young boy failed. Oh, the other Greeks laughed at him.

---

[33] Stalin was Georgian, not Russian, but Savitri's point was that he was not a Jew. Stalin's third wife, from 1934–38, was Rosa Kaganovich, the sister of Lazar Kaganovich (1893–1991) and Mikhail Kaganovich, both enthusiastic accomplices in Stalin's crimes. Stalin's daughter, Svetlana Alliluyeva (1926–2011), was from his second wife, Nadezhda Alliluyeva Stalin (1902–1932), who was apparently not a Jew.

"Why did he try business when he was not fit for it?" That's all. "Why did he try business? Serves him right." Jews would never have said that of him. They would've picked him up once, twice, three times.

Now every Jew in Lyons, every Jew in Saint-Étienne, France—I know those two towns very well—gives one-tenth of his income to Israel. If every person with an income—I wish I had one, I'm living on private lessons and have no fixed income—but if every person with an income could give even one-twentieth to these National Socialist organizations, to one National Socialist organization—it's a pity there are more than one—it would make a great difference. It would make a great difference. You cannot yet think of the head of the NSWPP becoming president of the United States. Why is that unthinkable? Why is it unthinkable, after all? Because you need an enormous quantity of money to get the television hours for the propaganda to be president.

9. *ANTHROPOS* AND MISANTHROPY

I am at home when I'm thinking of gods. I've never seen any gods, but I like to think of them. And the supreme. I'm at home with animals. I love all animals, especially felines. But I'm not afraid of them. I've caressed a tiger, a Bengal tiger 300 kilos in weight, twice in my life. I put my hand in the cage in the Calcutta zoo. I gave a tip to the guardian. The guardian, the keeper, was green with fear. I said, "No fear. I'll give you a tip." And I put my hand in and caressed the tiger. I'm not afraid. If I were going into the cage, I wouldn't be afraid. I love them. I love felines.[34]

And I don't mind serpents. I had two cobras in my house when I was living in Jallundhar. I used to give them milk. They never did a thing to me.

I love trees, and I love that German characteristic that is love of forests and trees. That's perfectly Germanic. I think it's one of the reasons why I'm so much in love with the old Germany of former days, when the country was covered with forests, the Germany of Hermann the Cheruscan.

---

[34] Cf. *Pilgrimage*, 316.

Well, the only creature that I cannot love is the stupid, average two-legged mammal who doesn't think for himself. He's supposed to think. He's supposed to look upwards. Man in Greek is called *anthropos*. Now if you decompose the word *anthropos*, it means "the one who looks above." If he doesn't look above, he's no *anthropos*. He's no man. And the majority of people who call themselves men, they are not men according to the Greek etymology of the word. A man is supposed to think. That's what he's supposed to have more than the animals. He's supposed to think. Ask your neighbors, ask yourself, all those people that you are around, that are all around you, how far they think.

They tell you, "Yes, there were six million Jews killed in the war by your Führer. Six million. It was on the television." It's on the television, therefore it's right. And they have the cheek of criticizing the people of the Middle Ages who would tell you, "The priest said it, therefore it's right. The church says it, therefore it's right. The church says the world is flat, not round; therefore, the church is right. And Galileo's wrong." There's no difference. If you listen to what the radio says, because the radio says it, the radio is gospel or veda. And you listen to the television, and what the television says must be true. The television says the Führer is wrong. He must be wrong. That's not thinking.

If a man doesn't think, he's no man. What we should develop among ourselves is thinking. And what is compatible with our National Socialist faith, and what is not compatible, we should know that. Try to analyze. We are given a theory or given a philosophy. We are asked to adhere to it, of course, by the one who does adhere to it. Is that philosophy compatible with our philosophy? And we should know our philosophy for that.

Nowadays, at least in this Yuga, and more and more as we go to the end of the Yuga, people are not, as a mass of people, race-conscious. And you can wash their brains so well that they can go against their race. I've seen pictures — I've never seen the thing itself, but I've seen pictures — of pro-Negro demonstrations in the USA, and half the people are White. What do those White people want in a pro-Negro demonstration for Negro rights? Of course, I have answered this long ago. And my answer is this:

"All right, you are White and you don't mind supporting the Blacks. Well, I'm a two-legged mammal. I don't mind supporting the other animals. I'll be for the animals against you, against the two-legged mammals. I'll be for the trees and for nature against man. That is no worse than you being against your own race among men." But of course, among men, I'm for my own race. And I would say, more than that, I think that if I were not an Aryan by birth—well, already I'm not a pure Nordic—but I would support a Nordic. And if I were a mongrel, or if I were anything, a perfect non-Aryan, I think I would support the Aryan race all the same for the very same reason I support felines: because it's beautiful. Beauty is everything for me. Beauty is my god and goddess. Visible beauty first and, as it's said in the *Banquet* by Plato, "From visible beauty go up to invisible beauty, to truth without a form."[35] All right, but the basis is visible beauty. I'm all for beauty. And the first reason why I feel proud of being an Aryan is that in general—not myself, of course—but in general, the race is beautiful.

10. PROPAGANDA

You allow yourself to be brainwashed. I was brainwashed too. We were all brainwashed. In school: the French Revolution, the French Revolution, the French Revolution. I didn't have the time for it. I wouldn't have it. Who obliges you to think what people tell you? Who obliges you to bow your head to authority? Rise up, stick up—in your mind at least. You can say, "Yes, yes, yes," for your job. I have a job at the United Nations here. I have a job teaching French to the personnel. If I say no, I would lose 400 rupees a month, and I would have nothing to live on. I have to accept. All right. But even to my pupils, I tell them, "The United Nations is rubbish." I tell them, and they say, "We think so the same, but we have to live. So we take a job here."

And I could've had a very good job in 1946 at the United Nations in New York, recommended by the Greek Consul in Lyons, my native town, who told me so. And he said, "You can have a very good job if you like. You know several languages, and you

---

[35] Plato, *Symposium*, 210a–211c.

can go there." You know what I answered? I was rude to him. I said, "United Nations? That organization? I'd rather be the head of a brothel. Not do the work myself, but have it done by dirty girls, and have the profit. And earn even more than at the United Nations. But I don't like that kind of work, nor do I like the work of the United Nations. I'm not going to go there." He said, "All right, as you like."

This man had given, during the war, false passports to Jews. He gave them passports as Greek citizens. And the priests had given certificates of christening. They made a traffic. They made pots of money. If you were a Jew and you wanted to get out of France under the Germans, you could go to the Greek Consulate. They could do it for you. But it was 300,000 francs. If you were a poor Jew you couldn't go there. Only the Jews who were prepared to give 3 or 400,000 francs in those days. They made pots of money. I disliked that. I was ashamed of it. But that was that. The black market. They did many things.

But you see, that idea of people believing what they're told, being brainwashed, I just can't understand it.

11. "THE" HOLOCAUST

I wouldn't say I was never taken in by propaganda. No, I believed it as the damn fool I probably was. I believed it all. The six million Jews. I believed the lie for years and decades. I just disbelieved it last year [1977] when I saw Butz's book.[36] But I didn't care. I didn't care because I had my love of animals. That protected me. I said, "As long as man commits such atrocities on animals in the name of science, in the name of sport, in the name of eating, in the name of whatever you like — the fur industry — I have no time for atrocities on human beings, especially on enemies. I don't care what happened to them." That was my reaction. It is not the reaction of the average human. The average two-legged mammal was anti-Nazi, and I was not. I could never be and could not again today. And I'm not making a fuss about, say, a man like Idi Amin Dada in Africa, especially when Idi

---

[36] Arthur Butz, *The Hoax of the Twentieth Century* (Torrance, California: Institute for Historical Review, 1976).

Amin Dada says he admires Hitler. A Negro admiring Hitler: I'm not very enthusiastic about that. He wouldn't be enthusiastic about it if he were alive. But anyhow, "Better a moral risk than an enemy,"[37] and he says that he was a really remarkable man and he would even like to erect a statue to him in Uganda. All right. Anyhow, what he does to those Ugandan compatriots, I couldn't care less. I couldn't care. And the ending for the Jews, for the six million: I said, "Pity it's not 16 million. If it were 16 million, it would be very good. The question would have been solved already long ago. Pity it wasn't 26 million."

I approved of it when they said they made experiments on people instead of animals. I said, "Good for them. That should be done all over the world." But the only thing I would disagree with was this. I was told that for experiments, they used to choose people who were the most anti-Nazi in the camps and sent them. I said, "If I had been the head of the camp and if they told me, 'All right, the government wants 25 people for experiments, can you send them from your camp?' I would say, 'All right, can you wait two days? Only two days. I'll send them day after tomorrow.'" And during these two days I would've given an essay to the whole camp to write: "What do you think of Pasteur?[38] What do you think of Claude Bernard?[39] What do you think of so-and-so and so-and-so. Men who have done experiments on animals in the interest of science and medical application?"

And if there was one man in the camp who would've said to me, "Pasteur, I consider that fellow as a criminal. He made so many hundreds of dogs and sheep and other animals suffer. For mankind? I don't care. He made them suffer. I consider that fellow a criminal." I would've done my best to get the man out of the camp. Even if he were a real anti-Nazi, unless he was really dangerous. If the man was in camp just for calling Hitler a

---

[37] This is probably a quote from Idi Amin.

[38] Louis Pasteur (1822–1895).

[39] Claude Bernard (1813–1878) is known as the father of modern experimental medicine, including the use of animals in medical experiments.

Schweinehund or something like that, and never did anything, I couldn't care less. Let him call him what he likes. I'd rather have a man who calls Hitler a *Schweinehund* and does nothing than a man who calls him outwardly *"mein Führer"* and puts dynamite under the trains to do real sabotage. I'd much rather have the first one, of course. The first one is harmless. He's a harmless fool.

So I would've seen those who were enthusiastic about experiments on animals, who say, "Oh, it's for mankind, all right." I would've called them one by one, 25, one after the other, "Come here. Sit down in the office. You really love mankind so much you think it's worth torturing animals for the benefit of mankind?" "Oh yes, we do." "You think you can cure these tropical diseases in Africa, sleeping sickness and all that, and by experiments you can save so many people?" I'd say, "All right. Then you are going to follow these gentlemen in the black uniforms, and you'll have the honor of suffering for what you love." I would have liked to see the chap's face.

If I were told today that, if I am vivisected, Germany would be reunited under a National Socialist government, I would accept at once. I wouldn't accept vivisection of an animal even for that, not for that. I should go, or my comrades, people who are conscious of what they do. Otherwise, the sacrifice of a victim who's not conscious, is no sacrifice. It has no effect really. For it to be effective they must be consenting. Consenting and enthusiastic.

The Aztecs knew that. They knew that. And the ancients knew that. The ancient Europeans of the Neolithic period, they had matriarchy, in Greece and all around the Mediterranean. And the king was killed every year. He consented of course. It was the custom. He was killed. The queen embraced him, took another husband, and he was offered to the gods. He had to die for his people. It was the custom. At the time of the sowing of the crops, for the crops to be good. And then, of course, the kings didn't always like that custom. They took prisoners of war, they took slaves, and they took animals. They gave less and less and less valuable things to the gods. That was decay. According to me that's decay. The gods should be very well-served.

But when I was told that that they did experiments on people instead of on animals I said, "Well, good for them. That's the best thing the Third Reich did." They couldn't get me. There was nothing that they could tell me that could've changed my mind. They couldn't tell me anything.

(One Communist, the most intelligent Communist I've ever met, told me, "You know, Lenin loved cats, and Krupskaya his wife also. They loved cats." I said, "All right, Horst Wessel adored them." I knew that. I've seen photos of Horst Wessel with cats on his arms and cats on his lap and all that. He loved cats. That's quite true. He was photographed with them. His aunt showed me the photo. On one of his birthdays. He had one or two cats. Boys gave him cats from the neighborhood to be photographed with.)

Supposing they had told this story of the six million and supposing the answer of the world to the six million was, "And what if? Doesn't matter." What could they have done? What could they have done? Nothing. And supposing they said, "The one who could organize all this killing of Jews, Himmler: Himmler was a monster." Supposing we answer, "Yes, we like this monster." All right. What could they have done? They could do nothing! And supposing the first election in Germany, they put as blanks in the voting booth, "NSDAP or nothing." What could they have done? They couldn't kill all the German people. I asked a German. When I said, "What would've happened if you did that?" He said, "We would've had an occupation regime *ad infinitum*."[40] Would they have an occupation regime *ad infinitum*, even now? With moral decay on the top of it? A lot of food, plenty of stuff that destroys people's health, with big bellies and difficult circulation of blood and this or that.

12. THE IDEALISTIC VERSUS THE APPETITIVE

I had a long talk one day with Heinrich Blume, who was *Oberregierungs- und Schulrat* under the Third Reich, and he told me, "In 1935, at the height of Germany before the war when we had great hopes and we were going forward without any oppo-

---

[40] See *Pilgrimage*, 232–33.

sition, there were about 300,000 National Socialists in the whole of Germany." I said, "Three hundred thousand? There were 14 million members of the party." "That doesn't make any difference," he said, "They could be members of the party for several reasons. One was a member of the party because the NSV gave him help for his 11 children. Another one was a member of the party because the party arranged to give him a flat. He had no flat. Another one was a member of the party because he thought it would give him advancement in his job, at his office. Different reasons." There were many.

And there is a record in 1969, a record in German of the materially satisfied Germany of 1969, the Germany that the occupying powers are trying to corrupt. According to the words of a Jew that I heard in 1948, Ben Topf, the stage manager of the dancing company of Ram Gopal, "What I want to see in Germany, is this: larders full and arsenals empty. No arms but plenty to eat and plenty to drink." That's what happened. That's the defeat of Germany. That's the defeat. Plenty to eat, plenty to drink, plenty to enjoy, sex films, sex books, sex magazines, whatever you like. And no enthusiasm for fighting at all, if possible. As little as possible. Perhaps fighting Bolshevism, because if the Russians come, of course, all these enjoyments will be stopped. But only on that ground, not for honor. This is the tactic of the Jew and the tactic of his servants, the occupying powers.

If we had freed ourselves from the idea of temptation, if we were not tempted, they would lose their power. Suppose — well, it's not possible for a whole country — it were possible for the whole country to say, "We don't want your goods. Keep them for yourselves." I remember a Greek slogan they used to chant in front of the palace in 1916, when the British were blockading the Greek ports for ten months. The Greeks had nothing to eat. They produced oil and raisins and wine, and you can't live on that. If they don't import they can't live. And the crowd was in front of the palace of Constantine, the brother-in-law of the German Kaiser whose sister, Sophia, he had married. And they were chanting, "Olives, olives and Constantine our King. Bread and salt and Constantine in the palace." Meaning, "You can give us what you like. We don't want it. We don't want your advantages. We don't want your riches. We want poverty and our king." The Greek royalists used to say of Greece of those days, "small but honorable." We don't want to get into your war. We were forced into the First World War. The Greek nation was forced into it, with the government of Venizelos. We couldn't even prevent that. Of course the territory was doubled after the war, but we didn't ask for that. As soon as they called back the king, the Allies tore the treaty of Sèvres into pieces.

So to come back to this record of 1969, in Germany, it's called "*Sauerkraut und Bier*." And it's for those people who love to eat a lot and to eat nice things. And it's the glorification of the Germany of plenty of 1969. Now you can't tell me, because human nature is human nature, that under the rule of the Führer, there were no Germans who wouldn't be ready to live for sauerkraut and beer. They were the same people. Among these people, some were idealists, and always it is a minority that is idealist, and the masses are the masses. Everywhere you go in the world, even the Aryan masses cannot come up to the élite. It's impossible, materially impossible. But we have to do what we can to bring them up as near to the élite as we can.

Therefore, give them what's necessary for them, and teach them at the same time that all this superfluous stuff that they are promised by our enemies is only promised to them to degrade them. For no other purpose. They don't do it out of love. The Allies don't give freedom of so many things. Freedom of sex as much as you like, and films on that. But freedom for the NSDAP? Do they allow the NSDAP to come back as a party? No. I'd much rather them to forbid all the pornographic stuff that they brought in and allow the NSDAP. In fact, pornographic stuff was forbidden under the Führer. And any manifestation of it was forbidden also. I could tell you of cases I heard of from friends of mine, how he treated those people who tried to spread immorality, not because it was immoral from the Christian point of view but because it was *weakening* from the Aryan point of view. From the point of view of race, it was weakening.

13. MULTI-RACIALISM AND COLONIALISM

I'm for a multi-racial world in which each race keeps to itself, in harmony with the other races. Like in a garden, you have flowerbeds of roses and flowerbeds of carnations and irises and different other flowers. They don't intermarry. They stay separate, and each one has its beauty. In the same way among human races each one has its beauty. I might prefer the beauty of the Aryan because I am an Aryan myself. But of course, a Negro would find a Negro very beautiful. Not in my opinion, but it's his. I have no objection to the Negro as long as he stays in his place. I don't want him to destroy nature. I don't want him to injure another race. But in his own surroundings, all right. Let them learn the respect of their surroundings, the respect of nature, of non-human nature, and live the best they can, each one in their surroundings.

I'm against colonialism for the reason that colonialism infects the master as well as the slave. It even infects the master more. You can see that with the English.

Of course I preferred India under the British. It was much better organized. You get a box of matches today in India, and half the matches break when you try to strike them. In those days it was better. In those days, if you wanted any kind of convenience, any kind of commodity for everyday life, you go into the Army and Navy stores, you got it, and it lasted for your lifetime. Now it isn't lasting. A pair of shoes: this pair I bought three or four months ago, 50 rupees. If you take a pair of shoes, five rupees or six, you can wear it three days or a week. You have to change it. Indian made is no good. The stuff we had under the English was very good, much better at least.

But, I have nothing against the fact that an Englishman was paid 2,000 rupees and an Indian bank clerk 35 rupees a month. What I have against it is that the Englishman with 2,000 rupees a month was the most non-entertaining person. He knew nothing. Nothing about history, nothing about mythology, nothing about religion. He knew all about dogs or all about gardening. That was his hobby. His work, his technical work, and dogs, especially dogs of a certain breed. Or all his work and gardening, or all his work and tennis or basketball or something else, some sport. It was dull. I never met an entertaining Britisher, under the British, hardly ever.

But I met very entertaining Indians. Upper caste Indians were entertaining. They knew something. Not all of them, of course, but some of them. Some were stupid. I met one once who was interested in Mexico, in the Maya, ancient America. I was interested in ancient America all my life. And this one said, "You see, the Hindus gave their civilization to ancient America." I said, "How is that?" He was a rich man, mind you, had a lot of property. The Hindu Mission sent me there to try to get money from him. And he gave us 50 rupees or something like that. He said, "Well, India is just opposite Mexico on the Earth. And they dug a hole, and they came out the other side. They went through." I said, "There is not any evidence of the hole." "Oh, it must've been stopped up by now. I don't know if I have any evidence." I said, "Nor do I." "Anyhow, it doesn't matter." But look at the stupid thing! Going through the earth like that. How can you imagine it? They were naïve. Many who wanted to prove something were very naïve. But next to that, you had very interesting Hindus. And you had the *sadhus*, the real ones. You have 10,000 quacks, 10,000 bogus monks walking the streets, but you have some real ones too.

My husband used to say, "I am a follower of Adolf Hitler because I am an orthodox Hindu, and first of all because I was born an orthodox Hindu, and because of that I went into both movements. Well, they're not two movements. It's the same movement, but applied to different countries and applied to different times. It's the same principle, the principle of the separation of races and government by Aryans, the government of a multi-racial world by Aryans in every country."

And if the British had done that, they would be still here. If they had said, "Out with Christianity. We're not Christians. We are Hindus. We are Kshatriyas, conquerors of the Kshatriya caste. We accept Hinduism. We marry among ourselves. Brahmins marry among themselves. At the most, at the top, we might marry a Kshatriya Indian, if she's fair. But even that wouldn't be very correct. And we govern. Kshatriyas are made to govern." And they construct Hindu temples of their own style. All right. They would be here still. They would be here still.

I much prefer now the pagans that we were, the pagan religion we had. We had several pagan religions: the Germanic,
the Celtic, the Greek, the Roman. The root was the same. The
root was the same: worship the sun. I imagine what the world
would be if pagan Europeans, pagan Aryans, had conquered the
world instead of Christians. America would be all right. Fight
the country, but respect the gods. All right.

The only conquerors I really like in India are the Greeks. They
didn't destroy. They kept to themselves. You take the lists of the
Greek kings who ruled India for 250 years, the immediate suc-
cessors, not of Alexander the Great, but of Seleucus Nikator,[41]
the general of Alexander the Great who had the biggest slice of
his empire after his death, from the Mediterranean to the Indus
valley, and beyond the Indus. Well, the big piece became two
pieces because one of the governors made himself independent,
and there was another one he appointed in Afghanistan. Afghanistan and India were the same in those days. There was a
capital at Baktra, a capital at Sialkot. Sialkot is Sagala in Punjab.
All right. Two kingdoms. They continued ruling for decades.
They kept to themselves. They married among themselves. They
married Greeks. But one of the last ones became a Buddhist, and
if you see their coins in the museum of Lahore, the first generation has Greek letters and Greek deities on both sides. Second
generation, Greek deities and Greek letters on one side, Hindu
deities and Hindu letters on the other side. And the third generation has Hindu deities and Hindu letters on both sides. But
they remained separate all the same. They were just Kshatriya
kings or Kshatriya caste conquerors. If the British had followed
their policy, they would be here today.

The Kshatriya caste was once perhaps the highest caste. It's
the caste of conquerors, of warriors, administrators. The Brahmins are the advisors. The temporal power is Kshatriya. Spiritual power is Brahmin. You should have both. You should have a
king, and his advisor is a Brahmin. All advisors of the old kings
of India were Brahmins. But some religious teachers — unortho-
dox, like the Buddha — were Kshatriyas.

---

[41] Seleucus "the Conqueror" (Nikator), d. 280 BC.

Chapter 5

"1953"

In 1953, before I went back to Germany, I stayed for some time in Greece, and it was the birthday of a *Kameradin* whom I had met in Werl, a so-called war criminal, Hertha Ehlert. Living in Bad Homburg now if she's alive. She's my age, six months older. She was born on the 26th of March, 1905. It was the 26th of March, and I was in Athens. I was free, under the sunshine. She, poor thing, was in Werl still. She only came out later. And I went into a place where you get yogurt and you can eat cakes and things like that. I had something to eat there. And it came to me. I thought of Hertha. I thought of her. I thought of her. And it came to me to write this poem.

And time rolls on . . . And every empty day
that slowly fades away,
as uneventful
as any other one, into the mist
of unrecorded history,
brings us along our strenuous way,
nearer the heart's desire of the revengeful;
nearer the doom of those whom we resist;
nearer the unfailing end of this atrocious night;
nearer the yet well-hidden goal for which we fight:
the one undying dream for which we live,
— while we never forget, never forgive!

And time rolls on . . . And every dreary hour
that passes by into eternity
glaringly shows the soundness of our claim,
and tells the world the inanity
of Thy enemies' victory,
while bringing Thy dismembered Nation
new strength and new prosperity,

new hopes of unity,
with the increasing certainty
of our return to power,
and *both* our persecutors, further fears
of unavoidable annihilation.

And thus we march invincibly
towards our lofty aim
along the Way of blood and tears.
It matters not how much we gave.
It matters not how much we shall yet give,
to see all those who hated Thee
descend into the grave
after they groan under our whip for years and years,
— for we never forget, never forgive!

And time rolls on . . . And every fleeting second
brings us further away
from the long nightmare of defeat;
nearer the glory of our dawning Day;
nearer the time we shall begin again;
nearer the morn of Thy unending Reign,
when Thy adoring people shall repeat,
in frenzied, spell-like cheers,
the now forbidden words of faith and pride,
and when, for countless scores of years,
the nations of the West that have refused to side with Thee, and
fight the common foe, and live,
will lie in ruins at our feet,
— while we never forget, never forgive!

And time rolls on . . . With us, they did not reckon,
when setting forth their vast utopian schemes.
They thought Thee dead, and us also.
They thought our faith had slackened.
They thought — the fools! — that they could rely
upon our loyalties to values which we hate.
They thought they could send us to die

without us ever asking why
when we had grown too weary to say "No."
They thought they had become the masters of our fate.
And here we rise, and here we stand,
and give the world to understand,
that we shall never fight
but for our same old dream:
for honor and for might,
and what we know is right;
for the joy of asserting
the privileges of our birth;
for Thee, for Greater Germany,
for Aryan rule upon this earth:
The Gospel of perennial Truth in its new form
which we came to proclaim, and which is more, to live,
—while we never forget, never forgive!

And time rolls on . . . Nothing can break our spirit,
nor alter our allegiance
to Thee and to the German Reich,
home of the best,
stronghold and hope of Aryan mankind in the West.
Of all Thy enemies can say or do to gain
our favor, that they so require,
nothing can shake our faith.
Nothing can ever mar
our loyalty to the old oath.
Nothing can kill our will to rise again.
Every new step the former "Great Allies"
take towards us, we meet with a new grievance.
No threat can force us to believe their lies.
No bribery can keep our hearts from hating *both*.

Happier as the storm draws nigh,
we wait, and watch events go by.
We wait, and watch the signs of war.
The hopes of liberation,
the coming chances of Thy nation

to seize the lead of Sunset Lands once more.
And we are confident in our own strength,
and we are grateful
to the immortal Gods who made us free,
serene, even in hell, and loving only Thee;
having nothing to lose and all to give,
"faithful, when all become unfaithful,"
— while we never forget, never forgive!

INDEX

ABOUT THE AUTHORESS

SAVITRI DEVI, 1905–1982, is one of the most original and influential National Socialist thinkers of the post-World War II era. Born Maximine Julia Portaz in Lyons, France on 30 September 1905, she was of English, Greek, and Italian ancestry and described her nationality as "Indo-European." She earned Master's Degrees in philosophy and chemistry and a Ph.D. in philosophy from the University of Lyons.

A self-described "nationalist of every nation" and an Indo-European pagan revivalist, Savitri Devi embraced National Socialism in 1929 while in Palestine. In 1935, she traveled to India to experience in Hinduism the last living Indo-European pagan religion. Settling eventually in Calcutta, she worked for the Hindu nationalist movement, married a Bengali Brahmin, the pro-Axis publisher Asit Krishna Mukherji, and spied for the Japanese during World War II.

After World War II, Savitri Devi embarked upon an itinerant, ascetic life. Her two chief activities were tireless witness on behalf of National Socialism and caring for homeless and abused animals.

Savitri Devi influenced such leading figures of post-war National Socialism as George Lincoln Rockwell, Colin Jordan, William Pierce, and Miguel Serrano. In 1962, she took part in the Cotswolds camp, where the World Union of National Socialists (WUNS) was formed.

Her books include *A Warning to the Hindus* (1939), *L'Etang aux lotus* (*The Lotus Pond*) (1940), *A Son of God: The Life and Philosophy of Akhnaton, King of Egypt* (1946), later republished as *Son of the Sun* (1956), *Akhnaton: A Play* (1948), *Defiance* (1951), *Gold in the Furnace* (1952), *The Lightning and the Sun* (1958), *Pilgrimage* (1958), *Impeachment of Man* (1959), *Long-Whiskers and the Two-Legged Goddess* (1965), *Souvenirs et réflexions d'une Aryenne* (*Memories and Reflections of an Aryan Woman*) (1976), and *Forever and Ever: Devotional Poems* (2012).

Savitri Devi died in England on 22 October 1982, at the age of 77.

www.ingramcontent.com/pod-product-compliance
Lightning Source LLC
Chambersburg PA
CBHW031506270326
41930CB00006B/283